TIME
LIFE ®
BOOKS

*This volume is one of a series that explains and demonstrates
how to prepare various types of food, and that offers in each
book an international anthology of great recipes.*

Cakes

BY
THE EDITORS OF TIME-LIFE BOOKS

TIME-LIFE BOOKS/ALEXANDRIA, VIRGINIA

Cover: Fragile chocolate shavings and a piped garland of sweetened whipped cream adorn a sumptuous four-tier Black Forest cake (recipe, page 153). Hidden from view until the cake is cut into wedges, the layers are sandwiched together with poached whole cherries and more whipped cream.

Time-Life Books Inc.
is a wholly owned subsidiary of
TIME INCORPORATED

Founder: Henry R. Luce 1898-1967
Editor-in-Chief: Henry Anatole Grunwald
President: J. Richard Munro
Chairman of the Board: Ralph P. Davidson
Corporate Editor: Ray Cave
Group Vice President, Books: Reginald K. Brack Jr.
Vice President, Books: George Artandi

TIME-LIFE BOOKS INC.

EDITOR: George Constable
Director of Design: Louis Klein
Director of Editorial Resources: Phyllis K. Wise
Acting Text Director: Ellen Phillips
Editorial Board: Russell B. Adams Jr., Dale M. Brown,
Roberta Conlan, Thomas H. Flaherty, Donia Ann Steele,
Rosalind Stubenberg, Kit van Tulleken, Henry Woodhead
Director of Photography and Research: John Conrad Weiser
Copy Chief: Diane Ullius *Editorial Operations:* Caroline A.
Boubin (manager) *Production:* Celia Beattie *Quality
Control:* James J. Cox (director) *Library:* Louise D. Forstall

PRESIDENT: Reginald K. Brack Jr.
Executive Vice Presidents: John M. Fahey Jr.,
Christopher T. Linen
Senior Vice Presidents: James L. Mercer,
Leopoldo Toralballa
Vice Presidents: Stephen L. Bair, Ralph J. Cuomo, Neal
Goff, Stephen L. Goldstein, Juanita T. James, Hallett
Johnson III, Robert H. Smith, Paul R. Stewart
Director of Production Services: Robert J. Passantino

THE GOOD COOK

The original version of this book was created in London for
Time-Life Books B.V.
European Editor: Kit van Tulleken *Design Director:*
Ed Skyner *Photography Director:* Pamela Marke *Chief of
Research:* Vanessa Kramer *Chief Sub-Editor:* Ilse Gray *Chief
of Editorial Production:* Ellen Brush *Quality Control:*
Douglas Whitworth

Staff for *Cakes: Series Editor:* Alan Lothian *Series
Coordinator:* Liz Timothy *Head Designer:* Rick Bowring
Text Director: Ann Tweedy *Anthology Editor:* Markie Benet
Staff Writers: Alexandra Carlier, Jay Ferguson, Mary
Harron, Thom Henvey *Designer:* Zaki Elia *Researchers:*
Ursula Beary, Nora Carey, Margaret Hall, Eleanor Lines,
Deborah Litton *Sub-Editors:* Katie Lloyd, Sally Rowland
Design Assistant: Cherry Doyle *Editorial Department:* Pat
Boag, Deborah Dick, Beverly Doe, Philip Garner, Brian
Sambrook, Molly Sutherland, Julia West, Helen Whitehorn

U.S. Staff for *Cakes: Series Editor:* Ellen Phillips (acting)
Designer: Ellen Robling *Chief Researcher:* Barbara Fleming
Picture Editor: Adrian Allen *Text Editor:* Mark Steele *Staff
Writer:* Leslie Marshall *Researchers:* Ann Ready
(techniques), Pamela Gould (anthology) *Assistant Designer:*
Peg Schreiber *Copy Coordinators:* Allan Fallow, Tonna
Gibert, Nancy Lendved, Bobbie C. Paradise *Art Assistant:*
Robert Herndon *Picture Coordinator:* Alvin Ferrell *Editorial
Assistants:* Brenda Harwell, Patricia Whiteford *Special
Contributors:* Norman Kolpas (text), Christine Bowie Dove
(research)

CHIEF SERIES CONSULTANT

Richard Olney, an American, has lived and worked for some three decades in France, where he is highly regarded as an authority on food and wine. Author of the award-winning *Simple French Food* and of *The French Menu Cookbook,* he has also contributed to a number of gastronomic magazines in France and the United States, including the influential journals *Cuisine et Vins de France* and *La Revue du Vin de France.* He has directed cooking courses in France and the United States and is a member of several distinguished gastronomic and oenological societies, including L'Académie Internationale du Vin, La Commanderie du Bontemps de Médoc et des Graves and La Confrérie des Chevaliers du Tastevin. Working in London with the series editorial staff, he has been basically responsible for the planning of this volume, and has supervised the final selection of recipes submitted by other consultants. The United States edition of The Good Cook has been revised by the Editors of Time-Life Books to bring it into complete accord with American customs and usage.

CHIEF AMERICAN CONSULTANT
Carol Cutler is the author of a number of cookbooks, among them the award-winning *Six-Minute Soufflé and Other Culinary Delights* (republished as *Cuisine Rapide*). During the 12 years she lived in France, she studied at the Cordon Bleu and the École des Trois Gourmandes, as well as with private chefs. She is a member of the Cercle des Gourmettes, a long-established French food society limited to 50 members, and is a charter member of Les Dames d'Escoffier, Washington Chapter.

SPECIAL CONSULTANTS
Jolene Worthington received degrees in pastry making and candymaking from the Culinary Institute of America in Hyde Park, New York, and worked as a restaurant pastry chef for many years. Formerly the Test Kitchen Chef in recipe development at *Cuisine* magazine, she contributes articles to food magazines and conducts classes in cooking and pastry making in Chicago. She has been largely responsible for the photographic sequences in this volume. *Amy Malone* received her Master Cake Decorator certificate from Wilton School of Cake Decorating in Chicago. Since 1977, she has run her own school of cake decoration in Virginia. She was responsible for a number of the technique demonstrations in this volume.

PHOTOGRAPHER
Aldo Tutino, a native of Italy, has worked in Milan, New York City and Washington, D.C. He has won a number of awards for his photographs from the New York Advertising Club.

INTERNATIONAL CONSULTANTS
GREAT BRITAIN: *Jane Grigson* has written a number of books about food and has been a cookery correspondent for the London *Observer* since 1968. *Alan Davidson* is the author of several cookbooks and the founder of Prospect Books, which specializes in scholarly publications about food and cookery. *Pat Alburey,* special consultant for this volume, is a member of the Association of Home Economists of Great Britain. She has been responsible for some of the step-by-step photographic sequences in this volume. *Alice Wooledge Salmon,* special consultant for this volume, is a chef who has worked at Ma Cuisine restaurant and at The Connaught Hotel in London. She is also a contributor to many publications, including the *Journal of the International Wine and Food Society.* FRANCE: *Michel Lemonnier,* the co-founder and vice president of Les Amitiés Gastronomiques Internationales, is a frequent lecturer on wine and vineyards. GERMANY: *Jochen Kuchenbecker* trained as a chef, but worked for 10 years as a food photographer in several European countries before opening his own restaurant in Hamburg. *Anne Brakemeier* is the co-author of a number of cookbooks. ITALY: *Massimo Alberini* is a well-known food writer and journalist, with a particular interest in culinary history. His many books include *Storia del Pranzo all'Italiana, 4000 Anni a Tavola* and *100 Ricette Storiche.* THE NETHERLANDS: *Hugh Jans* has published cookbooks and his recipes appear in several Dutch magazines. THE UNITED STATES: *Judith Olney,* the author of *Comforting Food* and *Summer Food,* received her culinary training in England and France. In addition to conducting cooking classes, she regularly writes for gastronomic magazines.

Correspondents: Elisabeth Kraemer-Singh (Bonn); Dorothy Bacon (London); Maria Vincenza Aloisi (Paris); Ann Natanson (Rome).
Valuable assistance was also provided by: Janny Hovinga (Amsterdam); Judy Aspinall (London); Bona Schmid, Maria Teresa Marenco (Milan); Carolyn T. Chubet, Miriam Hsia, Christina Lieberman (New York); Mimi Murphy (Rome).

Library of Congress CIP data, page 175.

CONTENTS

Symbols of Celebration

Towering wedding cakes festooned with frosting garlands, layered birthday cakes glowing with candles, fruited Christmas cakes moist and dark—all are symbols of celebration. So, on a less magnificent scale, is a seedcake baked for afternoon tea, or a cupcake shaped to please a small child. Cakes, in sum, are festive food, and the techniques for making them constitute one of the happier culinary arts.

This volume addresses the entire field of cakemaking. The following pages give some historical information about cakes and offer practical advice on using ovens for baking and on serving wine with cake. Next, a series of demonstrations explains the preparation of all the elements that decorate cakes: Step-by-step photographs show how to handle nuts, chocolate and other ingredients; how to mix icings and frostings; and how to use a pastry bag to pipe those icings and frostings into decorative borders, intricate leaves and many-petaled flowers. In this introductory section you also will find information on preparing baking pans so that cakes may be perfectly unmolded.

The chapters that follow deal with the making of particular types of cake. The lightest cakes—spongecakes, angel food, meringue and other cakes leavened by the air trapped in beaten eggs—are the subject of the first chapter. The second chapter addresses poundcakes, fruitcakes and other dense, moist confections leavened by air trapped in beaten butter. A third chapter teaches how to make cakes that are leavened not only by air in the batters, but also by the carbon dioxide that yeast, baking powder or baking soda releases. In this group are quickly made cakes such as gingerbread, as well as classic yeast cakes—savarin from France and panettone from Italy. A final chapter describes the assembly of special cakes, from rolled cakes such as butter-cream-filled yule logs to a three-tiered wedding cake.

Used in conjunction with the international anthology of recipes that makes up the second half of this volume, all of these demonstrations will help you to become skilled and versatile in a branch of cookery so distinguished that Urbain Dubois, a great 19th Century Parisian chef, characterized it as *"un art dans l'art"*—an art within art.

A little history

The cakes baked today are the end products of centuries of refinement, both of ingredients and of the way those ingredients are manipulated. Like bread, pastry and pasta, cakes made their appearance about 10,000 years ago as coarse mixtures of grain and water, flattened and cooked on hot stones by the early farming peoples of the Middle East. Sweet cakes eventually were produced by adding honey or fruit to the grain pastes. Evidence of growing sophistication in cakemaking is seen in a bas-relief on the tomb of the Third Millennium Egyptian pharaoh Ramses II at Thebes; it shows a bakery stocked with a variety of cakes formed into rings and various other shapes.

For centuries, cake baking remained confined to the Middle East, where cooks had a veritable treasury of ingredients. Sugar cane had been grown in the region since the Fourth Century B.C., and Arabs also had the spices and perfumes of the Orient to lend distinction to their desserts. Persians of the Seventh Century A.D., for instance, made cakes flavored with cinnamon, nutmeg, cloves, almonds, walnuts and rose water.

These delicacies spread slowly into Western Europe with the Muslim invasion of Spain in the Seventh Century, the Crusades of the 11th Century and the development of the great Eastern trade routes during the early Middle Ages. Because the most important Western ports were in Italy, Italians had the closest contact with Arab traders and were the first to translate and use their treatises on food and cooking. From Italy, the culinary arts spread into France—and many recipes from great French cooks acknowledge their Italian origin in their titles. That most famous of spongecakes, *génoise,* for instance, is named for its supposed city of origin, Genoa.

The egg-lightened *génoise,* however, appeared fairly late in the history of baking. Until the Renaissance was well advanced, European cakes were leavened by yeast; they were, in effect, sweetened breads. As late as 1660, Robert May, English author of *The Accomplisht Cook or The Art and Mystery of Cookery,* recorded a recipe called "To Make an Extraordinary Good Cake." The cake was leavened by yeast and contained no eggs. It did, however, contain generous quantities of almost everything else—half a bushel of flour, 3 pounds of butter, 14 ounces of currants, 3 quarts of cream, 2 pounds of sugar and 3 pints of ale.

The first recipe for true spongecake appeared in 1699 in a cookbook titled *Occasional Confectionery,* by Mistress Maria Schellhammer. This cake, known as "French Sweet Bread," was made by warming eggs, beating air into them, and then folding in flour and other ingredients in the manner still used today and demonstrated on pages 36-37.

Delicate yet rich, egg-lightened cakes quickly became a large and important group. As early cookbooks show, the use of eggs was nothing less than profligate. In *Home Cookery,* a book published in Boston in 1853, a Mrs. J. Chadwick specified 90 eggs for a wedding cake; an ordinary cake, she allowed, needed no more than 32. *Christianity in the Kitchen,* another American cookbook of the day, specified 20 eggs—and three hours of beating them—to make just one cake.

During the 19th Century, advances were made not only in cake-baking techniques but also in the ingredients that formed the batters, permitting the creation of a wider range of cakes than had ever been known. Flour—essential to almost every cake—was no longer the coarse, mealy mixture known in the Renaissance. Millers learned to sift it even finer, and in 1856, in Evansville, Indiana, a young miller named Addison Iglehart took soft winter wheat, ground it, sifted it, then ground it again.

The result was very fine, exceedingly light cake flour, now used to give many cakes—angel food cakes and spongecakes, in particular—their airy distinction.

Similar advances occurred in the manufacture of leavenings. Yeast cakes certainly were made in quantity before the 19th Century, but the formation of the yeast culture was a tedious process: First, flour was mixed with liquid to provide a growing medium; then the cook had to wait for airborne yeast cells to multiply in it, producing a spongy medium known as a starter that could be used to leaven cakes. In the 1850s, however, ready-made fresh yeast designed just for bakers was developed in Germany and brought to the United States. (Dried yeast did not appear until just before World War II.)

Chemical leavening also came into use during the 19th Century. The Arabs had leavened cakes with wood ash in the early Middle Ages: Mixed with acid liquids such as sour milk, the ash produced bubbles of carbon-dioxide gas, which helped raise cake batters. The effects of wood ash were unknown in the West, however, until the late 18th Century, when bakers discovered that a refined wood ash called pearl ash would produce carbon dioxide when mixed with an acidic ingredient such as sour milk. The use of pearl ash quickly became widespread, but it was confined to highly spiced cakes, such as gingerbread (pages 64-65), whose strong flavors would mask the unpleasant, soapy aftertaste of pearl ash.

Pearl ash was soon replaced by baking soda—sodium bicarbonate. And by the mid-19th Century, cooks could buy the first commercial baking powder. This was a mixture of baking soda and an acid (usually tartaric acid) that would activate it in the presence of moisture; to keep the mixture dry and prevent the soda and acid from interacting in storage, the leavening agent also included rice flour. The form of baking powder now available is called "double-acting" because, in addition to moisture-activated tartaric acid, it contains an acid that requires heat for reaction. Cake batters leavened with it rise somewhat during mixing, when the baking powder is liquefied, but most of the rising occurs during baking.

The stuff of ceremony

Except for bread, no food speaks so strongly of ritual as cake. In prehistoric times, cakes—symbols of the life-sustaining grain—were important sacrificial foods, and the eating of food thus sanctified was thought to confer magical benefits upon the eater. It is not surprising that even now almost every major religious festival—and private rites of passage such as birthdays and weddings—has its attendant cake. For example, All Hallows' Eve (October 31) has long been celebrated in Spain and Italy with the eating of Dead Man's Cake, a dark-chocolate confection (recipe, page 154). In Sicily, small, elongated cakes known as St. Joseph's Fingers are baked in honor of that saint's day (March 19); and Polish cooks, on November 11, bake St. Martin's Horseshoes, shaped to recall the hoofs of the mount of that much-traveled saint.

Christmas is celebrated everywhere with cakes. In Ireland, Christmas Eve is known in Gaelic as Oidhche na Ceapairi; the name means "night of cakes." The classic English Christmas fruitcake (pages 52-53) is a dark confection filled with dried fruits—and sometimes with small favors such as rings and coins that bring luck to the diners who receive them. In France, the traditional Christmas confection is a spongecake rolled around a filling and frosted to resemble a yule log. German Christmas confections, called Stollen or fruit loaves, are yeast cakes shaped into oblongs and dusted with sugar to imitate the Christ Child in swaddling clothes.

Birthday cakes, too, are rich in tradition. In classical times, the birthdays of Roman emperors were marked not only by the offering of cakes to the gods but also by the donation of cakes to all and sundry. Early Christians banned the celebration of birthdays, along with all of the other evidences of pagan festivities, but during the Middle Ages birthday cakes reappeared in a new guise: People received rich yeast cakes on the feast days of the saints for whom they were named.

The first candle-covered birthday cakes seem to have appeared in Germany during the late Middle Ages; the candles were themselves a dim reminder of ancient votive candles. The German birthday cake of the period bore a large, central candle called the Lebenslicht, or "light of life," surrounded by smaller candles, one for each year of the honored person's life. For luck, the celebrant blew out the Lebenslicht and its surrounding candles, making a wish at the same time; the number of puffs required to extinguish the candles denoted the number of months it would take for the wish to come true.

Weddings and cakes have been paired since antiquity. At a Roman wedding, a cake was broken over the heads of the bridal pair as a sign of plenty, and all of the guests took some cake to share in the good fortune. That custom survived well into modern times. Here, for instance, is a description of a wedding from the 18th Century English novel Humphrey Clinker by Tobias

Smollet: "A cake being broken over the head of Mrs. Tabitha Lismahago, the fragments were distributed among the bystanders . . . on the supposition that every person who ate of the hallowed cake should that night have a vision of the man or woman whom Heaven designed should be his or her wedded mate." Today, guests take pieces of wedding cake—sliced, not crumbled—home to eat or, perhaps, to dream on.

Knowing ingredients

Most cake batters are mixtures of flour, sugar, moisture and fat, interlaced with myriad tiny air bubbles produced by beating. Moisture causes a complex of flour proteins called gluten to develop into an elastic network that strengthens cakes; fat and sugar prevent the gluten from overdeveloping and toughening the cakes. During baking, the cake is puffed up by steam from the batter's moisture, by the expansion of air bubbles, and perhaps by the release of carbon dioxide from baking powder, baking soda or yeast.

The very lightest cakes are made with fine-textured cake flour; other cakes are made with heavier, all-purpose flour. All-purpose flour may be substituted in recipes calling for cake flour if 2 tablespoons [30 ml.] of flour are removed from each cup specified, to allow for the greater firmness of all-purpose flour. Whatever the flour, most cake recipes are written on the assumption that it is sifted before it is measured; since the aeration caused by sifting significantly increases volume, be sure to follow this sequence unless a recipe specifies otherwise.

Sugar in cakes is usually simple granulated sugar, although recipes for very light cakes may specify superfine or confectioners' sugar for easier mixing. The moisture and some of the fat in cakes is provided by eggs; use eggs graded "large" unless another size is called for in a recipe. Most cakes are enriched with butter—fresh unsalted butter should be used. The exceptions are a few old-fashioned cakes enriched with meat fat *(recipe, page 132)* and some cakes, such as chiffon cakes, that derive richness and lightness—but not flavor—from vegetable oil.

Know your oven

No equipment is more important for cakemaking than the oven. Oven thermostats are often inaccurate, so temperatures should be monitored with an oven thermometer bought at a kitchen-supply store: Preheat the oven to the desired temperature, and move the thermometer to various positions within to be sure the oven is heating accurately and evenly.

Quite possibly, your oven will have hotter and cooler areas; the hot areas most commonly are found in the top or back. If that is the case, bake cakes on the lower oven racks—rather than on the center one, as you would in an evenly heating oven—and turn the cakes around during baking to ensure that they cook evenly. You cannot, however, bake very light cakes such as angel food in ovens that heat unevenly: Moving the cakes during baking might cause them to collapse.

Do not bake more than three cakes or cake layers at a time: Otherwise, the circulation of heat in the oven will be impaired, and the cakes will bake unevenly. If you bake several layers, stagger the pans on the oven racks.

High altitude baking

Lowered air pressure at high altitudes necessitates some adjustments in cake recipes: Under such conditions, heated liquids evaporate more rapidly than at sea level, and heated air and gases expand more dramatically. Without changes in cake recipes designed for baking at sea level, cakes baked at high altitudes will emerge overinflated, dry and coarse-textured. You will have to experiment with recipe adjustments to achieve perfect results. The following guidelines for baking cakes at altitudes higher than 3,000 feet [914 meters] above sea level, however, should aid your experiments:
● If a cake recipe specifies large amounts of butter—as in a poundcake—reduce the total amount of butter by 1 to 2 tablespoons [15 to 30 ml.].
● Each cup [¼ liter] of sugar in a cake recipe should be reduced by 1 to 3 tablespoons [15 to 45 ml.].
● Each cup of liquid such as milk should be increased by 1 to 4 tablespoons [15 to 60 ml.].
● If a recipe includes baking powder, each teaspoon [5 ml.] of the powder should be reduced by ⅛ to ¼ teaspoon [½ to 1 ml.].

Wines and other beverages

When a cake is served at the end of a meal that has been accompanied by a succession of wines, the cake, too, should have its wine—a white, sweet dessert wine such as French Sauternes or Barsac, German *Beerenauslese* or sweet Hungarian Tokay. To prevent the wines from tasting oversweet, chill them in the refrigerator for three hours or in an ice bucket for one hour.

Cakes should always be less sweet than the wine served with them; otherwise the wine will taste thin and acidic. Some

cakes are made with ingredients that preclude serving them with wine. Chocolate overwhelms a wine, and an abundance of cream may have a dulling effect. Acid fruits such as strawberries or currants may clash with a sweet wine, but cakes that contain apples, pears, peaches or almonds make excellent foils for dessert wines.

There are so many different kinds of cakes and so many different occasions to enjoy them that it is pointless to lay down too many strictures. Coffee may seem the ideal beverage for cakes served at midmorning, and there is no question about the drink that should accompany cakes at afternoon tea. A homemade layer cake and a glass of milk are a pairing hallowed by American children. And a wedding cake would be unthinkable without Champagne. In these and many other cases, common sense and the occasion itself will lead to the correct choice.

Sugar: The Substance of Toppings

To make icings and frostings you must understand the behavior of sugar: All of these toppings contain sugar, and some are composed almost entirely of it.

Simple glacé icing *(box, below; recipe, page 165)*, for instance, is made by stirring warm liquid—water or fruit juice—into confectioners' sugar. While it is still fluid, the icing can be poured over cakes to give them a glossy finish. Other toppings begin with a solution of granulated sugar and water. If the solution is merely brought to a boil, the sugar will dissolve into a syrup that can be flavored *(recipe, page 164)* and used as a glittering glaze for cake layers or for fruit-topped cakes.

Continued boiling will evaporate the water in the syrup, making the syrup progressively denser and thus suitable for thicker icings and frostings. The density of the syrup can be measured with a candy thermometer: As the water evaporates, the temperature rises. To ensure that a syrup has reached a particular density, apply the tests shown here.

A syrup boiled to 217° to 220° F. [103° to 105° C.] will fall from a spoon in wispy threads. This small-thread syrup is thick enough to give body to butter cream *(pages 12-13)*. If the syrup is boiled to 234° to 240° F. [112° to 116° C.], it will form a pliable lump in ice water; this soft-ball syrup is used for boiled icing *(pages 10-11)* and for fondant *(Steps 4-7)*.

For fondant, the syrup is manipulated so that tiny sugar crystals and air bubbles are trapped in it, turning it into a white paste. The paste is melted, thinned and flavored *(recipe, page 164)* for an icing that sets to a hard, shiny coating.

In cooking any syrup, you must guard against crystallization—the formation of coarse sugar crystals. Prepare syrup in a smooth-surfaced pan and remove sugar grains on the pan before the syrup boils: Rough surfaces can cause crystallization. Do not stir the syrup after it boils. And add to the syrup an ingredient that interferes chemically with crystal formation. Cream of tartar has this effect: Its acid converts some sugar molecules into a substance that inhibits crystallization.

1 **Forming syrup.** Dissolve sugar and water in a pan. Add cream of tartar. Set the pan over low heat and brush down crystals that form on the sides, using a pastry brush dipped in hot water. Bring the syrup to a boil, stirring occasionally. To use the syrup as a glaze, remove the pan from the heat when the syrup boils; add flavorings. Otherwise, leave the pan on the heat.

A Simple Glaze from Confectioners' Sugar

Dissolving the sugar. Sift confectioners' sugar into a bowl. Make a well in the center of the sugar with the back of a spoon. A spoonful at a time, pour warm water into the well *(above, left)* and stir the mixture from the center outward to dissolve the sugar. Add enough water to give the glacé icing the consistency of heavy cream *(right)*. Use the icing immediately.

5 **Folding the syrup.** With a dampened flat spatula or a pastry scraper, as shown here, repeatedly scoop up the edges of the syrup and fold them into the center. Work for only two or three minutes, until the syrup is glossy and viscous.

2 **Testing for a small thread.** Place a candy thermometer—warmed in hot water to keep it from breaking—in the pan. Boil the syrup without stirring until the temperature reaches 217° to 220° F. [103° to 105° C.]. Pour some syrup from a spoon. If it falls in a thin wisp, the syrup has reached the small-thread stage. If you want to use the syrup now, dip the pan in ice water to arrest cooking.

3 **Testing for a soft ball.** Continue to boil the syrup to 234° to 240° F. [112° to 116° C.]. Test the syrup by dropping a spoonful into ice water. Lift out the lump of syrup when it solidifies, an almost instantaneous process. If the lump feels malleable when rolled between your fingers, the syrup has reached the soft-ball stage. Dip the pan into ice water to arrest cooking.

4 **Pouring the syrup.** Immediately pour the syrup onto a cool work surface that has been sprinkled with cold water to prevent sticking; a marble slab is used here, but a metal baking sheet is suitable. Allow the syrup to cool for two or three minutes.

6 **Completing the folding.** Using the scraper, work the mass of syrup in a figure-8 pattern, repeatedly folding and turning it on the cold surface. After about 15 minutes, the syrup will be opaque, white and too stiff to stir.

7 **Kneading.** Knead the syrup with your hands for about 10 minutes, folding it over on itself and pressing it flat until it is smooth, white and firm. The fondant paste may now be enclosed in plastic wrap, placed in an airtight container and stored indefinitely.

8 **Preparing icing.** Half-fill a saucepan with water. Place the fondant paste in a heatproof bowl and set the bowl over the water. Place the pan over low heat. When the fondant begins to melt, gradually stir in warm small-thread syrup, a little at a time. Continue to stir until the icing has the consistency of heavy cream, then use it at once.

A Trio of Icings Based on Egg Whites

Beating egg whites with sugar aerates them and puffs them up into snowy, meringue-like icings *(recipes, pages 164-165)*. Different effects can be achieved by varying the method of adding the sugar, but certain rules apply in all cases.

Egg whites to be beaten should always be at room temperature: The proteins they contain will be more elastic at 70° F. [20° C.] than at 40° F. [5° C.], and the whites will thus absorb much more air. Even a trace of fat will keep the whites from mounting properly; use care when separating whites from yolks, which contain fat, and make sure that all implements used for beating are clean.

Beat the egg whites in a large copper, glass, ceramic or stainless-steel bowl; do not use aluminum, which would discolor them. The acid in copper interacts with egg whites, strengthening them so that they remain fluffy; if you do not use a copper bowl, strengthen the whites by adding tartaric acid in the form of cream of tartar, allowing ¼ teaspoon [1 ml.] for every four whites.

To make very light icings that will be firm and satiny when they set, heat the whites: Heating partly coagulates the proteins in the whites and helps them stiffen. One way to do this *(right, top)* is to beat the whites until they are fully aerated, then beat in hot soft-ball sugar syrup *(pages 8-9)*; the result is called boiled icing. For a similar effect without sugar syrup, make a seven-minute icing *(opposite, bottom)*: Combine whites with granulated sugar and water, and beat them over gentle heat until they are puffy. Either icing may be flavored with liqueur, fruit juice or extract, and colored with liquid food coloring: Beat in these fluids drop by drop, until the desired flavor and color are achieved.

Another egg-white icing can be formed by beating unheated whites with large amounts of confectioners' sugar. The sugar prevents the whites from absorbing much air, yielding an icing dense enough to pipe from a pastry bag into freestanding decorations *(pages 24-27)*. This icing, known as royal icing, becomes hard when it dries, so the decorations keep their shape. Royal icing may replace molding butter cream and may be colored in the same way *(pages 12-13)*.

Boiled Icing: Beating In Sugar Syrup

1 **Separating eggs.** Pour an egg yolk between the halves of its cracked shell, dropping the white into a small bowl. Set the yolk aside for another use. Pour the white into a mixing bowl. Repeat with the remaining eggs, dropping each white first into the small bowl so that if one yolk breaks it will not contaminate the whole batch of whites.

2 **Beating.** With a wire whisk, beat the whites in an elliptical motion—lifting the mass high to incorporate as much air as possible. With an electric mixer, beat the whites in a circular motion at medium speed. If you are not using a copper bowl, add cream of tartar to the whites while they are still loose and foamy to help strengthen them.

Royal Icing: Mixing without Cooking

1 **Adding sugar.** Beat egg whites with a metal spoon—the mixture will stick to wood—while you add spoonfuls of sifted confectioners' sugar, making sure each batch is incorporated before adding the next. Beat in lemon juice to help coagulate the egg whites.

2 **Checking consistency.** Continue to beat in sugar until the icing is thick enough to mound in the spoon. It is now ready for coloring and piping and should be used immediately, because it will quickly harden.

3 **Testing for soft peaks.** When the whites begin to look glossy and feel thick, lift the beater from the bowl. A peak should form on the surface of the mass of whites and fall back on itself almost immediately. If no peak forms, beat a few more strokes and test again.

4 **Adding syrup.** Dampen a towel and twist it to form a ring on a work surface. Set the bowl of whites in the ring to steady it and free both of your hands. Continue to beat the whites vigorously as you pour into them a thin stream of hot soft-ball sugar syrup.

5 **Testing consistency.** Continue beating in syrup until the mixture has a satiny gloss and the whites stand in stiff peaks that do not fall back on themselves. Beat in a few drops of flavoring or food coloring, if you like. Immediately spread the frosting on a cake; it will dry and stiffen if it is left standing more than five minutes.

Seven-Minute Icing: Blending over Heat

1 **Combining ingredients.** Half-fill a small saucepan with water, set the pan over low heat, and bring the water to a simmer. On top of the pan set a heatproof glass, copper or stainless-steel bowl containing egg whites, sugar, water and salt. Immediately begin to beat this mixture vigorously.

2 **Testing for consistency.** Beat the egg-white mixture for about seven minutes, until the whites form stiff, unwavering peaks when the beater is lifted from the mass.

3 **Flavoring.** Remove the bowl from the heat, set it on a dampened, twisted towel. Then, when there is no danger of its alcohol evaporating, beat in flavoring—here, vanilla extract—and, if you like, food coloring. Use the icing at once.

Butter Creams Suited to Frosting and Molding

The two smooth pastes known as butter cream serve quite different purposes in cake decoration: One is used as a cake frosting and sets to a delectably rich, soft coating; the other is used as a molding medium for freestanding cake decorations such as flowers *(pages 26-27)* and sets to a firm consistency, ensuring that the decorations hold their shape. The different characters of the two butter-cream mixtures are determined by the ingredients used to form them.

Butter cream for frosting is made by combining hot sugar syrup with beaten egg, most often egg yolks, then beating the mixture into butter that has been creamed—aerated and fluffed by beating. The hot syrup cooks the yolks slightly, coagulating them and thickening the frosting; the butter contributes flavor and extra richness. Egg yolks produce a yellow frosting; for a lighter, ivory frosting, you can replace some of the yolks with egg whites, and for a white frosting you can replace all of the yolks with whites *(recipe, page 166)*.

Any of the frosting butter creams may be flavored with such ingredients as liqueur, melted chocolate, chopped nuts or grated citrus peel. White butter cream may be colored as shown in the box opposite, but do not try to color ivory or yellow butter creams: Because of their color they will not take on true tints. The rich butter creams are spread with a spatula and are dense enough to be piped into border decorations *(pages 22-23)*.

To make intricate shapes, however, molding butter cream must be made with hydrogenated vegetable shortening; unlike butter, the shortening will set to a firm, relatively dry consistency. To make a molding butter cream, the shortening is beaten with hot water and confectioners' sugar, which gives it stiffness. It may be flavored with a few drops of flavoring extract such as almond or vanilla.

Egg Yolks and Butter for a Silky Finish

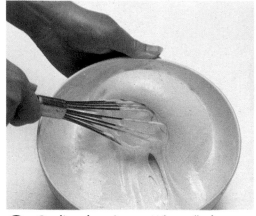

1 **Mixing yolks and syrup.** Separate eggs; reserve the whites for another use. Beat the yolks until they are thick and creamy—this takes five to seven minutes by hand or two minutes with an electric mixer. Continue to beat while you pour hot small-thread syrup in a thin stream over the yolks.

2 **Cooling the mixture.** When all of the syrup has been incorporated, continue to beat the mixture until it is tepid in temperature and fluffy in texture—this will take about 15 minutes of beating by hand or five minutes with an electric mixer.

A Sturdy Mixture for Piping

1 **Softening shortening.** Sift confectioners' sugar. Put hydrogenated vegetable shortening into a mixing bowl and beat until it is soft and creamy—about three minutes by hand or one minute with an electric mixer. Beat in a little hot tap water to soften the shortening and ease mixing.

2 **Forming butter cream.** Still beating, gradually add the confectioners' sugar. When all of the sugar has been added, the butter cream will be thick and stiff. Colorings may be added. The butter cream may be shaped now or stored—tightly covered with plastic wrap—in the refrigerator for up to six months.

3 Creaming butter. In a separate bowl and using a wooden spoon, mash tepid butter to make it malleable. Then beat the butter to aerate it and give it a smooth, creamy texture. This will take about 10 minutes by hand or three minutes with an electric mixer.

4 Blending the ingredients. Pour the cooled egg-and-sugar mixture into the creamed butter in a thin stream, beating the ingredients together constantly with a wooden spoon.

5 Finishing. When the egg mixture is thoroughly incorporated, the butter cream will be smooth, thick and shiny. Colorings and flavorings may be beaten in at this point. You may use the butter cream immediately, or store it, tightly covered with plastic wrap or foil, for as long as one week in the refrigerator.

A Compatible Paste Coloring

Both rich and molding butter cream may be colored, but you must take care in your choice of colorings and the way you add them to ensure that the butter cream maintains the proper consistency and achieves the right hue. Liquid food colorings would dilute the frosting, spoiling the consistency of a butter cream used for frosting or preventing a molding mixture from setting to the perfect hardness.

A highly concentrated food coloring paste, however—the pastes are sold at cakemaking-supply stores—is ideal for both kinds of butter cream, and, as shown at right, is added to either kind by the same method. A small quantity of the paste is drawn across the surface of a portion of butter cream with a wooden pick or small knife, then thoroughly worked in. By adding a little more of the paste coloring or of the butter cream, the desired shade can be achieved with precision.

Blending in the coloring. Put a little butter cream— molding butter cream here—in a mixing bowl. With a wooden pick, draw a little paste food coloring through the butter cream *(above, left)*. Mash the color into the frosting with a rubber spatula *(right)* until the color is evenly blended. The color will darken slightly with time, so cover the butter cream and leave it for a few minutes. Then check the color and, as necessary, work in more butter cream or coloring to achieve a lighter or darker shade.

Chocolate Toppings, Thick and Thin

Dark and luxuriously rich, chocolate can be used to produce a range of coatings for cakes *(recipes, pages 165-166)*. It can simply be melted with cream or butter to produce thin, satiny glazes, and these glazes may be whipped to aerate them to frothy thickness. Or, with careful cooking, the chocolate can become a dense, candy-like fudge frosting.

The chocolate used for any glaze or frosting is widely available in block form; it is sold unsweetened, or with sugar added as semisweet or sweet chocolate. The three types may be used interchangeably in recipes. If altering the type of chocolate called for, you must, of course, adjust the proportions of sugar in a recipe to suit your taste. Any type of chocolate must be melted with care over gentle heat: Overheated chocolate will scorch and stiffen into an unusable, lumpy mass. The method for melting the chocolate depends on the ingredients it is to be combined with.

Chocolate will melt easily, with little danger of scorching, when it is broken or chopped into small pieces and surrounded by liquid such as cream or milk; to make a glaze with these ingredients, simply heat the liquid in a heavy saucepan, add chopped chocolate and stir the mixture over low heat until the chocolate melts *(right, top)*. For a slightly thicker glaze made with butter, exercise more care in melting the ingredients: Butter provides less protection against scorching. To make a butter glaze, melt the chocolate and butter over hot water. Do not let the water reach a simmer, lest rising steam stiffen the chocolate.

Either of these glazes can be poured immediately over a cake; they will quickly harden to thin, shiny coatings. Or the glazes may be chilled for one hour, then when they are thick enough to trap air they are beaten to aerate them, producing thick, fluffy frostings.

For an even thicker chocolate frosting, you can make fudge. The principle is similar to the one for forming fondant *(pages 8-9)*: The chocolate is cooked with milk, butter and sugar until the mixture thickens to the soft-ball stage; then it is beaten. The agitation of beating causes the formation of minute sugar crystals, giving the frosting a dense and slightly grainy consistency.

Melting Chocolate in Cream

1 **Heating the ingredients.** Pour heavy cream into a heavy saucepan. Over low heat, bring the cream just to a boil. Add chunks of chocolate—semisweet chocolate was used for this demonstration—and begin to stir the ingredients with a wooden spoon.

2 **Melting the chocolate.** Continue stirring until the chocolate melts and the mixture is smooth and thickly coats the spoon. Use the glaze at once or it will harden and become unpourable.

Fashioning Fudge

1 **Melting the mixture.** Put pieces of chocolate—semisweet is shown above—sugar, salt, milk and butter in a heavy saucepan. Place the pan over medium heat and stir the ingredients with a wooden spoon.

2 **Boiling the mixture.** Continue stirring until the chocolate and butter have melted and the ingredients are thoroughly blended. When the mixture comes to a boil, place a warmed candy thermometer in the pan. Cook the mixture until it registers a temperature of 234° to 240° F. [112° to 116° C.]—the soft-ball stage.

Combining Chocolate with Butter

1 **Melting the chocolate.** Fill a pan a quarter full with water and heat it until the water reaches a simmer; adjust the heat to very low so that the water remains hot but does not simmer. Break chocolate—here, semisweet—into a heatproof bowl and set it over the water. Stir with a wooden spoon as the chocolate begins to melt.

2 **Adding butter.** Continue stirring until the chocolate is completely melted. Then add chunks of butter and stir as they begin to melt.

3 **Completing the glaze.** Stir the chocolate and butter until the butter melts and the mixture is stiff and shiny (above). Use the glaze immediately.

3 **Adding vanilla extract.** Remove the pan from the heat and let it cool for several minutes. Then stir in vanilla extract (above). If added earlier, the flavor of the alcohol-based extract would be dissipated by the heat.

4 **Thickening the fudge.** With a wooden spoon, beat the fudge mixture vigorously for about five minutes to cool it and thicken it.

5 **Checking consistency.** Beat the fudge for at least five minutes more, until it is fairly cool and thick and has a smooth, matte finish (above). Use the fudge frosting immediately; if beaten too long or left to stand, it will become too hard to spread.

Ornamental Forms for Chocolate

In addition to serving as a base for frostings, chocolate can be used to create pretty cake decorations. Simple chocolate gratings and shavings (box, opposite) can be formed from the same solid cooking chocolate used for frostings. Fancier shapes made from melted chocolate, however, should set to a smooth, glossy finish, something regular cooking chocolate will not always do.

To make these shapes, it is best to use dipping chocolate, which is available in both semisweet- and milk-chocolate flavors at cakemaking-supply stores. Dipping chocolate contains large amounts of cocoa butter, which gives the chocolate its sheen; because of the cocoa butter, the chocolate requires a special melting technique known as tempering.

The cocoa butter in unmelted dipping chocolate is made up of stable fat crystals. When the chocolate melts, these crystals dissolve, and as the chocolate cools, the fat can recrystallize in two forms—first, the original stable crystals and later, new unstable crystals that will rise to the surface of the chocolate, forming gray streaks.

To keep unstable crystals from forming, the chocolate is carefully melted, then removed from the heat. Unmelted grated dipping chocolate is stirred into it at once. The stable crystals in this chocolate act as seeds, prompting the fat to recrystallize only in its stable form. The tempering process continues until the chocolate cools to 86° to 90° F. [30° to 32° C.] for semisweet or 83° to 88° F. [29° to 31° C.] for milk chocolate. The dipping chocolate is now ready for use.

The melted chocolate, still soft, can be molded onto nicely shaped leaves. When the chocolate hardens and the leaves are peeled away, the chocolate will have assumed their shape (right, below). Or the chocolate can be spread out on a cool surface, left until partially set and then shaved with a metal spatula; it will curl into delicate scrolls (opposite, below). A thin sheet of chocolate left to set hard can be cut with a knife or cookie cutters into geometric shapes (right, top).

You can use any of these decorations at once. Alternatively you may store them in an airtight container in a cool place for as long as two weeks.

Cutting Geometric Shapes

1 **Tempering.** Chop dipping chocolate; grate a quarter as much. Stir the chopped chocolate in a bowl set over hot water. When the chocolate reaches 110° F. [43° C.], remove the bowl from the heat. Stir in small amounts of the grated chocolate until the chocolate cools to 86° to 90° F. [30° to 32° C.].

2 **Spreading the chocolate.** Using a spatula, spread the melted chocolate on parchment paper on which you have drawn a series of parallel lines 1½ inches [4 cm.] apart as cutting guides. Smooth the chocolate from the center out, to give it a thickness of about ⅛ inch [3 mm.]. Leave guidelines visible at both ends of the chocolate sheet.

Molding Leaves

1 **Coating a leaf.** Wash and dry leaves—here, rose leaves. Temper dipping chocolate (Step 1, above) and spread it on a flat plate. Hold each leaf by the stem and draw its shiny top surface through the chocolate so that the surface is coated completely.

2 **Peeling the leaf.** Allow the leaves to dry, either spread out flat on parchment paper or curled, chocolate side up, over a rolling pin. When the chocolate is firm, peel off each leaf, starting from the stem.

Curling and Grating

3 **Decorating the surface.** Before the melted chocolate sets, gently pull a fork or a decorating comb—available at cakemaking-supply stores—across its surface to give it a rippled finish. Let the chocolate harden; this will take five to 10 minutes.

4 **Cutting the chocolate.** Using a long, sharp knife and following the guidelines, cut the chocolate into 1½-inch [4-cm.] strips. For semicircles, center a round cookie cutter over the incisions and stamp out the shape. For triangles, cut the strips into squares and halve these diagonally. Transfer the shapes to a baking sheet.

Making curls of chocolate. Hold a block of chocolate over a plate. Draw the blade of a vegetable peeler upward along the thin edge of the block. Chocolate at room temperature, as used here, yields longer shavings than chilled, hard chocolate.

Shaving Scrolls

1 **Spreading the chocolate.** Pour tempered dipping chocolate (Step 1, opposite, above) onto a work surface—here, marble. Use a flexible metal spatula to spread the chocolate ⅛ inch [3 mm.] thick.

2 **Forming scrolls.** Let the chocolate cool for two to three minutes, until it is firm but not completely hard. Push a pastry scraper or a wide, sharp-edged spatula such as the one shown here under the chocolate; the blade will lift up the chocolate in scrolls.

Grating chocolate. Chill a block of chocolate to harden it: Warm chocolate would clog a grater. Rest one side of a grater on a plate (above) and rub the chocolate on the grater, letting the shreds fall onto the plate.

The Basics of Nut Preparation

Nuts add distinction to cakes. Left whole or chopped, they make elegant decorations. Ground, they can be folded into batters and frostings or turned into a rich, sweetened flavoring paste. No matter how you use nuts, you will get the best results if you buy fresh ones and prepare them at home as you need them.

All fresh nuts must first be shelled—a simple procedure with the help of an efficient nutcracker. The next step is to remove the inner skins, which could spoil the color of many preparations. The skins of most nuts will loosen if the nuts are toasted for 10 minutes in a 350° F. [180° C.] oven *(right, top)*. The clinging skins of almonds and pistachios, however, are more easily loosened by blanching the nuts in boiling water *(box, opposite)*.

To chop nuts, use a sharp, heavy knife. If you plan to use the chopped nuts as a decoration, sift them to remove the dust-like particles that could spoil the appearance of a cake; save the sifted particles to flavor batters or frostings. To add color and bring out flavor, toast the chopped nuts in a 350° F. [180° C.] oven for a minute or two, turning them frequently to prevent burning.

To grind nuts, use a mortar and pestle, a nut grinder or a food processor fitted with a metal blade. If you use a processor, operate it in short spurts to ensure that the heat generated by the speed of the blade does not draw out the nuts' oils and turn them into a sticky mass. Finely ground nuts will blend smoothly into a batter or frosting.

Ground nuts—usually almonds—are also the basis of the rich nut pastes often called marzipan *(right, below)*. Mixing the nuts with egg, confectioners' sugar, lemon juice and flavorings produces a smooth confection that can be used as a filling between cake layers or as a flavoring to enrich and strengthen cake batters *(pages 54-55)*.

Roasting and Peeling Loose-skinned Varieties

1 **Toasting the nuts.** Spread shelled nuts—hazelnuts, here—in a single layer on a baking sheet. Toast the nuts in a preheated 350° F. [180° C.] oven for 10 minutes; then, protecting your hand with a glove, push the nuts from the sides of the sheet toward the center so that they all toast evenly.

2 **Peeling the nuts.** After another five minutes, when the nuts' skins are blistered and brittle, remove them from the oven. A few dozen at a time, fold the nuts in a towel; press down and rub back and forth to remove their skins. Use your finger tips to remove any remaining skin that clings to the nuts.

A Paste from Pounded Almonds

1 **Mixing nuts and sugar.** Squeeze half a lemon and strain the juice. In a small bowl, lightly whisk an egg. Blanch and peel almonds, then grind them in a food processor. In a large bowl, mix the ground nuts, superfine sugar and confectioners' sugar.

2 **Adding lemon juice and egg.** Use a knife to stir the lemon juice into the almonds and sugar; the mixture would stick to a spoon. Add just enough beaten egg—a little at a time—to make a stiff paste. If the mixture is very sticky, add a little more confectioners' sugar.

3 **Chopping the nuts.** Put the peeled nuts on a work surface and chop a small batch at a time. Grip the handle of a large, heavy knife with one hand and steady the tip of the blade with the other; rock the blade rhythmically with even pressure on the nuts to chop them.

4 **Sifting the nuts.** For even nut pieces to coat a cake, shake the chopped nuts in a strainer. Reserve the powdery nuts that drop through the strainer for use in batters or frostings.

3 **Completing the mixture.** Steady the bowl with one hand and use the other to gather the ingredients gently together. Handle the paste lightly—overworking will draw out the oil from the almonds and make the paste greasy.

4 **Kneading.** Sprinkle a work surface with confectioners' sugar to prevent sticking. Knead the almond paste until smooth and pliable, then shape it into a ball *(above)*. Use immediately or store in plastic wrap or foil in a refrigerator for up to two weeks.

Blanching Almonds

The skins of some nuts—particularly almonds and pistachios—are so tight that toasting will not loosen them. These nuts can be skinned easily, however, by blanching.

A brief soaking in boiling water makes the skins loose enough to be slipped off by hand. Because some of the water is absorbed by the nuts, they should be dried for a few minutes in a preheated 350° F. [180° C.] oven after peeling. If you do not want them toasted, however, keep a close eye on the nuts so that you can remove them before they brown.

1 **Softening the skins.** Pour shelled nuts—almonds, here—into boiling water. After a minute, remove a nut. If the skin slips off easily, drain the nuts.

2 **Removing the skins.** With your fingers, slip the loosened skins off the nuts. Drop the peeled almonds in a bowl of cold water to keep them white. To dry the nuts, spread them on a baking sheet and place them in a preheated 325° F. [160° C.] oven for about five minutes.

Piping Decorations: The Basic Tools

A cone-shaped bag fitted with a metal tube is the preeminent tool for cake decorating. Filled with frosting and gently squeezed, the bag produces a strand of frosting in a shape determined by the tube. With an assortment of tubes, you can use the bag to pipe decorations as diverse as the ribbons, flowers and filigrees shown on the following pages.

The bag you choose depends on the decorating job at hand. Canvas bags 8 to 10 inches [20 to 25 cm.] deep hold large quantities of frosting. These bags usually are sold in kits, accompanied by a selection of tubes and sometimes by a coupling device—a plastic collar that fits inside the bag's opening to narrow it for use with very small tubes.

For working with small quantities of frosting, with frostings of various colors, or with an assortment of tubes, homemade parchment-paper bags *(below)* are ideal. And unlike canvas bags, which require washing, paper bags can simply be made as you need them and discarded after one use. To pipe plain lines of frosting, snip an opening in the cone's tip after you fill it; for more elaborate effects, snip off the tip of the empty cone and drop in a decorating tube, as for a canvas bag.

Once equipped with the appropriate bag and decorating tubes *(box, opposite)*, you have only to choose the proper frosting for the decoration you plan. To make the tracery referred to as stringwork *(pages 24-25)*, you will need a fluid icing such as fondant, melted chocolate or butter cream thinned with a little corn syrup. Most border decorations and simple flowers *(pages 22-23)* require a frosting firm enough to keep its shape when it is piped—rich butter creams are excellent. Freestanding flowers *(pages 26-27)* require a stiff molding butter cream or royal icing. The molding butter cream used in the demonstrations that follow is an inexpensive and reusable medium for practicing the making of decorations.

Using a Canvas Pastry Bag

1 **Inserting the tube.** Fold down a collar at the top of the pastry bag. Select a decorating tube—in this case, a star tube. Push the tube—tip down—into the opening at the base of the bag. Half of the tube should protrude; if it does not, remove the tube and widen the bag opening with scissors.

Making a Paper Pastry Bag

1 **Making the bag.** Cut a 10-inch [25-cm.] square of parchment paper diagonally in half to make two triangles. Holding the right-angled point of one triangle, curl one short side of the triangle until the underside of its oblique-angled point meets the right angle, thus forming a cone *(above, left)*. Hold the points together and curl the other half of the paper around the cone *(center)* until all three points meet. Fold the points into the open end of the cone to secure it *(right)*.

2 **Filling the bag.** Using a small spatula, scoop frosting into the bag, pushing it to the bottom and scraping it off the spatula against the side of the bag. Fill the bag no more than halfway.

2 **Filling the bag.** With the tube in place, hold the bag just below the collar with one hand. Using a small spatula, put frosting into the bag; as you do so, push the frosting down to the tube to eliminate any air pockets.

3 **Closing the bag.** Fill the bag halfway with frosting. Gather the open edges of the bag together in one hand and, with your other hand, push the frosting down toward the tube to eliminate any remaining air pockets.

4 **Preparing to pipe.** Gather the bag together just above the frosting with one hand; hold the filled portion of the bag with your other hand. Twist the top of the bag away from you and the bottom toward you to pack the frosting. To pipe, press from the top of the bag, twisting the bag as it empties.

3 **Closing the bag.** Fold the open end of the bag several times to enclose the frosting tightly. Before piping, snip off the tip of the bag with scissors.

A Selection of Piping Tubes

Tubes for pastry bags are sold in two different standardized series. A large series consists of four basic tubes—plain, open star, closed star and an intricate star tube designated *B*. Each tube is available in 10 different sizes, which are numbered from 0 to 9. A sec-ond series, numbered from 1 to 200, consists of small versions of the basic tubes plus a variety of special tubes used for making leaves and flowers.

All of the tubes are sold in sets and also individually. The most commonly used tubes are described below.

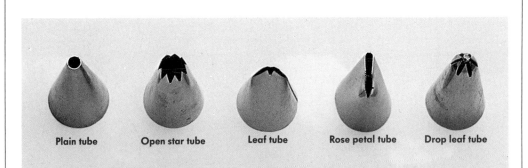

Plain tube   Open star tube   Leaf tube   Rose petal tube   Drop leaf tube

Choosing the right tube. Use a plain tube for writing, stringwork or simple figures. A star tube, either open as shown or closed, gives a ridged effect to piped borders and rosettes. For ribbed leaves, use a notched leaf tube. A rose petal tube has an angled slit that shapes delicately curved petals. Flowers are made with one squeeze of a pastry bag fitted with a drop leaf tube.

Piping Decorations: Borders

Decorative cake borders are most often made with star tubes, which produce cylinders of frosting with elegant, fluted finishes. By altering the way you move the pastry bag, you can use this tube to make borders as varied in appearance as the five demonstrated here.

For borders, tube sizes are chosen according to the size of the cake being decorated: The larger the cake, the broader its borders should be, and the wider the tube's opening. A No. 22 star tube is used in this demonstration; it produces a cylinder of frosting about ½ inch [1 cm.] wide, appropriate for a cake that is 8 to 10 inches [20 to 25 cm.] in diameter. For a tiered cake, such as a wedding cake *(pages 80-84)*, borders are made with tubes of graduated sizes so that the borders for the small upper tiers are narrower than those for the larger lower tiers and the cake appears balanced. Always make the top borders first to reduce the chance of accidentally spoiling a border.

Before you pipe any border onto a cake, practice piping it on a baking sheet until you can comfortably coordinate the pressure you exert on the pastry bag with the movements of your hands. Some borders are perfected quickly: Stars *(right, top)* and shells *(opposite, top)* require only a series of brief squeezes on the bag and small hand movements. Other borders demand greater deftness, but still can be mastered easily. And practice borders need not go to waste: Just scrape up the icing and return it to the pastry bag.

A Series of Stars

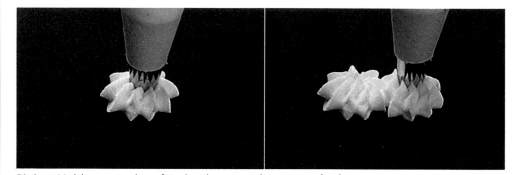

Piping. Hold a pastry bag fitted with a star tube perpendicular to the work surface and ¼ inch [6 mm.] above it. Squeeze the bag above the frosting to pipe a star *(above, left)*. Stop squeezing and lift the bag. Pipe another star next to the first *(right)*.

A Serpentine Ribbon

Reversing directions. Hold a bag fitted with a star tube at a 45-degree angle ½ inch [1 cm.] above the work surface. Pipe a short line of frosting; reverse direction and pipe a second line next to the first *(above, left)*. Repeat this motion *(right)*.

A Two-Strand Border

1 **Forming loops.** Holding the bag at a 45-degree angle, draw the tube toward you *(above, left)*; then lift the tube and shift to the right *(center)* forming a curve. Pipe back toward you, lowering the tube to make a strand equal to the first.

A Chain of Shells

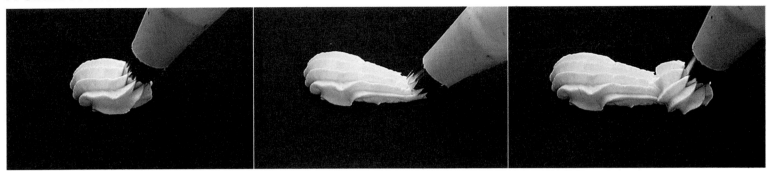

Varying pressure. Hold a bag fitted with a star tube at a 45-degree angle ½ inch [1 cm.] above the work surface. Pipe a mound *(above, left)*; reduce pressure as you draw the tube down to make a teardrop *(center)*. Repeat at the teardrop base *(right)*.

A Band of Alternating Shells

Making curves. Holding the bag at a 45-degree angle, pipe a mound *(above, left)*; ease pressure as you move the bag to one side to form a curve *(center)*. At the end of the curve, pipe a mound, then a curve in the opposite direction *(right)*.

2 **Overlapping loops.** Hold the tube under the first curve. Pipe a line next to the second strand *(above, left)*; then shift to the right to make a curve *(center)*, then pipe back toward you. Repeat *(right)*.

Piping Decorations: Simple Flowers, Leaves and Stringwork

With only a small selection of decorating tubes, you can add all kinds of fancy flourishes to your cakes—from elegant lilies to diminutive wild flowers, from robust rosettes to finely formed rosebuds and delicate traceries of stringwork.

Before you apply any of these decorations to a cake, practice making them on a baking sheet until you are satisfied that you can pipe them perfectly. A flat, three-petaled lily *(right, top)*, made with a star tube, is most easily piped directly onto a cake. The other decorations shown at right can also be piped directly onto cakes. Or, for convenience, they can be shaped on wax paper, lifted with a spatula, and glued to the cake with a dab of frosting. Some are relatively simple creations: A daisy-like flower *(opposite, top)*, made with a drop leaf tube, requires just a squeeze of the piping bag and a twist of the wrist; its yellow center is piped in with a plain tube. A rosette *(right, center)*, made with a star tube, is a rising swirl of icing.

More control and practice are required to form delicate, three-petaled rosebuds with a rose petal tube *(opposite, center)* or leaves with a leaf tube *(right, bottom)*; both demand coordination of wrist movement with the amount of pressure exerted on the piping bag. And delicate stringwork, made with a plain tube *(opposite, bottom)*, is best achieved with the guidance of a carefully drawn design. The stringwork pattern can be piped onto wax paper laid over the design, allowed to harden, and then transferred to a cake. Only with experience will you be able to pipe such tracery directly on a cake.

Any decorations piped onto wax paper can be stored easily. Leave them in a cool dry place until their surfaces form a protective crust—at least overnight. Then store them in an airtight container; they will keep for a week.

A Three-petaled Lily

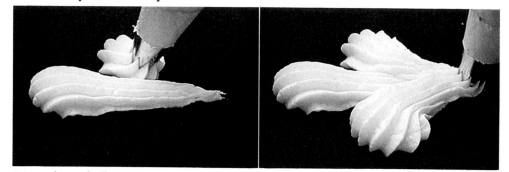

Piping three shells. Using a pastry bag fitted with a star tube, pipe an elongated shell shape *(page 23)*. Next to it on the right, pipe a shorter reverse shell *(page 23; above, left)*, curving right to left. On the left side, pipe a shell curving left to right *(right)*.

A Mounded Rosette

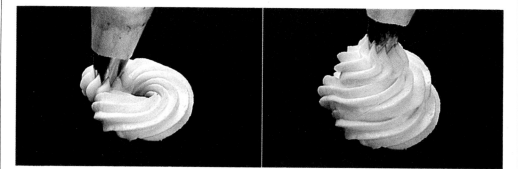

Swirling the icing. Use a star tube. With even pressure, pipe the frosting in a circle *(above, left)* and then, without stopping, spiral frosting on top in a smaller circle, finally ending the swirl in a peak as you ease the pressure.

A Rippled Leaf

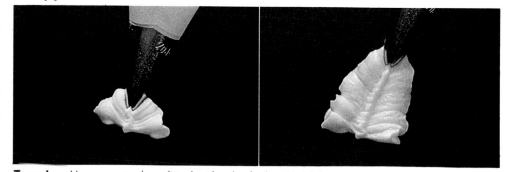

Tapering. Use a pastry bag fitted with a leaf tube. Hold the bag with the tube slit down. Press on the bag to build a mound as the leaf's base *(above, left)*; then draw the tube toward yourself, releasing pressure to taper the leaf *(right)*.

A Dainty Wild Flower

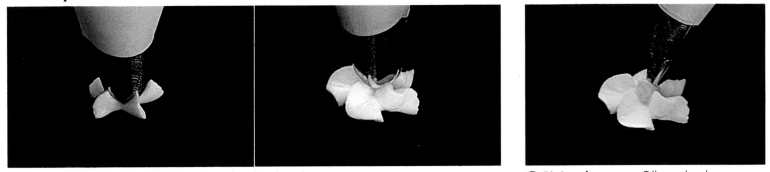

1 **Forming the flower.** Use a pastry bag fitted with a drop leaf tube. Hold it perpendicular to and touching the work surface. Pivot the tube 180 degrees to pipe curved petals *(above, left)*; then lift the tube *(center)*.

2 **Piping the center.** Fill another bag with frosting of a contrasting color. Pipe frosting into the center of the flower.

A Furled Bud

Piping petals. Use a rose petal tube. With the wide end of the slit touching the surface, pipe a petal flat and then curled up. From its center, pipe a petal curving left and then up and right. Pipe a petal around the first two.

A Delicate Tracery

Following a design. Draw a pattern on white paper; place wax paper on top. Hold a plain tube above one end of the design. Apply even pressure and move the tube along the pattern so that the frosting—here, chocolate—falls in the pattern.

Piping Decorations: Elaborate Flowers

Some frosting flowers are so intricate that they are difficult to form by guiding a pastry bag over a stationary surface. These blossoms are most easily shaped on a small, readily manipulated platform called a rose nail. By piping frosting onto the platform with one hand and turning the platform with the other, you can fashion lovely, lifelike flowers.

Shaped like large nails with oversized heads, rose nails are sold in a range of sizes. For making a flower, the platform is covered with a square of wax or parchment paper held in place with frosting. The flower is formed on the paper from molding butter cream *(pages 12-13)* or royal icing, which are the only frostings stiff enough to hold a three-dimensional shape. Once the flower has been shaped, it can be moved—on the paper—to a baking sheet to set overnight. The flowers will keep for up to a week before they are glued to a cake with frosting.

The simplest flower made on a rose nail is a flat daisy *(right):* To position each new petal, the nail is turned after each stroke of the pastry bag. A wild rose *(box, center)* consists of two layers of several petals each; the nail is slowly turned during piping so that the petals overlap. A full-blown rose *(box, bottom)* is a masterpiece of rose-nail work. To make it, layers of petals are built on a core of frosting until the flower blooms in full glory.

A Radiant Daisy

1 **Anchoring the paper.** Pipe a dab of molding butter cream onto the center of a rose nail. Center a square of wax paper on top and press it firmly down.

A Rustic Wild Rose

1 **Piping a petal.** Use a rose petal tube. Hold its wide end above the paper-covered nail; pipe and turn the nail 90 degrees counterclockwise.

2 **Overlapping the petal.** Pipe another petal in the same way, just overlapping the first and to the right of it.

3 **Forming a flower.** Pipe three more overlapping petals, turning the nail after each. For a simple blossom, use a plain tube to pipe a yellow-icing center.

A Perfect Tea Rose

1 **Building a cone of icing.** Use a plain tube to build up a cone-shaped mound of butter cream in the center of the paper-covered rose nail.

2 **Wrapping.** Use a rose petal tube. Pipe a long ribbon onto the cone top; draw the tube away and turn the nail to wrap the ribbon around the cone top.

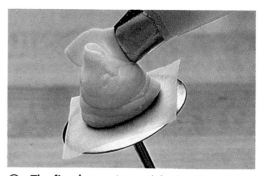

3 **The first layer.** Around the bud's base, pipe three overlapping petals: Turn the nail 120 degrees for each and keep the tube's wide end on the cone.

2 **Piping petals.** Use a rose petal tube, the narrow end down. Pipe petals at right angles to each other, turning the nail a quarter turn for each.

3 **Filling in more petals.** In each quadrant of the daisy, pipe two more petals, to form 12 petals in all.

4 **Adding a center.** Use a plain tube and yellow frosting to pipe a center in the daisy. Transfer the flower on the paper to a baking sheet.

4 **Starting a second layer.** For a wild rose, pipe a smaller petal on top of the first layer; center it on the juncture of two petals in the bottom layer.

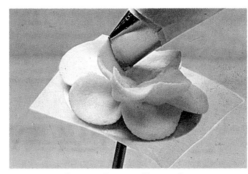

5 **Completing the small petals.** In the same way, pipe three more small, overlapping petals to complete the upper layer of the flower.

6 **Piping the center.** Use a plain tube to pipe a yellow center in the wild rose. Remove the flower from the nail and set it aside to dry.

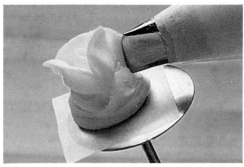

4 **A second layer.** Hold the bag at a less acute angle so that the petals stand out more. Pipe five larger, overlapping petals closer to the cone base.

5 **A third layer.** Farther down the cone, pipe a third layer of overlapping petals, centering each on a juncture of petals in the row above.

6 **Completing the rose.** Pipe petals down to the base. For each layer, hold the bag closer to a horizontal position so that the petals billow out.

Tailor-made Linings for Baking

All cakes are baked in pans, and to facilitate removal of the cakes after baking, almost all pans must be prepared before they are filled with batter. The method of preparation varies according to the pan and to the batter.

Most cakes are baked in round layer-cake pans 1½ inches [4 cm.] deep or in round cake pans 2½ inches [6 cm.] deep. When baking a separated-egg or butter-sponge batter *(pages 34-37),* the bottom of the pan should be buttered, floured and lined with parchment paper *(right, top);* this will help keep the bottom of the cake moist and prevent it from sticking during removal. The sides of the pan should be left unprepared: The light batter must cling to the sides for support as it rises. When the cake is done, it pulls away from the pan sides, making removal easier.

The batter for a creamed or one-bowl cake *(pages 50-51)* may also be baked in a shallow pan. The pan bottom and sides should be buttered and floured before the bottom is lined with parchment paper. A creamed cake rises less than a sponge-cake and its sugary batter sticks more than a sponge batter does, making removal difficult if the sides of the pan are not prepared.

Deep pans are frequently used to hold creamed-cake batters and require extra preparation. A dense batter baked in a large, deep pan requires long baking; unprotected, the sides of the cake would brown too much. To protect the cake, the pan is completely lined with parchment paper. A straight-sided spring-form pan should be buttered before it is lined, but it should not be floured on the sides *(right, below):* The paper would fall into the center of the pan before the batter was poured in. A sloping-sided loaf pan, however, can be both buttered and floured before it is lined *(opposite, below).*

Some cakes are baked in unprepared pans. An upside-down cake *(pages 62-63)* provides its own preparation. Cakes leavened by egg whites must cling to the pans as they rise, and the method of unmolding prevents sticking on the bottom.

Cupcakes are a special case. While the general rules for suiting the pan preparation to the batter can apply, cupcake pans usually are lined with frilled paper cases.

Covering the Bottom of a Shallow Pan

1 **Cutting out the paper.** Place a cake pan on a sheet of parchment paper. Hold the pan firmly down with one hand and outline its base on the paper with a pencil; remove the pan. With scissors, cut around the paper just inside the pencil line to produce a shape that will fit the pan bottom neatly. Cut as many parchment-paper shapes as you have pans.

Shielding the Sides for Longer Cooking

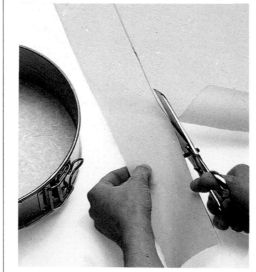

1 **Cutting the paper.** Butter the bottom and sides of a spring-form pan. Cut a parchment-paper disk to fit the bottom and place it inside. Cut a strip of paper slightly longer than the pan's circumference and as wide as its height.

2 **Lining the side.** Place the long strip of paper against the buttered sides of the pan. Butter one paper end and overlap the other on it. Press the paper firmly into place.

2 **Buttering the pan.** Melt butter in a small pan. Brush a thin layer of butter on each cake-pan bottom; for a creamed cake, brush the pan sides too. Sprinkle flour into the pan; shake the pan to distribute the flour, then invert the pan and tap it to remove the excess.

3 **Fitting in the paper.** Lay the shaped parchment-paper sheet on the base of each prepared pan; smooth the paper down with your hand.

A Neat Fit for a Rectangular Shape

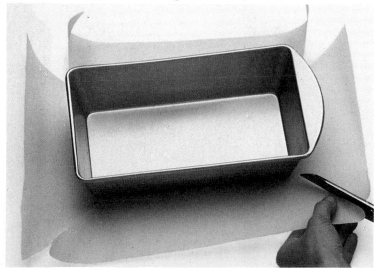

1 **Cutting corners.** On a work surface, lay a sheet of parchment paper long enough to cover the base and the sides of the pan. Set the pan at its center. With scissors, cut the paper from each corner to the nearest corner of the pan.

2 **Fitting the paper.** Brush the bottom and sides of the pan with melted butter and dust them with flour. Lay the paper in the pan *(above)* and press it securely against the sides and the base, overlapping the corner flaps neatly. Brush the undersides of the top flaps with more melted butter so that the lining sticks neatly to the corners of the pan.

1
Egg-Foam Cakes
Delicate Confections from Airy Batters

A metal cake tester is inserted halfway down into a lemon chiffon cake *(pages 40-41)* to test the cake for doneness. If the tester comes out clean—indicating that the batter in the center is no longer liquid—the cake is done. The cake's golden brown crust, and the fact that its sides have begun to pull away from the edges of the pan, are further clues that the cake is ready.

Most cakes rise because air trapped in their batters expands during baking. The most delicate of cakes—a group appropriately known as egg-foam cakes—are leavened by the air trapped in beaten eggs. For some of these cakes, egg whites alone provide the leavening: Angel food cakes, made with egg whites, sugar and flour *(pages 32-33),* are cakes of this type, as are meringue cakes, whose layers are composed only of beaten egg whites and sugar, sometimes enriched with nuts *(pages 42-43).* Richer egg-foam cakes, often called spongecakes *(pages 34-39),* contain both beaten whites and beaten yolks. These cakes may be made moister by adding butter to the batters, producing a confection known as *génoise* from its supposed origin in Genoa. Or the textures may be altered by substituting nuts or bread crumbs for the flour *(pages 44-47).*

No matter what the combination of ingredients, the success of all these cakes depends on aerating the eggs by beating them properly and by making sure that they do not lose their aeration when they are combined with other ingredients. Eggs—whether separated into whites and yolks or used whole—should be at room temperature when they are beaten: They will then hold three times as much air as chilled eggs because the protein they contain will be more elastic.

If you are planning to make an egg-foam cake, therefore, remove the eggs from the refrigerator at least 30 minutes before you begin mixing. As always, when beating egg whites alone, be sure that there is not a speck of yolk and that all the utensils used are absolutely free of fat.

Once the eggs have been aerated, the batters should be formed and baked quickly: If the eggs are allowed to stand, the air incorporated into them will begin to escape. Before you begin beating the eggs, have the cake pans prepared and the other ingredients measured and ready to use.

Egg-foam cakes are distinguished by their lightness, and this should be kept in mind when garnishing them. The airiest of these cakes—angel food and chiffon cakes—can support nothing heavier than simple fruit glazes, thin poured icings, such as glacé icing, or meringue-like boiled or seven-minute icing. Richer cakes may be decorated more elaborately with frostings such as butter cream, but the frostings should be applied with restraint: Thick, heavy coatings would only obscure the delectable qualities of the cakes beneath.

Angel Food: An Ethereal Structure from Egg Whites

Wonderfully light, an angel food cake is merely beaten egg whites, sugar, flour and flavorings (recipe, page 86). Careful handling ensures that the air in the whites puffs the batter properly.

The dry ingredients should be fine-grained: Use superfine sugar and cake flour, aerating each by repeated sifting and by stirring a little of the sugar into the flour to help keep the flour particles discrete and the mass of flour light.

As much air as they can hold should be beaten into the egg whites—they should triple in volume. But they must not be overbeaten, lest they become so dry and difficult to blend with the other ingredients that they lose air during the blending and thus produce a heavy cake. The rules for beating whites on pages 10-11 should be scrupulously obeyed. As insurance against drying, water or lemon juice can be added to the whites early in the beating process. The sugar added during the later stages of beating will dissolve into an elastic syrup that strengthens the whites and helps them hold air.

When the whites reach their fluffiest, they should be blended with the other ingredients. Bake the batter immediately to minimize air loss.

The batters for angel food cakes double in volume during baking and require deep pans. For small cakes, use loaf pans. A large cake should be baked in a tube cake pan. The tube conducts heat to the center of the batter; without it, large angel food cakes will dry out on the edges before the center bakes through.

An angel food cake is always hung upside down in its pan to cool so that the steam inside can condense on the bottom of the pan and help prevent sticking. The rims of some tube cake pans have legs that hold the pans in the air. If not, suspend the cake by sliding the tube onto the neck of a bottle or inverted funnel. If you are using loaf pans, balance the rims across the bottoms of two inverted pans.

These lightest of cakes should have the lightest of garnishes—glacé icing (pages 8-9), whipped cream or the fresh, juicy fruit used here.

1 **Sifting dry ingredients.** Measure sugar and sift it twice; sift and then measure flour. Add a little sugar and salt to the flour. Sift this mixture three times. Use two large bowls for this process, and choose a large spoon to transfer the flour-and-sugar mixture from the bowl to the sifter between successive siftings.

5 **Filling the pan.** Use a spatula to transfer the batter in dollops from the bowl to a clean, dry, high-sided cake pan. Deposit the dollops of batter as close together as possible in order to prevent large air pockets from forming holes in the finished cake.

6 **Eliminating air pockets.** Run a knife or spatula around the inside edge of the pan, around the tube, and through the middle of the batter to eliminate any large air pockets that may have formed. Bake the cake in a preheated 350° F. [180° C.] oven for about 45 minutes, or until a cake tester inserted in its center comes out clean.

7 **Cooling the cake.** Immediately invert the baked cake and allow it to cool upside down in the pan for an hour and a half, or until it feels cool to the touch.

2 **Beating egg whites.** Using a wire whisk, beat egg whites until they are frothy; if you are not using a copper bowl, add a little cream of tartar at this stage to help stabilize the egg whites. Then add a little tepid water and continue whisking until the egg whites form soft peaks. Fold in flavorings—here, vanilla and almond extracts.

3 **Adding dry ingredients.** Continue whisking the egg whites, adding sugar about a tablespoon [15 ml.] at a time until all of the sugar is incorporated. Sift a little of the sifted flour mixture evenly over the egg whites. Use a rubber spatula or your hand to gently fold in the flour.

4 **Finishing the batter.** Continue to sift and fold the flour-and-sugar mixture into the egg whites. Fold the mixture gently and quickly after each addition, stirring in a smooth, circular motion from the bottom of the bowl, up the side and over the top of the batter, until all of the flour has been absorbed.

8 **Turning out the cake.** Turn the cake pan right side up. To loosen the cake, run a knife around the inside edges of the pan. Invert the pan and tap it gently to turn out the cake onto the work surface. If the cake sticks, place the pan in a preheated 200° F. [100° C.] oven for five minutes to melt the sugar encrusted on the bottom.

9 **Serving the cake.** If you plan to serve the cake unfrosted, use your hand to gently rub away the brown crust—called the sugar bloom—to give the cake an even, white exterior *(inset)*. Transfer the cake to a serving plate; use a serrated knife—pressing only lightly—to cut the cake into wedges. Garnish the wedges; sugared strawberries are used for this demonstration.

Including Yolks for Moistness and Color

Richer and denser than angel food cakes because their batters contain egg yolks, spongecakes *(recipes, pages 92-103)* are nevertheless quite light. Like angel food cakes, spongecakes are leavened by air trapped in eggs—but in the yolks as well as the whites. As demonstrated here and on the following pages, different methods may be used to ensure the maximum aeration of both yolks and whites.

The lightest spongecakes are known as separated-egg spongecakes because of the method of forming them: Eggs are separated and the yolks are beaten with sugar until they double in volume from aeration. Beating can take as long as 20 minutes if done by hand; an electric mixer will reduce the time to 10 minutes. The whites are beaten with sugar until they form firm peaks and triple in volume; the whites may be beaten to a slightly drier stage than for angel food cakes because the batter receives additional moisture from egg yolks. To form the batter, the aerated whites are folded into the yolks along with sifted flour.

The batters for separated-egg spongecakes can be flavored with the grated peel of citrus fruits or with cocoa powder or chopped nuts. To allow citrus oils to permeate the batter, add the fruit peel to the yolk-and-sugar mixture. To make a chocolate cake, replace a third of the flour specified in a recipe with cocoa powder; cocoa powder is lightweight enough to be sifted into the batter with flour. Heavier flavorings such as chopped nuts are best folded in at the last moment.

The batter can be baked, as here, in layer-cake pans; it can be baked in jelly-roll pans to form thin sheets *(pages 72-73)*; and it makes excellent cupcakes. Any of the pans should be buttered and floured on the bottom, then lined with parchment paper to keep the egg-yolk-enriched batter from sticking.

Garnishes depend on the imagination of the cook: These versatile cakes can be matched with almost any filling or frosting. They make appealing presentations when simply garnished. Here, for instance, two spongecake layers are sandwiched together with jam. The topping is simple also—a patterned dusting of confectioners' sugar made with the aid of a parchment-paper stencil.

1 **Whisking yolks.** Separate eggs, dropping the whites into one bowl and the yolks into another. Gradually add sugar to the yolks and whisk the mixture until it falls from the whisk in a ribbon. Whisk the whites to the soft-peak stage, then add sugar gradually, whisking until the whites form firm peaks.

2 **Adding flour and whites.** Measure sifted cake flour, and sift half of the flour into the yolk mixture. Gently fold it in. Fold in a little of the whites to lighten the batter, then fold in half of the whites. Fold in more flour, then more whites, until all the ingredients are blended.

6 **Spreading a jam filling.** Heat fruit jam—in this case, raspberry jam—until it melts, then strain it. Use a narrow-bladed spatula to spread a thick layer of the jam over the exposed bottom surface of one of the cake layers *(above)*. Set the second layer on the first; its flat bottom will form a smooth top for the cake.

3 **Filling the pans.** Scrape the batter into prepared layer-cake pans, and gently smooth the top of the batter to make even layers. Place the pans in a preheated 350° F. [180° C.] oven and bake for 20 to 25 minutes.

4 **Testing for doneness.** When the cakes are golden and begin to shrink from the pans, press the center of each with your finger tips; it should feel springy and firm. An inserted tester should come out clean. Let the cakes cool in their pans on racks for about 10 minutes; then run a knife around the inner edge of each pan.

5 **Turning out the cakes.** Place a wire rack upside down over one cake layer. Holding the pan sandwiched between the racks, lift and turn the assembly upside down to turn out the cake. Lift off the pan and peel away the lining. Turn out the second layer. Let both layers cool for about 30 minutes.

7 **Stenciling.** Evenly space four strips of paper—each cut about 1 inch [2½ cm.] wide and slightly longer than the cake's diameter—across the cake. Sift confectioners' sugar over the surface and then lift away the paper.

8 **Serving.** Use a pastry brush to paint stripes of the jam in the areas between the stripes of sugar. Let the jam set. Slide the cake onto a plate, slice it into wedges, and serve (right).

A Classic Spongecake Enhanced with Butter

Instead of beating egg yolks and whites separately to achieve maximum aeration for a spongecake, you can leave the eggs whole and heat them gently while you beat; the heat partially coagulates the protein in the eggs and thus transforms them into an elastic mass, able to trap and hold large quantities of air. The fluffy, aerated mixture can then be folded together with melted butter, flour and flavorings to produce an especially rich butter-sponge batter (recipe, page 94).

Gentleness is the rule when heating the eggs: If they become too hot, they will form clots. The safest procedure is to whisk eggs and sugar over hot water in the top of a double boiler or in a heatproof bowl that can be suspended snugly inside a saucepan.

In either case, the vessel holding the eggs should rest above, not in, the water, and the water container should be set over low heat. The water must never be allowed to boil. As soon as the sugar has dissolved into the yolks and the mixture

is cream-colored, remove it from the heat and continue whisking—or beating with an electric mixer—until the volume of the egg mixture triples.

As with any spongecake, the egg mixture and other ingredients must be gently and quickly folded together to prevent loss of air. The batter may be flavored by any of the means—and baked in any of the pans—that are used for separated-egg spongecakes. Because butter spongecakes are moist, and thus unlikely to tear when sliced, the batter need not be baked in layer pans. Instead, it may be baked in one pan 2 inches [5 cm.] deep; the cake can then be trimmed and sliced into horizontal layers for decorating.

Like the other spongecakes, a butter spongecake lends itself to a variety of garnishes. In the demonstration on the following pages, a butter spongecake is metamorphosed into an elaborate, three-layer confection filled and frosted with chocolate-flavored rich butter cream and decorated with chopped nuts.

Finishing a cake of this type is not too difficult a task; a few pieces of special equipment, which can be purchased at a cakemaking-supply store, will ensure a professional result. Cardboard cake circles, which are available in standard cake diameters, provide a firm foundation for the bottom layer, allowing you to support the cake in one hand while you apply frosting and garnishes to the sides. A flexible, narrow-bladed spatula is useful for spreading the frosting.

For the later stages of frosting—covering the top of the cake and smoothing the top and sides, as well as applying borders—a cake-decorating wheel is invaluable. The wheel is a round, flat platform that may be rotated on a standing base so that you can trim the cake evenly on all sides. Surface decorations can be made with a pastry bag filled with frosting and fitted with any of a variety of tubes. The techniques for forming different decorations with a pastry bag are demonstrated on pages 22-25.

3 **Folding in flour and butter.** Draw a spatula along the bottom of the bowl, and bring it up around the sides to fold the flour gently into the egg-and-sugar mixture (above, left). Then add a little melted butter that has been cooled to room temperature (right), and use the same motion to distribute it. In two more stages, alternately add the remaining flour and butter, folding gently after each addition until the ingredients are well blended.

4 **Filling the pan.** Pour the batter into a pan that has been buttered and floured on the bottom, then lined on the bottom with parchment paper. Bake the cake in a preheated 350° F. [180° C.] oven for 35 to 40 minutes, until it feels springy to the touch and begins to shrink from the sides of the pan.

1 **Beating eggs and sugar.** In a large bowl, whisk eggs and sugar together. Pour hot water into a saucepan, set the pan over low heat and place the bowl on top. Whisk the mixture *(above, left)*—for five to 10 minutes, until it begins to thicken. Remove the saucepan and bowl from the heat, and continue to beat the mixture until it triples in bulk and falls in a thick ribbon *(right)*—this will take about 20 minutes by hand or 10 minutes with an electric mixer.

2 **Adding flour.** Beat flavoring into the egg-and-sugar mixture—almond extract was used here. Then sift in about one third of the flour required, distributing it evenly.

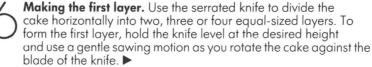

5 **Removing the sugar bloom.** Cool the cake for about 10 minutes, then turn it out of the pan and peel off the lining. Let the cake cool completely; invert it so that its brown top crust is uppermost. With a serrated knife, cut away the crust—the sugar bloom—to make a flat surface.

6 **Making the first layer.** Use the serrated knife to divide the cake horizontally into two, three or four equal-sized layers. To form the first layer, hold the knife level at the desired height and use a gentle sawing motion as you rotate the cake against the blade of the knife. ▶

7 **Providing support.** Slide the first layer of cake onto a cardboard cake circle of a diameter ½ inch [1 cm.] greater than the cake's. Slice the remaining cake into two layers. Make brandy-flavored sugar syrup *(recipe, page 164)*. Make frosting—in this case, rich butter cream flavored with half the usual chocolate *(recipe, page 166)*.

8 **Glazing the layers.** To add flavor and moisture to the cake, use a pastry brush to paint a thin coat of the flavored sugar syrup over the top and sides of the cake layer on the cake circle.

9 **Filling between layers.** Use a flexible, narrow-bladed metal spatula to spread a coat of butter cream about ¼ inch [6 mm.] thick over the top of the glazed layer. Gently position the center layer on top of the first; glaze it with sugar syrup *(Step 8)* and spread butter cream over its top.

12 **Combing.** Hold a decorating comb against the side of the cake, and turn the wheel to move the cake against the comb. To groove the top, begin with one end of the comb in the center and make one complete turn of the wheel; then reposition the comb over the ungrooved area, aligning its teeth with existing grooves *(above)*, and make a second complete turn.

13 **Piping a shell border.** Fit a pastry bag with a large No. 2B star tube *(pages 20-21)* and half-fill the bag with butter cream. Holding the pastry bag at an oblique angle to the edge of the cake, squeeze it with an even pressure as you turn the wheel to make a shell border around the edge of the cake.

10 **Frosting the sides.** Invert the final cake layer onto the cake; its flat bottom forms a smooth top for frosting. Slide a spatula under the cake circle, and raise it so that you can lift the cake up on one hand. Rotate the cake circle as you apply butter cream all around the sides of the cake, smoothing it with the spatula.

11 **Frosting the top.** Transfer the cake to a decorating wheel. Turn the wheel slowly as you spread butter cream across the top of the cake (above, left). When the cake is completely frosted, hold the spatula vertically, with its blade flush against the projecting edge of the cake circle, and turn the wheel to remove excess frosting from the sides of the cake. Smooth the top of the cake. Then use the spatula to sweep excess butter cream around the edge of the top inward, spreading it across the top (right).

14 **Decorating with nuts.** Blanch, peel, coarsely chop, and toast almonds (pages 18-19). Sprinkle a few almonds on top of the cake. Lift the cake in one hand, supporting the cake circle at its base. Use your free hand to scoop up some of the chopped nuts and press them gently into the side of the cake along its bottom (right). Continue all the way around the cake; place the finished cake on a serving plate.

Chiffon Cake: A Marriage of Methods

Invented in the 1920s as an easy-to-make variation of angel food cake *(pages 32-33)*, chiffon cake includes ingredients and techniques drawn from the baking of both angel food cakes and spongecakes. Chiffon-cake batter rises almost as high as angel food batter because it is leavened not only by the air in beaten egg whites, but also by the carbon dioxide that baking powder produces and by the steam rising from the liquid in the exceptionally moist batter. Much of the liquid used in a chiffon-cake batter is in the form of vegetable oil, and the fat in the oil—as well as the fat in egg yolks, which are also included in chiffon cakes—gives the finished cake a moisture and richness similar to that of a butter spongecake.

The characteristics of these various ingredients help to make the formation of a chiffon-cake batter a simple affair in-deed. The presence of baking powder, for instance, eliminates the need to aerate the flour and sugar by repeated siftings, as required for angel food batters: The dry ingredients are sifted together only once, to blend them and remove any lumps. Nor do the egg yolks require the lengthy beating used to incorporate air into a spongecake. The yolks are mixed with flavorless vegetable oil, then stirred into the dry ingredients without further ado. The batter thus quickly formed is further lightened by beaten egg whites.

Batters of this type may be flavored in any of a variety of ways *(recipes, pages 91-92)*. Vanilla or almond extract may be added to some; others, as in this demonstration, are flavored with fruit juice and grated fruit peel. For a chocolate chiffon cake, cocoa powder may be substituted for part of the flour.

Because chiffon batters increase tremendously in volume during their baking, chiffon cakes should be baked in the same deep pans used for baking angel food cakes. And, as for angel food cakes, the pans should be unbuttered so that the rising batters can cling to the sides.

Again like angel food cakes, chiffon cakes should be cooled upside down in their pans. However, these cakes do not peak quite so high as angel food cakes, so the pans can simply be inverted onto racks for cooling—there is no danger of the racks crushing the top of the cakes.

As their name implies, chiffon cakes are very light confections and are best complemented by light garnishes. Fresh fruit, whipped cream, ice cream or the simple glacé icing *(page 8)* used in the demonstration on these pages all make appropriate accompaniments.

3 **Baking the cake.** Pour the batter into a deep, unbuttered cake pan—a fluted tube pan is used in this demonstration. Bake the cake in a preheated 325° F. [160° C.] oven for 55 minutes, or until a tester inserted into the center of the cake comes out clean.

4 **Cooling the cake.** Remove the cake from the oven and immediately invert the pan onto a rack. Allow the cake to cool upside down in the pan for about an hour. Turn the cake right side up, and carefully run a knife or skewer around the inside edges of the pan to loosen the cake; turn the cake out onto a rack set over a large baking pan.

5 **Mixing icing.** Sift confectioners' sugar into a bowl. Gradually stir in water or fruit juice and a flavoring—in this case, strained fresh lemon juice and grated lemon peel *(recipe, page 165)*. The icing is ready when it is creamy and coats the back of a metal spoon—if it is too thin, add more sugar; if it is too thick, add more juice.

1 **Combining egg yolks and flour.** Sift flour, sugar, baking powder and salt into a large bowl. Make a well in the center of the mound. Stir lightly beaten egg yolks into flavorless vegetable oil, pour this mixture into the well and, to prevent lumps, use a flat wire whisk or a fork to stir it into the dry ingredients. Add lemon juice, water and grated lemon peel, and stir until smooth.

2 **Folding in egg whites.** Beat egg whites until they form stiff peaks, adding cream of tartar at the foamy stage if you are not using a copper bowl. Spoon a quarter of the beaten whites into the batter (above, left) folding them in with a spatula to lighten the batter. Then add the remaining egg whites, and gently but thoroughly fold them in (right).

6 **Icing the cake.** Spoon the glacé icing over the top of the cake (above), allowing it to drip down the sides; the baking pan will catch excess icing. Leave the cake on the rack for about 15 minutes, until the icing has set and is firm to the touch. Then transfer the cake to a serving plate. Use a serrated knife to divide the cake into wedges for serving (right).

Crisp Meringue Layers Swathed in Butter Cream

Many cakes based on beaten eggs or egg whites derive a delectably light texture from batters made without flour. The lightest of these are meringue cakes *(recipes, pages 87-90)*. These are formed by beating egg whites with sugar until they form a stiff meringue that, baked in thin sheets, produces cake layers.

The meringue used to make the layers includes large proportions of sugar for strength: Allow 4 tablespoons [60 ml.] of sugar for each egg white. The meringue may be flavored with any extract, with ground hazelnuts or almonds as shown here, or with shredded coconut. Chocolate meringue is made by folding cocoa powder into the beaten sugar and whites.

The layers are formed on baking sheets lined with parchment paper and may be given any shape or size you please— circles, squares, diamonds or, as shown here, hearts. You may make as many layers as you want; for this demonstration, three layers are made from a meringue containing four egg whites. To ensure that all of the layers match, form them with the aid of a cardboard template cut in the appropriate shape. Use the template as a guide to trace the outlines for the layers on the parchment paper lining the baking sheets. You can spread the meringue on the sheets with a spatula, but piping it from a pastry bag is neater.

The cooking of meringue layers is a process of drying them out: Long periods in a slow oven are needed to make the layers firm, crisp and cream-colored— not brown. The baked layers are brittle and must be handled carefully. However, cracked layers can be patched with frosting when the cake is assembled.

The choice of fillings, frostings and garnishes for the cakes is up to the cook. But a crisp meringue makes a fine foil for rich, creamy mixtures such as whipped cream or rich butter cream of any flavor or color *(recipe, page 166)*. In this demonstration, the layers are sandwiched together and frosted with vanilla-flavored rich butter cream. The top is dusted with cocoa powder to add color, then it is decorated with confectioners' sugar in a design made with a stencil purchased at an art-supply store. Chocolate curls *(pages 16-17)* garnish the sides of the cake.

1 Drawing guidelines. Line three baking sheets with parchment paper. Using a template—a cardboard heart is shown—draw the outline of each layer on the lining of each sheet. Reserve the template. To keep the meringue from sticking, brush the area inside the outline with melted butter and then dust the area with cornstarch.

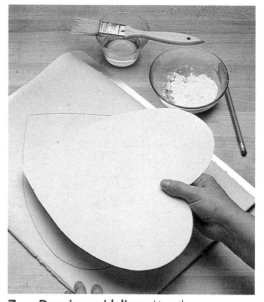

2 Preparing the meringue. Grind nuts—blanched and peeled almonds are used here—to a fine consistency *(pages 18-19)* and mix the nuts with sugar. In a large bowl, whisk egg whites until they form soft peaks. Keep whisking, gradually adding sugar, until the whites form stiff, glossy peaks. Gently fold in the sugar-and-nut mixture, a little at a time.

6 Frosting the sides. Slip a spatula under the template and raise it so that you can support the cake on one hand. Gently spread butter cream evenly around the sides of the cake.

7 Dusting the top. Transfer the cake to a decorating wheel to frost the top and to remove any excess frosting from the sides and top *(page 39, Step 11)*. When the entire cake is smoothly frosted, sift cocoa powder over the top *(above)*.

3 **Piping outlines.** Gently scoop the meringue mixture into a pastry bag fitted with a large No. 4 plain tube *(pages 20-21)*, filling the bag half-full. Following the pattern drawn on each paper-lined baking sheet, outline the shape with meringue piped in a cylinder ½ inch [1 cm.] high. To ensure even thickness, pipe a second cylinder of meringue in the center of the pattern.

4 **Filling the outlines.** Using a narrow-bladed spatula, gently place dollops of meringue inside the piped outlines on each baking sheet, and spread the meringue within the outlines to make layers that are level and smooth. Bake the layers in a preheated 170° F. [75° C.] oven for one hour, or until they are firm and dry. Transfer the meringue layers to racks to cool completely.

5 **Filling the layers.** Make a vanilla-flavored rich butter cream. Gently place one of the meringue layers on the cardboard template, and use a spatula to spread frosting ¼ to ½ inch [6 mm. to 1 cm.] thick. Position a second meringue layer on the first and cover the second layer with butter cream. Set the last meringue layer on top.

8 **Stenciling.** Position a paper stencil—in this case, of a rose—on the cake top; the cocoa powder will keep the stencil from sticking. Sift confectioners' sugar over the stencil *(above)*. Take care not to let any sugar fall on the exposed cocoa powder.

9 **Serving.** Remove the stencil and transfer the cake to a serving plate. Press chocolate curls around the base. Chill the cake for two hours to let the meringue soften. Serve in wedges.

Luxurious Replacements for Flour

A cake made without flour achieves distinctive richness when its batter includes egg yolks as well as whites and when the flour is replaced—as it is in many Austrian recipes—by ingredients such as plain cookie, cracker or bread crumbs, ground nuts, or a combination of these ingredients *(recipes, pages 98, 134-135)*. Batters of this type are formed in much the same way as a batter for a separated-egg spongecake *(pages 34-35)*; that is, the yolks and whites are beaten separately in order to aerate them as much as possible, and are then folded together with the other ingredients to form a batter. In the demonstration on these pages, the batter contains ground hazelnuts *(pages 18-19)* and bread crumbs made from crustless, firm, homemade-type white bread in a food processor.

The batter may be baked in round, deep cake pans, then sliced horizontal-ly to form layers, or it may be baked in layer-cake pans. To shape a rectangular cake, spread the batter in a jelly-roll pan; after baking, the thin sheet of cake can be sliced into strips to form the cake layers.

The textured, nut-laden cake layers can be filled and covered with any type of smooth, creamy frosting—a rich butter cream is used here. Cakes of this type are traditionally decorated in a fashion that marks off individual portions, a reflection of the fact that, in European pastry shops, the cakes are displayed whole but sold by the piece. In this demonstration, for instance, the long bottom edges of the cake display a border of semicircular chocolate shapes, each the width of a cake slice *(pages 16-17)*.

On the top of the cake, a hazelnut dipped in chocolate and set in the center of a piped butter-cream button marks the center of each slice.

1 **Aerating eggs.** Separate eggs. Beat the yolks with sugar until they are smooth and thick, and stir into them freshly grated lemon peel mixed with lemon juice. Beat the whites with sugar until they form stiff peaks. Fold bread crumbs and a small amount of the whites into the yolks, then fold in a sprinkling of ground nuts—here, hazelnuts.

5 **Assembling the layers.** Prepare a vanilla-flavored rich butter cream *(recipe, page 98)*. Set a cake layer on a serving board, and use a flexible metal spatula to spread butter cream on it to a depth of ¼ to ½ inch [6 mm. to 1 cm.]. Stack and frost the remaining layers in turn, leaving the last layer unfrosted.

6 **Frosting the sides and top.** Spread dollops of butter cream around the sides of the cake; then frost the top. Remove excess frosting from the sides and top of the cake.

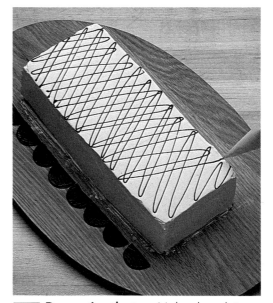

7 **Decorating the top.** Make chocolate semicircles, each as wide as the cake slices are to be. Make a paper pastry bag, fill it with melted chocolate, and decorate the cake top with stringwork *(page 25)*. With a damp towel, clean frosting from the serving board. Press the semicircles into the base of the cake along each side.

2 **Folding ingredients in.** Fold in the remaining egg whites and ground nuts alternately until all of the ingredients are combined. Fold gently, and stop folding when no streaks of white show.

3 **Filling the pan.** Pour the batter into a jelly-roll pan that has been buttered, floured and lined with parchment paper *(pages 28-29)*. With a spatula, spread the batter into a level layer. Bake in a preheated 350° F. [180° C.] oven for 15 to 20 minutes, until the cake springs back when gently pressed. Cool it in the pan for five minutes, then turn it out and peel off the paper.

4 **Cutting out layers.** Let the cake cool completely—this takes about 30 minutes. With a ruler as a guide and a long serrated knife, cut off ¼ inch [6 mm.] all around the cake to make the edges even. Then position the ruler along one long edge, and slice across the cake at equal intervals to divide it into four identical rectangular sections.

8 **Marking slices.** Insert wooden picks as marks in the center of the cake top, aligning each with the center of a chocolate semicircle. Remove each pick, pipe butter cream in its place, using a large No. 1 plain tube, and top with a chocolate-dipped hazelnut.

9 **Serving.** Using the side and top decorations as guides, cut the cake into cross sections. Each slice should have a hazelnut centered on top.

Opulence from Chestnuts and Chocolate

When fresh chestnuts take the place of flour in the batter for a separated-egg spongecake *(recipe, page 96)*, the resulting cake is dense, moist and particularly rich: Chestnuts are high in both starch and liquid. If the cake is not to become too heavy, the chestnuts—available in November and December—must be carefully prepared.

The first step—shelling the nuts—is the most time-consuming. The usual procedure for shelling chestnuts is to cut a cross in each shell, then boil the nuts for a few minutes to soften and loosen the shells and bitter inner skins. However, when the chestnuts are treated this way, the flesh absorbs water and becomes too moist for use in a cake batter. Instead, the nuts should be left uncut and boiled for 20 minutes, after which the shells and skins will be soft and loose enough to be peeled off with the aid of a sharp knife.

To blend easily into the batter, the nut meat must be puréed, but the puréeing must be done in such a way that the flesh

is aerated: Chestnut meat that is puréed in a food processor or with a mortar and pestle will become a heavy mass. Instead, force the chestnuts through a coarse-meshed sieve or a food mill that is fitted with a coarse disk, or press the chestnuts through a potato ricer to get long, light strands of flesh.

With the preparation of the nuts complete, the forming of the batter procceds as for that of a separated-egg spongecake. Egg yolks and egg whites are beaten separately, then folded together with the chestnuts and any other flavorings. Ground almonds and rum are used here, but you could substitute ground hazelnuts, chopped candied fruits or grated chocolate, and brandy or bourbon.

Any icing or frosting will enhance the cake and, for extra flavor, the cake may be given a thin coat of fruit glaze before it is decorated. Rich and sweet, the cake has an affinity for chocolate: In this demonstration, a thin chocolate icing provides both filling and coating.

1 Peeling the chestnuts. Boil unshelled, uncut chestnuts in water for 20 minutes. Take the pan off the heat and lift out the chestnuts one at a time, leaving the rest to soak in the pan. Use a small, sharp knife to slit the shell of each chestnut and cut it away; use the knife or your fingernails to peel away any skin that does not pull away with the shell.

4 Baking. Transfer the batter to a springform pan that has been buttered, floured and lined on the bottom. Bake in a preheated 350° F. [180° C.] oven for 45 to 60 minutes, or until a tester comes out clean. Cool the cake for five minutes. Remove the pan sides and cool the cake for 20 minutes. Invert it onto a rack, remove the pan bottom and paper, and cool completely.

5 Layering the cake. Make thin chocolate icing *(recipe, page 165)*. Keep half of the icing warm; chill the rest and beat it until it is thick and fluffy. Split the cake into two layers *(page 37, Step 6)*. Set the bottom layer, split side up, on a cardboard cake circle. Cover it with the whipped chocolate icing.

6 Glazing the cake. Place the second layer on top of the first. Place the cake on a wire rack set over a piece of wax paper, and use a pastry brush to coat the top and sides of the cake with apricot jam glaze *(recipe, page 167)*. Let the glaze firm for 20 minutes.

2 **Ricing the chestnuts.** Press the chestnuts through a ricer into a bowl *(inset)* and sprinkle them with rum. In a large mixing bowl, beat egg yolks with sugar until the mixture is pale and thick. Sprinkle the riced chestnuts over the yolks a little at a time *(above)*, folding gently with a rubber spatula after each addition. Fold in blanched, peeled and ground almonds.

3 **Folding in egg whites.** Beat egg whites until they are stiff but not dry. Fold about a third of the beaten whites into the egg-yolk mixture to lighten it; then gently fold in the remaining whites.

7 **Frosting.** Place the cake on its rack over a pan, and pour the reserved, warm icing over it *(inset)*. If necessary, use a spatula to spread the icing. Let the icing set for 10 minutes. Transfer the cake to a serving plate; chill it for an hour to harden the icing. Garnish the cake with a candied chestnut that has been dipped in confectioners' sugar. Serve the cake in wedges *(right)*.

2
Creamed Cakes
Melting Richness from Beaten Butter

How to trap air in butter
Dealing with dried fruits
Making the most of a coconut
Reddening chocolate for devil's food

When a large proportion of butter is included in a batter, the resulting cake is rich, dense, moist and long-keeping. Batters of this type are too heavy to be leavened with beaten eggs. Instead, the butter itself provides the primary means of leavening: It is creamed with sugar—beaten and folded so that it entraps as much air as possible—before it is combined with such other ingredients as eggs, flour and flavorings to make a batter. During baking, the air in the butter expands and the moisture in the eggs turns to steam, raising and lightening the cake.

Among creamed cakes, poundcake *(pages 50-51)* is the paradigm. It takes its name from its classic recipe, which includes 1 pound [½ kg.] each of butter, sugar, eggs and flour; in France, the same cake is known as *quatre-quarts,* or "four quarters," because each of the four ingredients makes up a quarter of the batter. Buttery, moist and strong, poundcake lends itself to a number of interesting variations. The thick batter, for instance, can easily support the large amounts of dried fruits and nuts required to make a traditional fruitcake *(pages 52-53),* and the finished cake will be cohesive enough that it will not disintegrate when soaked in the rum or brandy that gives fruitcake extra fragrance. If a basic pound-cake batter is further strengthened with almond paste, it can be baked with such heavy toppings as fresh fruit: The density of the batter prevents the fruit from sinking into the cake during baking, and the result is a handsome confection that comes out of the oven with a juicy, ready-made garnish *(opposite and pages 54-55).*

Classic creamed cakes certainly can hold up heavy fillings and frostings such as fudge, but the assemblies would be cloyingly rich if garnished in this fashion; these cakes are better finished with sprinklings of sugar or with clear fruit glazes. Cakes firm enough for the thick frostings traditional to American layer cakes—but relatively light in texture—are made by slightly reducing the amount of butter in a creamed-cake batter. Less butter means that less air can be incorporated into the cake mixture: These cakes require a little help in leavening from baking powder, which releases carbon dioxide during baking to further lighten the batter. The three-layer cake filled and coated with coconut frosting demonstrated on pages 56-57 is a cake of this type; so are the chocolate cupcakes shown on pages 58-59.

Half of a pitted red plum is gently placed amidst the walnuts adorning a creamed-cake batter. Rich in butter and eggs, the batter was further fortified with almond paste to give it the strength necessary to keep the heavy fruit afloat during baking.

A Traditional Poundcake

Like the many creamed cakes it exemplifies, a poundcake *(recipe, page 103)* acquires richness from butter and lightness from air trapped in the butter. The secret of its success lies in creaming the butter—or handling it in a way that forces it to incorporate the most air possible—before other ingredients are added.

The butter should be just at room temperature: Chilled butter will be too rigid to manipulate; butter allowed to warm to the melting point will be too liquid to hold air. For the right malleability, remove the butter from the refrigerator about 30 minutes before you start mixing the cake. When the butter is ready, it will feel firm and cool, and a finger tip pressed onto the top will leave an indentation.

Creaming is essentially a repeated, rapid folding of the mass of butter; each folding action traps and distributes air bubbles. As soon as the butter is fluffy enough to fold easily—this takes only moments—sugar is folded in. The sugar provides sweetness, of course, but it has another advantage: The sharp edges of the crystals cut into the butter, creating minute pockets for air.

Creaming should take no longer than five minutes. When it is complete, the sweetened butter will be pale and almost doubled in volume. The butter is now ready for the addition of other ingredients: eggs, which provide extra leavening during baking in the forms of steam and of air trapped in the yolks; flour; and any of the flavorings commonly used in poundcakes—grated lemon peel and juice or vanilla extract, for instance.

The best implements for forming a creamed-cake batter are a wooden paddle or spoon and a strong arm. The textured wood surface roughens the butter, creating tiny depressions that hold air, and the development of the batter is most easily controlled when working by hand. It is possible to use an electric mixer to form the batter; indeed, some batters are so dense that a mixer is a necessity *(pages 54-55)*. Mixers, however, work so quickly that they can easily overbeat the batter, causing the butter to melt and the eggs to separate from the other ingredients; the result will be a heavy, lumpy cake. This can be prevented by operating a mixer in spurts and checking the batter after each mixing.

Dense creamed-cake batters require relatively long baking times, and the oven temperature must be kept low to prevent overbrowning. If you bake the cakes in shallow layer-cake pans—thus reducing the baking time required—the buttered and floured pans need no more than a bottom lining of parchment paper *(pages 28-29)*. However, cakes baked in deep loaf, tube cake or spring-form pans will spend lengthy periods in the oven. To prevent the cake surfaces from absorbing too much heat from the pans and overbrowning, line the pans completely.

4 **Filling the baking pan.** With a rubber spatula, scoop the poundcake batter into a buttered, floured and lined loaf pan. Spread the batter with the spatula to keep it of an even thickness and fill the pan no more than two thirds full. Smooth the top of the batter. Rap the pan on the work surface to eliminate air pockets.

5 **Baking and cooling.** Bake the cake in a preheated 300° F. [150° C.] oven for one and one half hours, or until a tester inserted in the center comes out clean. Transfer the pan to a rack and let the cake cool in the pan. Turn the cooled cake out onto your hand, lift off the pan, and peel off the parchment paper.

1 **Creaming butter and sugar.** With a wooden paddle, as here, or a spoon, mash softened butter against the side of a bowl. Then fold the mass over itself into the center of the bowl. Mash and fold for about one minute, until the butter is fluffy. Then sprinkle in sugar, a little at a time, continuing the creaming strokes after each addition.

2 **Adding eggs.** Cream the butter and sugar for about five minutes, until they are pale and light. Then break an egg into the mixture and beat it in, lifting the bottom of the mass to the top. Repeat with the remaining eggs, making sure each egg is incorporated before adding the next. Beat in flavoring— vanilla extract was used here.

3 **Stirring in flour.** Beat the mixture for about five minutes more, until it is again light, pale and fluffy. Then sift in flour, a little at a time, stirring the batter gently after each addition just enough to incorporate the flour: Further vigorous beating at this stage would release air from the batter and reduce the volume of the finished cake.

6 **Slicing and serving.** Turn the cake right side up onto a serving board and, if you like, garnish the top with confectioners' sugar or a jam glaze (recipe, page 167). Use a serrated knife to cut the cake into slices that are ½ to 1½ inches [1 to 4 cm.] thick. Stale leftover poundcake can be toasted and served with butter, cinnamon and sugar.

An Extravaganza Packed with Fruit

The flavorings for many creamed cakes are as simple as grated lemon peel or vanilla extract, but the dense batters can support extravagant quantities of heavy dried and candied fruits and nuts. The finished cakes are both porous and strong, easily absorbing spirits such as brandy, which, like dried fruits and nuts, are ingredients included in traditional fruitcakes *(recipes, pages 124-130)*. Their batters are formed as are those for other creamed cakes *(pages 50-51)*; careful handling of the fruits and nuts ensures an even texture, and preparing the pans lets the cakes cook to just the right stage.

Small dried fruits such as raisins do not require special preparation. Larger dried fruits such as apricots should be cut up, and nuts should be blanched and peeled *(pages 18-19)*. Candied fruits and peel contain large amounts of sugar syrup. If they are sticky, blanch them in boiling water, then drain and dry the fruits and peel. To keep fruits and nuts scattered throughout the batter rather than clinging together and sinking, chop them fine and toss them with flour.

Like most dense cakes, fruitcakes require long, slow baking; they are so high in sugar that the oven temperature must be gradually reduced to prevent overbrowning. As additional insurance, the pan should be lined with parchment paper *(pages 28-29)*. If the batter comes to within 2 inches [5 cm.] of the rim, a high paper collar should be wrapped around the pan *(Step 6)* to deflect heat from the top of the cake. This acts as a guarantee against overbrowning and also prevents the development of a high dome, which would make decorating difficult.

Fruitcakes are so moist that they will keep, properly wrapped *(Step 7)*, for up to a year. The cakes should, in fact, be stored for at least two weeks before serving to let their flavors develop. For added flavor and moisture, they may be sprinkled with brandy, whiskey or rum after they have been baked and cooled, and at frequent intervals during their storage.

Matured fruitcakes can be served with a sprinkling of confectioners' sugar or, as here, with fruit decorations and glaze. English fruitcake *(recipe, page 130)* is traditionally covered with a layer of almond paste and a coat of royal icing.

1 Preparing fruit. Chop candied orange peel and peeled, blanched almonds, and cut candied cherries into halves or quarters. Place these in a large bowl. Add dark and golden raisins and dried currants. Sprinkle a few spoonfuls of flour over the mixture and, with your hands, toss the fruits and nuts to coat them with flour.

2 Creaming. Beat eggs to make them easier to incorporate into the extremely dense batter. Grate fresh lemon and orange peels into a small bowl. In a large bowl, cream together butter and brown sugar until the mixture lightens in color and doubles in volume *(page 51, Step 1)*. Beat in molasses. Beat in the grated peels and the eggs.

6 Baking. Cut a long strip of brown paper 1 inch [2½ cm.] wider than the cake pan is tall, wrap it around the outside of the pan, and secure it with string. Transfer the cake pan to a preheated 325° F. [160° C.] oven. After 20 minutes, reduce the heat to 300° F. [150° C.]. Bake for 40 minutes more, then reduce the heat to 275° F. [140° C.]. Bake the cake for one hour or so longer; it is done when a tester inserted into the center comes out clean.

7 Brushing on liquor. Let the cake cool in the pan for about an hour. Place a sheet of foil on a work surface and cover the foil with a double thickness of cheesecloth. Turn out the cake onto the cheesecloth and permit it to cool completely. Pierce the top all over and brush on rum, brandy or whiskey. Wrap the cake in the cheesecloth and brush more spirits onto the cloth. Wrap the cake in foil and store it in the refrigerator for at least two weeks.

3 **Adding dry ingredients.** Sift together flour, salt, grated nutmeg, and mixed spices such as the ground cinnamon and cloves used here. Sift the mixture over the butter and eggs, a little at a time, stirring the batter just enough to blend it after each addition. After the flour is incorporated, stir in rum.

4 **Adding fruits and nuts.** Scoop up the flour-dusted fruit-and-nut mixture and sprinkle it over the batter, two large spoonfuls at a time. Blending gently with a wooden spoon or paddle, spread the mixture evenly through the batter. Continue adding and blending until all of the fruits and nuts are incorporated.

5 **Filling the pan.** Scoop the batter into a deep cake pan or, as here, a spring-form pan that has been buttered and lined with parchment paper (pages 28-29). After dropping each spoonful of batter into the pan, smooth it out evenly. Rap the pan on the work surface to eliminate air pockets.

8 **Decorating and serving.** Set the matured cake on a rack and decorate the top with candied fruit slices. Brush apricot jam glaze over the cake and fruit (above). Let the glaze set for 30 minutes before putting the cake on a platter for serving (inset).

Fortifying Butter with Almond Paste

Almond paste *(recipe, page 167)*—a mixture of ground almonds, sugar and eggs that is rich in structure-building protein—enhances the taste of creamed-cake batters and also gives them great tensile strength. Batters fortified in this manner can keep afloat such heavy additions as the baked-on topping of fruit shown here; the finished cakes are dense and close-grained enough to be cut into the small, sharp-edged shapes required to construct petits fours.

The use of almond paste dictates some changes in the methods of creaming and mixing normally used for creamed cakes. The paste is so hard and cohesive that it must be broken into crumbs and the grainy crumbs must be partially dissolved before they can be combined with other batter ingredients. Beating sugar and egg white into the paste accomplishes both tasks: The sharp sugar crystals help to break up the paste, and the moisture from the egg white dissolves it.

Batters that include almond paste are so stiff that only the strongest cooks can work in by hand enough air for leavening. For most cooks, an electric mixer is a necessity. Because the mixer works so quickly, there is a danger of overbeating the batter and melting the butter, thereby losing entrapped air. To minimize mixing time, do not cream the butter separately before adding other ingredients; instead, working in rapid spurts, beat the butter directly into the prepared almond paste and add the eggs in quick succession. Stop beating as soon as the batter looks light and fluffy, then mix in the flour; as with hand-mixing, the flour must be added gradually and stirred in gently to prevent the escape of air.

A batter of this type may be baked in a loaf pan as a poundcake is *(pages 50-51)*, in a deep cake pan as is a fruitcake *(pages 52-53)*, in a jelly-roll pan to form thin sheets for petits fours *(pages 76-77)*, or in layer-cake pans. For a topping, the batter in the pan may be decorated with firm fruits—halved nectarines or plums and sliced apples or pears, for instance.

The finished cake is so rich that toppings and fillings should be light. Use jam glazes *(recipe, page 167)* or dustings of granulated or confectioners' sugar for garnishes.

1 Preparing almond paste. Place almond paste and sugar in a large bowl. Using an electric mixer, beat the ingredients at low speed until the paste is reduced to coarse crumbs. Separate an egg and blend the white into the mixture; reserve the yolk.

2 Beating. Add softened butter to the blended paste, and beat the mixture at low speed until the butter is just blended in. Similarly, beat in whole eggs and the reserved egg yolk, one at a time. Add grated lemon peel. Increase the speed of the mixer to medium, and beat the batter until it just lightens in color and becomes fluffy in texture.

6 Glazing the fruit. Place confectioners' sugar in a sieve set over a bowl. Make apricot jam glaze. With a pastry brush, paint the tops of the plum halves with a thin, even coat of the apricot jam glaze.

7 Sprinkling on sugar. Holding the sieve containing the confectioners' sugar about 4 inches [10 cm.] above the top of the cake, shake it gently to dust the cake with the sugar. The sugar should cover the top completely to a depth of about ¼ inch [6 mm.].

3 **Adding flour.** Decrease the speed of the mixer to low. Add sifted flour, a little at a time, beating after each addition just enough to moisten the flour and disperse it. After all of the flour has been incorporated, divide the batter between two layer-cake pans that have been buttered and floured, then lined on the bottom.

4 **Topping and baking.** Arrange walnut halves evenly on one layer; place plum halves, round sides up, among the nuts. Bake the layers in a preheated 350° F. [180° C.] oven for 30 minutes, or until a tester inserted in the center of each layer comes out clean. The fruit-covered layer may need a few minutes more than the plain one.

5 **Assembling the cake.** Cool the layers in the pans, then invert them onto racks; finally invert them again onto cardboard cake circles for easy handling. Spread the plain layer with a thick, even coat of warmed jam—plum is used here. Carefully lift the fruited layer and slide it off the cardboard onto the top of the first layer.

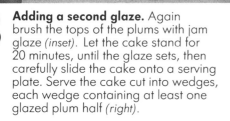

8 **Adding a second glaze.** Again brush the tops of the plums with jam glaze *(inset)*. Let the cake stand for 20 minutes, until the glaze sets, then carefully slide the cake onto a serving plate. Serve the cake cut into wedges, each wedge containing at least one glazed plum half *(right)*.

An Old-fashioned American Layer Cake

A layer cake that is to be garnished with the sort of thick, rich frosting traditional to birthday and wedding cakes must be dense and strong enough to provide support. However, to keep the decorated assemblies from being cloying, the layers should be made from a creamed-cake batter that contains lower proportions of butter and eggs than the batters for cakes such as poundcake and fruitcake.

Reducing the amounts of butter and eggs requires some other modifications in the composition of the batters. Classic creamed cakes, for instance, depend primarily on eggs for the liquid that moistens their batters. Cakes containing reduced numbers of eggs need extra liquid in the form of cream, milk or fruit juice, depending on the flavor of the cake. For the coconut cake at right, the extra liquid is coconut milk, made by steeping grated fresh coconut in hot water (box, below).

Creamed cakes are lightened primarily by air trapped in butter (pages 50-51); when butter proportions are reduced, the batters will contain less air and will require supplementary leavening. The leavening often added is baking powder, a mixture of baking soda and tartaric acid. When liquefied in batter and heated during baking, the soda and acid interact to produce bubbles of carbon dioxide, which help to lighten the cake.

The cake batters may be flavored in any of a variety of ways. The batters are usually baked in layers and, while any frosting or icing may be used to garnish them, they are particularly suited to rich mixtures such as the boiled icing that is shown here, seven-minute icing, rich butter cream, and fudge frosting (recipes, pages 164-166). Extra garnishes to accompany the icing or frosting can include chopped nuts and candied fruit peel; the cake in this demonstration is garnished with a sprinkling of grated coconut.

1 **Creaming the butter.** Place butter in a large bowl and cream it, gradually adding sugar until the mixture becomes light and fluffy. Add eggs—beaten, as here, for easier mixing—a small quantity at a time, or beat in whole eggs one at a time.

Meat and Milk from a Coconut

1 **Freeing the flesh.** With a skewer, pierce the three fleshy spots in one end of a ripe coconut—one whose liquid gurgles. Drain the liquid, then crack open the nut with a cleaver near the end opposite the holes. Pry the flesh away from the shell with a knife; peel the papery skin from the flesh.

2 **Steeping the coconut.** Grate half of the peeled flesh into a bowl. The rest can be grated and reserved for garnishing the cake demonstrated here. Pour boiling water over the flesh, allowing ½ cup [125 ml.] for each 1 cup [¼ liter] of flesh. Let the mixture steep for at least 10 minutes.

3 **Straining the milk.** Line a strainer with muslin or cheesecloth and set it over a bowl. Pour the steeped mixture into it, and let the coconut milk drain into the bowl. Then gather the cloth into a bag around the grated flesh; set the strainer aside and squeeze the bag to extract the last of the milk. Discard the flesh.

2 **Completing the batter.** Sift flour, salt and baking powder together, then sift a little of the mixture over the batter and stir it in gently. Stir in a little coconut milk *(box, opposite)*. Alternate additions of the flour and the milk until both are used up, then stir in grated lime peel and vanilla extract.

3 **Baking.** Divide the batter between two layer-cake pans that have been buttered and floured and lined on the bottoms. Bake in a preheated 350° F. [180° C.] oven for 30 minutes, or until a tester inserted in the layers comes out clean. Let the layers cool for 10 minutes. Turn them out onto racks.

4 **Assembling.** Transfer one cooled layer to a cardboard cake circle. Spread it with boiled icing. Place the second layer on the first. Support the cake circle on one hand, rotating it as you spread icing on the cake sides with a narrow-bladed spatula. Then place the cake on a decorating wheel.

5 **Garnishing and serving.** Spread icing over the top of the cake, then sprinkle grated fresh coconut *(box, opposite)* over the top and sides *(left)*. Serve the cake in wedges *(inset)*.

A Triple Leavening for Perfect Cupcakes

Recipes for the lighter creamed cakes—those with reduced amounts of butter and eggs—specify several means for providing the supplementary moisture and leavening that these cakes require. Some cakes, such as the coconut cake demonstrated on pages 56-57, use baking powder for leavening and sweet ingredients such as coconut milk, milk or cream as moisteners. Old-fashioned cakes often contain baking soda—discovered long before baking powder—for the leavening and acidic liquids such as buttermilk or sour milk for the moistener: These liquids provide the acid necessary to stimulate the production of carbon dioxide in the baking soda, and also neutralize the soda's somewhat soapy taste.

The combination of buttermilk or sour milk and soda also ensures a cake's tenderness and lightens its color—a chocolate cake that includes these ingredients will acquire the reddish hue that accounts for the name devil's food *(recipe, page 151)*. That is why these ingredients often appear in creamed-cake recipes, even when, as in this demonstration, the amount of acid liquid is too small to activate enough baking soda for adequate leavening—and the batter must include baking powder as well as baking soda.

Some of these cakes also incorporate extra entrapped air in the form of beaten egg whites, as here. The extra air is particularly important when making cupcakes from a creamed-cake batter because air expands during baking to give cupcakes their characteristic dome.

Cupcakes are frosted and decorated with the same frostings and icings used for other cakes, but their small size—and the fact that they are held in the hands for eating—dictates that they be decorated only on their tops. For the whimsical presentation shown here, the cupcake domes are sliced off, split and attached to the frosted cake tops at an angle that makes them look like butterfly wings. Frosting piped between the wings gives each butterfly a body.

1 **Creaming the butter.** Cream butter in a large bowl. Gradually add sugar, continuing to cream until the mixture becomes light and fluffy. Separate eggs, reserve the whites, and add the yolks one by one to the creamed mixture; beat until the mixture again lightens and is fluffy.

2 **Adding baking soda.** In a small bowl, whisk baking soda into buttermilk. The mixture will foam slightly as an indication that the alkaline soda is reacting with the acids in the buttermilk. Set the mixture aside.

6 **Baking the cupcakes.** Drop a paper liner into each cup of a muffin pan, as here, or butter the cups and dust them with flour. Spoon the batter into the pan, filling each cup about two thirds full. Place the pan in a preheated 350° F. [180° C.] oven and bake for about 20 minutes, or until a tester inserted in the cakes comes out clean.

7 **Making wings.** Cool the cupcakes in the pan for 10 minutes, then transfer them to a rack and let them cool completely; this takes about 30 minutes. With a serrated knife, slice the domed tops off the cupcakes and cut across each top to divide it into semicircles that can be used for butterfly wings.

3 **Sifting the flour.** Set a sifter in a dry bowl. Pour flour into the sifter, then add baking powder and sift the ingredients together into the bowl.

4 **Flavoring the batter.** Dissolve cocoa powder in hot water. Add small amounts of the dissolved cocoa, the buttermilk-and-baking-soda mixture and the sifted dry ingredients alternately to the creamed batter, gently stirring after each addition just enough to incorporate it. Stir in vanilla extract.

5 **Folding in egg whites.** Beat the reserved egg whites until they are stiff but not dry. Using a rubber spatula, scoop about one third of the egg whites into the batter and fold them in well to lighten the batter; gently fold in the remaining whites using a cutting-and-turning motion.

8 **Decorating.** Fit a pastry bag with a large No. 6 closed star tube and half-fill the bag with frosting—here, sweetened whipped cream. Pipe it over the cut surfaces of each cupcake (inset), then embed the wings in the cream, tilting them slightly. Pipe a cylinder of cream between the wings for the butterfly's body (right).

3
Blended and Yeast-leavened Cakes
Exploiting Ready-made Lightening Agents

Two types of cakes—blended cakes and yeast cakes—are lightened not by the trapped air and steam that form the primary leavening for egg-foam cakes and creamed cakes, but by carbon dioxide, an odorless, tasteless gas. The carbon dioxide that leavens blended cakes comes from ingredients quite different from those in yeast cakes, and the two types of cakes differ greatly in the preparations they require and in the characteristics they display.

Blended cakes—variously called "dump," "quick-mix," "lightning" and "one-bowl" cakes according to the mixing method employed in making them—are designed for economy: They contain relatively small amounts of eggs and butter. In addition, their batters are easily made, since large amounts of liquids facilitate speedy dispersal of the ingredients. Lacking enough fat to trap air for leavening, these cakes must be leavened chemically with the carbon dioxide produced either by baking soda or by baking powder, depending on the other ingredients in the batter. The results are neither as light as spongecakes nor as rich as creamed cakes; these firm yet tender confections do, however, supply foundations for a pleasing array of coffeecakes, shortcakes and glazed, fruit-topped upside-down cakes *(pages 62-63)*.

Yeast, consisting of one-celled organisms that produce carbon dioxide when nourished by liquid and such ingredients as flour and sugar, is the most ancient of leavens. In the realm of cakemaking, it is used for creations as lavish as French babas and savarins, German *Kugelhopfe* and Italian panettones, all of them festive cousins of everyday bread. The organic release of carbon dioxide from yeast is a slower, more complex process than the quick chemical reaction of baking soda or baking powder, and results vary according to the density of the cake batter. For instance, when a very liquid yeast batter is beaten and allowed to rise briefly, it yields savarin, a delicate, porous cake that is traditionally transformed into a syrup-soaked showcase for fruit or cream fillings *(pages 66-67)*. A stiffer yeast dough that is kneaded and allowed to rise for longer time periods produces the Italian Christmas cake known as panettone, whose full flavor and fine, dense texture—as well as the fruits that are incorporated into the dough—make any additional embellishments unnecessary.

Tiny ring-shaped savarins, which have been filled with pineapple, kiwi fruit, strawberries, oranges and grapes, receive a coat of apricot jam glaze. The glaze will set to give these leavened cakes a glossy veneer.

The Simplest Cake of All

A blended cake is simplicity itself to make: The ingredients are stirred together in one bowl, and the resulting batter is poured into a pan and baked. For properly light results, however, meticulous attention must be paid to the details of preparation.

First, recipes should be followed precisely: The success of any blended-cake recipe depends on a careful balance of its components. The batters, for instance, contain relatively small amounts of eggs and butter; to supply the tenderness that these ingredients would otherwise provide, recipes specify large amounts of sugar. Altering the proportions of the ingredients can produce a dry, heavy cake.

For the requisite smooth batter, all ingredients should be at room temperature: Chilled liquids or eggs can cause lumps. Dry ingredients should first be sifted together for uniform blending; liquid ingredients should be incorporated a little at a time for even absorption.

Because the ingredients are simply stirred together in a bowl, blended batters receive little of the aeration that provides the primary leavening in egg-foam and creamed cakes. Leavening for most blended cakes is supplied by baking powder—baking soda mixed with an acid that will activate it to produce carbon dioxide during baking, thus raising and lightening the cake. Baking powder is called double-acting because it releases a small quantity of carbon dioxide when it is first moistened in the batter—thereby lightening the batter and promoting even blending—and then releases the remainder of the gas during baking.

Because they are low in the fats supplied by eggs and butter, blended cakes quickly dry out after they are baked. They are best eaten warm, and certainly should be eaten the day they are made. Rich or juicy toppings and garnishes—lightly whipped cream, syrups or fresh fruit—provide extra moisture.

One of the most appealing ways to give a blended cake a moist topping is to make an upside-down cake—an option demonstrated here (recipe, page 112). As a first step in the preparation of the topping, butter and sugar are melted together to form a moist glaze for the cake pan. Next, trimmed fresh fruit—nectarines in this case, but peaches, pears, apples or cherries could be used—are pressed into the glaze. The blended batter is poured over this assembly. During baking, the fruit and glaze adhere to the cake, and afterward, the cake is inverted onto a platter to expose a sweet, handsome covering.

4 **Adding the batter.** Pour the batter over the arranged fruit, using a rubber spatula to scrape all of the batter from the bowl. Bake the assembled cake in a preheated 350° F. [180° C.] oven for 25 to 35 minutes, or until the top has browned slightly and the sides of the cake have begun to shrink from the pan.

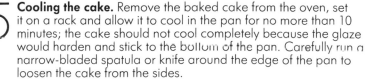

5 **Cooling the cake.** Remove the baked cake from the oven, set it on a rack and allow it to cool in the pan for no more than 10 minutes; the cake should not cool completely because the glaze would harden and stick to the bottom of the pan. Carefully run a narrow-bladed spatula or knife around the edge of the pan to loosen the cake from the sides.

1 **Mixing the batter.** Measure flour, sugar, salt and baking powder, and sift them together into a large bowl. Add softened butter. Measure milk and pour half of it into the bowl; stir the mixture until it is thick and smooth. Then stir in an egg and the remaining milk to produce a batter that has a consistency similar to heavy cream.

2 **Preparing the glaze.** Combine butter and brown sugar in a small saucepan. Stir the mixture over low heat until the butter has melted and the sugar has completely dissolved into a syrup. Pour the mixture into a cake pan to make an even layer, and let it cool and thicken for about five minutes.

3 **Arranging the topping.** Prepare fruit—pitted and sliced fresh nectarines are shown, their skin left on to add color. Arrange the fruit pieces on the glaze in the cake pan. The fruit pieces should cover the glaze almost completely and should be packed closely to allow for shrinkage.

6 **Serving.** Immediately place a serving plate upside down over the top of the pan. Holding the rack, pan and inverted plate together, lift and turn them to reverse the cake onto the serving plate (*above*). Cut the finished cake into wedges for serving (*right*).

A Molten Mixture of Sugar and Spice

Many spicy blended cakes—the ginger-bread shown at right is one—acquire their rich, full flavors and dark colors from liquid sweeteners such as molasses or honey. Cake batters sweetened with liquids require a leavening and a mixing technique different from those used for other blended cakes.

Because molasses and honey are comparatively high in acid, baking powder is an inappropriate leavening: It would produce overly dense cakes with acidic flavors. Plain baking soda, which is alkaline, is used instead. The acid in the sweetener will not only encourage the soda to produce carbon dioxide, but will also get rid of the soda's somewhat soapy taste. These cakes often contain other acidic ingredients to bolster the leavening effect; here, for example, buttermilk and orange juice are used in a molasses-sweetened batter (recipe, page 140).

Molasses and honey are so thick that they cannot be readily mixed with other ingredients, but a simple preliminary measure provides a solution. For smooth blending, stir the liquid sweeteners together with any other ingredients that can be melted—butter and sugar, for instance—and heat the mixture until it becomes thin and syrupy. Before using it to form the batter, let the mixture cool slightly, lest it curdle the eggs.

To ensure that the cake batter rises properly, bake the cake immediately after the batter is mixed. Baking soda begins to produce carbon dioxide the moment it is liquefied and mixed with acid; if the batter were allowed to stand before baking, it might release so much carbon dioxide into the air that too little would be left to leaven the cake.

Like other blended cakes, these spice-cakes dry quickly after they are baked, and therefore should be eaten soon afterward. They make excellent foundations for moist garnishes such as juicy fruit, whipped cream and ice cream.

1 **Melting molasses.** Combine molasses, brown sugar and butter in a small saucepan. Stir the mixture over low heat until the butter and sugar have melted and the mixture is thin and syrupy. Remove the saucepan from the heat and let the mixture cool slightly.

4 **Mixing all the ingredients.** Add the buttermilk to the bowl (left), and stir until the buttermilk and flour are blended. Then stir in the beaten eggs and, finally, the orange juice (above). Immediately pour the batter into a buttered and floured pan, and bake the cake in a preheated 350° F. [180° C.] oven for about 30 minutes.

2 **Combining the dry ingredients.** Sift flour and baking soda together into a large mixing bowl. Measure flavorings—ground ginger, cinnamon, nutmeg, cloves and salt are used in this demonstration—and stir them into the flour.

3 **Adding the molasses mixture to the flour.** Make a well in the center of the flour and pour the cooled molasses mixture into the well. Measure buttermilk and strained fresh orange juice. Beat eggs until they are foamy.

5 **Cooling and serving.** Cool the cake in the pan for about 10 minutes. Then run a knife around the edges of the pan, turn the cake out and set it on a rack. To serve the cake—warm or cooled—cut it into squares. Serve each square garnished with a dollop of whipped cream and, if you like, with a piece of preserved ginger *(right)*.

A High-Liquid Batter for a Spongy Texture

Cakes leavened with yeast vary widely in character, but they all are formed by the same basic method: Fresh cake or active dry yeast is softened in tepid liquid, then mixed with additional liquid, flour and sugar to make a dough. Feeding on the sugar and the starch in the flour, the yeast cells ferment and grow, producing the bubbles of carbon dioxide that raise and lighten the cake. The differences among yeast cakes depend on how much liquid is used in the dough, and how the dough is handled after it is formed.

Light, porous cakes such as the savarin demonstrated here (recipe, page 157), for instance, are the easiest yeast cakes to make: Softened yeast is simply mixed with flour, eggs and a large amount of milk, and allowed to rise. The raised dough is enriched with a liberal amount of butter—the fat in butter used in large quantities would inhibit the growth of the yeast if the butter was added earlier.

In copious liquid, the yeast develops quickly and disperses evenly throughout the dough. Kneading, which is used in drier doughs to break up carbon-dioxide bubbles and spread them evenly, is unnecessary. The liquid also turns to steam during the baking process, providing additional lightness for the cake. The result is a delicate confection with a unique, honeycombed interior.

The texture of the finished cake and the shape it takes from the large 9-inch [23-cm.] molds or small 3-inch [8-cm.] molds traditionally used for baking it make savarin a fine vehicle for imaginative flavoring and garnishing. Savarins and similar cakes usually are soaked in spirit-flavored sugar syrup before they are served. The porous cakes absorb the sweet liquid, becoming very moist and soft. The saturated cakes can then become containers for fresh fruit, sweetened whipped cream, ice cream or pastry cream. And any of the cakes, once assembled, can be glazed for a glittering finish.

1 **Softening yeast.** Measure flour; set out eggs and allow them to warm to room temperature. In a large mixing bowl, soften active dry yeast in a little tepid water mixed with a little sugar. Heat milk until it is just tepid, and then add a little sugar to it (above). After about 10 minutes, when the yeast looks frothy, stir in the sweetened milk.

5 **Soaking with rum sauce.** While the savarins bake, make a sugar syrup and flavor it with rum or kirsch. Turn the baked savarins out of their molds, set them with their wells up in a baking pan and let them cool briefly. Prick the cakes all over with a skewer and pour the syrup over them. Let them stand for about 30 minutes.

6 **Filling the centers.** Use a metal spatula to transfer the savarins from the baking pan to a wire cake rack, where excess syrup will drain. Garnish the center of each cake with a decorative filling—in this case, a fresh fruit arrangement that includes a notched slice of pineapple, an orange segment, a kiwi slice, a strawberry and a green grape.

2 **Letting the batter rise.** Stir the flour and eggs into the yeast mixture. Then beat the mixture for about two minutes, or until it forms a cohesive mass. Cover the bowl with a towel, and set it aside in a warm place (70° to 85° F. [20° to 30° C.]) for 20 to 40 minutes, until the dough has doubled in bulk.

3 **Adding butter and salt.** Punch the dough with your fist to deflate it. Then add salt and cooled melted butter, and work them into the dough. Butter ring molds—either small ones, as used in this demonstration, or a single large one.

4 **Filling molds.** Spoon the dough into the buttered molds, filling each by two thirds. Cover the molds and allow the dough to rise until it fills the molds, about 20 minutes. Set the molds on a baking sheet and bake the cakes in a preheated 400° F. [200° C.] oven; allow about 15 minutes for small molds and 25 minutes for a large one.

7 **Glazing the cakes.** Heat apricot jam and strain it to make an apricot glaze. Use a pastry brush to coat each savarin and its filling with the glaze. Then transfer the finished savarins to a platter. Allow one small savarin per serving, or cut a large one into wedges.

Kneading for a Breadlike Cake

A yeast-leavened cake made with a low proportion of liquid requires time and kneading, but the breadlike result—exhibited here with Italian panettone *(recipe, page 161)*—is well worth the effort.

The initial formation of the dough proceeds much as it does for savarin *(pages 66-67):* Yeast is mixed with sugar and water, then combined with other ingredients—milk, a little butter, flavorings, eggs and flour. However, the dough is relatively dry, and the yeast must be dispersed by manual means. Kneading breaks up carbon-dioxide bubbles formed by the yeast and helps distribute them, ensuring that the cake has a smooth texture and rises evenly. Solid flavorings such as candied fruit can be worked into the dough after it has risen: Added earlier, they might interfere with rising.

This dough expands a great deal during baking: The uncooked dough should fill its pan only halfway. To allow the cake to dry and firm slightly, cool it completely, wrap it in foil and store it overnight before serving.

1 **Combining milk and butter.** Mix softened yeast with a little sugar and tepid water. Set the mixture aside in a warm place for about 10 minutes to allow it to triple in bulk. In the meantime, scald milk in a small saucepan, remove the pan from the heat and stir in chunks of butter. When the butter melts, add sugar and salt, stirring until the dry ingredients dissolve.

2 **Adding flavorings.** Transfer the milk-and-butter mixture to a large bowl. Add vanilla extract and grated lemon peel *(above)*, and stir with a wooden spoon until the flavorings are evenly distributed throughout the mixture. Allow the mixture to cool until it reaches room temperature before proceeding.

6 **Letting the dough rise.** Form the dough into a smooth ball, and turn and twirl it in the bottom of the mixing bowl until the dough is well buttered *(above)*. Cover the bowl, and set it in a warm place until the dough has nearly tripled in bulk—three to four hours, depending on the temperature.

7 **Adding fruits.** Punch the dough to deflate it, and turn it onto the work surface—which need not be floured because the butter-coated dough will not stick. Flatten the dough into a round about 1 inch [2½ cm.] thick. Sprinkle raisins and slivered candied citron over the dough. Knead the dough until the fruits are evenly dispersed.

8 **Glazing the cake.** Place the dough in a well-buttered baking pan—in this case, a charlotte mold. Cover the pan with a towel, and set it aside in a warm place until the dough has doubled in size—generally about an hour. Then glaze the top by brushing the dough with a lightly beaten mixture of egg yolk, water and sugar.

3 **Starting to mix.** Use an electric mixer to beat about a quarter of the flour required by the recipe into the milk-and-butter mixture *(above)*. Continue to beat with the mixer as you add the yeast mixture and a little more flour. Then add eggs, one at a time, beating after each addition; add a single egg white to give the cake extra lightness.

4 **Adding more flour.** The mixture will now be smooth and too stiff for the mixer. Use a wooden spoon to work in all but about 1 cup [¼ liter] of the remaining flour. Scrape the sides of the bowl, and fold the dough over and over with the spoon until the flour is absorbed and the dough forms a shaggy mass. Flour a clean, dry work surface and empty the dough onto it.

5 **Kneading the dough.** Knead the dough by repeatedly folding it over on itself and pushing it away from you, working in the last cup of flour as you go. Continue kneading for six to eight minutes, until all of the flour has been absorbed and the dough is smooth and elastic. Wash out and dry the mixing bowl, and then lightly butter it.

9 **Baking.** For a decorative crust, cut a cross in the top of the dough *(inset)*. Place the pan in a preheated 400° F. [200° C.] oven. After 10 minutes, place butter in the cross to color the surface; reduce the heat to 375° F. [190° C.]. After 10 minutes, reduce the heat to 350° F. [180° C.] and bake the cake for about 30 minutes, until a tester inserted in the center comes out clean. Let the cake ripen overnight before serving *(right)*.

Special Presentations
Glories of the Baker's Art

As symbols of celebration, cakes lend themselves to the elaborate and fanciful. Madame Bovary's wedding cake in Gustave Flaubert's 19th Century novel, for instance, had as its base a cardboard temple, which supported a cake castle. On top of the castle was depicted a meadow with—among other decorations—lakes of jam, boats made from nutshells and "a small Cupid balancing himself on a chocolate swing."

That cake was, in culinary terms, guilty of extremism. But the cakemaker's art offers many proofs that elaboration and elegance can be entirely compatible. This chapter deals with such cakes, all based on the various batters shown in earlier chapters of this book; the cakes acquire distinction from the ways those batters are baked, shaped and garnished.

Most cake batters can be baked in jelly-roll pans to produce large, thin sheets. A flexible sheet made from a sponge batter may be rolled into a cylinder around a filling, which will be revealed as concentric rings when the cake is sliced into cross sections for serving. The most spectacular of rolled cakes, the French *bûche de Noël,* is coiled around a rich butter cream, then frosted and decorated to resemble a fallen log—bark, knots, mushrooms and all *(pages 72-73).*

A firmer cake sheet—poundcake, for instance—is inflexible, but it has enough strength to hold its shape when it is divided into tiny petits fours—rich and dainty morsels whose name derives from the fact that the cakes were first baked in brick ovens *("fours"* in French) after larger and supposedly more important cakes had finished cooking.

Another group of assembled cakes are created by techniques akin to engineering. Among them are ice-cream cakes *(opposite and pages 78-79),* constructed so that the cake layers and their chilly, creamy fillings remain distinct. Also in this category are cakes whose interiors can be hollowed to make room for large amounts of fillings such as fruit *(pages 74-75).* And the most brilliantly engineered structure of all is a traditional wedding cake, an ivory pyramid festooned with swags and flowers of frosting. Despite its intricacy, such a tiered cake can be made at home with little more than time, a few simple anchoring devices for the tiers, and some practice with the decorating techniques demonstrated at the beginning of this volume. And the results will be pretty and flowery enough to grace the happiest wedding day.

Its green, white and brown strata perfectly delineated, a wedge of ice-cream cake is lifted to a plate. To make the cake, layers of pistachio ice cream were frozen, interleaved with layers of chocolate butter spongecake, frosted with whipped cream and decorated with pistachios.

A Triumph of Trompe l'Oeil

Spread out in a jelly-roll pan, batter quickly bakes to a thin sheet that can be shaped into a variety of different cakes. Among the prettiest are rolled cakes, which are made by spreading a sheet with filling, then rolling it into a cylinder and garnishing it. The sheet used to make such a cake should be light and flexible enough to roll easily without cracking. The best choice in batters is one for a separated spongecake *(pages 34-35);* for a richer cake, you may use a butter-spongecake batter *(pages 36-37).*

As for the fillings and garnishes, the choice is infinite. Simple fillings include jam, jelly or whipped cream—the latter perhaps combined with chopped nuts or fresh fruits. Garnishes may be as elemental as a dusting of confectioners' sugar or a blanket of whipped cream. But far more elaborate effects are also possible. One spectacular creation is the traditional French Christmas cake known as *bûche de Noël* (yule log) *(recipe, page 96)*—demonstrated at right. The cake is filled with chocolate-flavored rich butter cream *(recipe, page 166),* and vanilla and chocolate-flavored rich butter creams are piped on the roll to make it resemble a tree trunk. Small meringue mushrooms *(box, opposite)* complete the whimsical effect *(recipe, page 167).*

The sheet for any rolled cake must be shaped into a roll while it is still warm and flexible, but the point at which filling is added depends on the type chosen. If you plan to fill the cake with jam, warm the jam first in a saucepan set over low heat so that it will be easier to spread. Cover the sheet of cake with jam while both are still warm, then roll the cake.

Fillings such as whipped cream or butter cream, which have high fat contents, would become oily if they were spread over a warm cake. Before adding these fillings, shape the warm cake by rolling it around a sheet of parchment paper; if your cake is a slightly less flexible butter sponge, roll it around a damp towel to prevent cracking. In either case, let the rolled cake cool under a damp towel. The interior parchment paper or towel prevents the cake from sticking to itself and enables you to unroll it easily to fill it when it cools; the covering towel will keep the cake moist and flexible.

1 Baking. Butter, flour and line a jelly-roll pan. Make a separated-sponge mixture. Pour the mixture into the pan, smoothing it so that it will cook evenly. Bake the spongecake in a preheated 450° F. [230° C.] oven for 12 minutes, or until it is springy and golden brown.

2 Turning out the cake. Spread a kitchen towel on a work surface. Cover it with parchment paper, and sprinkle the paper with confectioners' sugar. Invert the pan, protecting your hand with a towel, and ease the cake onto the sugared paper. Peel off the paper used to line the pan.

4 Rolling the filled cake. In a large bowl, prepare rich butter cream; put about one fifth of it in a smaller bowl. Melt some chocolate and stir it into the large bowl of butter cream. Unroll the spongecake, remove the top layer of paper, and brush sugar syrup—here, flavored with orange liqueur *(recipe, page 164)*—over it. With a spatula, cover the cake with some of the chocolate-flavored butter cream and roll it up *(above).*

Mushrooms from Meringue

Dusting with cocoa. Spread parchment paper on a baking sheet. Pipe meringue into various-sized circles for caps and strips for stalks. Dust the shapes with sifted cocoa powder. Bake the meringue at 200° F. [100° C.] for three hours, or until it is crisp and dry.

3 **Rolling the cake.** Trim the crusty edges of the cake with a knife. To make the cake easier to roll at the start, cut a shallow groove along its short side about 1 inch [2½ cm.] from the edge *(inset)*. Cover the cake with parchment paper. Fold the cake over at the groove. Grasp the ends of the towel and roll up the spongecake around the top layer of paper *(above)*. Set the rolled cake seam side down, cover it with a damp towel, and let it cool.

5 **Applying butter cream.** Set the roll on a plate, with the seam underneath the cake. With a spatula, cover both ends with vanilla butter cream and use the rest to make a mound *(above)*. When completely decorated, the mound will resemble a sawed-off branch.

6 **Making a branch.** Fit a pastry bag with a large No. 4 open star tube and pipe chocolate-flavored butter cream over the cake. Use a small plain No. 4 tube to pipe rings at each end. Chill the cake for 30 minutes. With a warm knife, slice off the top of the mound *(above)*.

7 **Decorating the log.** Make the mushroom stems and caps from molding meringue *(box, above)*; assemble them by pressing them together with a little rich butter cream. Place the mushrooms on top of the log. Slice the cake into rounds and serve.

Showcases for Fresh Fruit

Light on the palate and tempting to the eye, fresh fruit makes fine cake fillings and decorations. A very light-textured cake such as angel food cake may simply be garnished with spoonfuls of fresh fruit *(pages 32-33)*. Firmer confections such as separated-egg spongecakes and butter spongecakes *(recipes, pages 94-95)* can be shaped and filled in more elaborate ways. For example, you can roll such a cake around a fruit filling, as described on pages 72-73. Or, as demonstrated here, you can hollow out a cake and fill it with fruit *(right, top)* or layer a cake with a fresh-fruit filling *(right, bottom)*.

To retain the most natural flavor, preliminary preparations of the fruit should be kept simple. Soft fruits, such as berries or ripe peaches, need only be washed, peeled or cut up as required, and sweetened to taste. Firmer fruits, such as apples or pears, should be poached in sugar syrup *(pages 8-9)* until their flesh is tender, then drained and cooled thoroughly before they are used.

Because fruit will render juice that could make a cake soggy, all surfaces exposed to the fruit should be sealed with a glaze. Sugar syrup flavored with a fruit liqueur makes a suitable glaze. Alternatively, you can use melted jelly or melted, strained jam.

Using fruit in a cake limits the other types of fillings and frostings that can be included in the assembly: The acid in fruit would cause butter creams, fondants and glacé icings to separate. To give fruited assemblies a glittering finish, however, you can use glazes. For richness, you can use whipped cream and, for an airy surface, you can cover a cake with meringue *(recipe, page 167)*. Although neither meringue nor whipped cream will be affected by contact with fruit, both preparations tend to separate, and they should be applied to a cake no more than two hours before serving.

A Hidden Filling of Blackberries

1 Cutting a lid. Freeze a cake—here, a 9-inch [23-cm.] butter spongecake *(recipe, page 94)*—for an hour. Set it on a cake circle. Cut a circle 1 inch [2½ cm.] deep 1 inch inside the cake's rim. Cut horizontally to the center of the circle at a depth of ¼ inch [6 mm.]. Turn the cake to free the circle.

2 Glazing. Remove the cake under the lid to a depth of 1 inch [2½ cm.] by slicing it into blocks, then cutting out each block. Do not cut into the cake bottom. Heat jelly—here, ½ cup [125 ml.] of red currant jelly—until it coats the back of a metal spoon. Brush this glaze over the entire inner surface of the cake.

A Glittering Mosaic

1 Glazing. Cut a sheet of butter spongecake into two equal squares. Set one on a baking sheet. Brush each square with glaze—simple sugar syrup is used here. Whip heavy cream to make 2 cups [½ liter], flavoring it with sugar. Trim about 4 cups [1 liter] of strawberries.

2 Filling. Spread whipped cream over the square of cake on the baking sheet. Into the cream, set rows of whole strawberries, pointed ends up. Cover them with whipped cream. Place the second square of cake, glazed side down, on the filling. Refrigerate the cake for an hour to firm the filling.

3 **Filling the cake.** Brush the underside of the cake lid with currant jelly glaze. Then set freshly washed and drained fruit—about 3 cups [¾ liter] of blackberries are used for this cake—in concentric circles to fill the hollowed-out cake. Place the lid of the cake, glazed side down, over the berries.

4 **Frosting.** Make 2 cups [½ liter] of meringue. With a spatula, spread the meringue over the cake, dipping the spatula in hot water after each application to prevent sticking. Smooth the frosting. Use a pastry bag to pipe a meringue design on the cake.

5 **Browning the meringue.** Slide the cake onto a baking sheet and set it in a preheated 375° F. [190° C.] oven for five minutes, or until the meringue design is golden brown. Just before serving, garnish the cake with additional berries.

3 **Trimming the cake.** With a sharp, serrated knife, trim about ¼ inch [6 mm.] from each side of the cake to expose the rows of strawberries within. Melt about ½ cup [125 ml.] of apricot jam over low heat, then force the jam through a strainer.

4 **Decorating the cake.** Spread the top of the cake with about half of the jam glaze, and arrange a geometric design of fruit on top. Halved strawberries, whole grapes and sliced bananas are used for this demonstration.

5 **Finishing the cake.** To give the cake a glossy surface, brush the top of the fruit with the remaining apricot jam glaze. If you do not use the glaze, brush the bananas with strained fresh lemon juice to prevent them from browning. Refrigerate the cake until serving time.

Gleaming Gems of Cake and Fondant

Making the miniature layer cakes called petits fours is not very complicated: Thin sheets of cake are sandwiched together with a glaze, then cut into tiny diamonds, squares or circles, and coated with shiny fondant icing. But care must be taken to ensure that the cakes retain the proper shape after their extensive handling.

The basic layers must be formed of a smooth cake dense enough to be cut into clearly defined shapes and strong enough to withstand the weighting needed to make the layers adhere. A creamed cake such as a poundcake *(recipe, page 103)* is the perfect choice; the one used here derives extra flavor and strength from including almond paste in the batter. For even more flavor—and sharper edges— a sheet of almond paste *(recipe, page 167)* is rolled onto the top of the cake layers.

You can frost petits fours by either dipping them in fondant *(recipe, page 164)* or, to avoid potential damage, pouring the fondant over them. Possible garnishes include candied flowers, nuts or, as here, thin, piped stripes of a different-colored icing *(page 25)*.

1 **Glazing the layers.** Bake three thin poundcake layers for about 20 minutes in prepared jelly-roll pans; cool them in the pans. With a spatula, spread one layer with a thin coat of apricot jam glaze *(recipe, page 167)*, scraping off all excess glaze. Invert a second layer onto the first, remove the pan and parchment paper, and glaze this layer. Repeat with the third layer.

2 **Adding almond paste.** Roll almond paste into a rectangle slightly larger than the layers. Roll the paste around the rolling pin, then unroll it onto the cake and trim it to fit. Invert a jelly-roll pan over the assembly in its pan, then invert the pans so that the paste is on the bottom. Place 3 or 4 pounds [1½ or 2 kg.] of weights on top and refrigerate overnight.

6 **Adding white icing.** Transfer the cylinders to a rack set over a pan. Make 3 cups [¾ liter] of plain fondant icing; spoon it over the cylinders until they are coated, letting the excess drip into the pan. Allow the cylinders to dry for 30 minutes on the rack, until the icing is dry, then transfer them to a baking sheet lined with parchment paper.

7 **Adding pink icing.** Return the dripped icing to the icing pan. Set about ¼ cup [50 ml.] of plain fondant icing aside and color the rest pink. Transfer the diamond-shaped cakes to the rack and spoon the pink icing over them. Let the cakes dry, then transfer them to the baking sheet. Return the dripped fondant to the icing pan.

8 **Coating with chocolate.** Melt 4 ounces [125 g.] of unsweetened chocolate. Stir small amounts of it into the pink fondant icing until the icing is as dark as you wish. Keep the unused chocolate warm. Transfer the square cakes to the rack, coat them with chocolate icing, let them dry, and place them on the baking sheet.

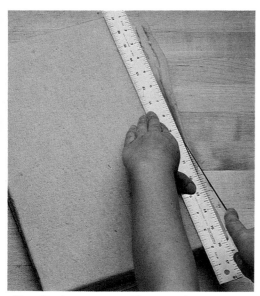

3 **Cutting squares.** The next day, invert the cake onto a work surface covered with a sheet of parchment paper. Lay a ruler along one long edge of the cake and use it as a guide in trimming that edge to perfect evenness (above). Cut a strip 1½ inches [4 cm.] wide from the trimmed side of the cake, and divide the strip into 1½-inch squares. Transfer the squares to a baking sheet.

4 **Cutting diamonds.** Cut a second strip of cake 1½ inches [4 cm.] wide. Make a diamond-shaped cardboard template, sized so that two of its edges align with the edges of the strip. Use the template as a guide to slice the strip of cake into diamond shapes. Transfer the diamond-shaped cakes to the baking sheet.

5 **Cutting cylinders.** Using a round cookie cutter 1½ inches [4 cm.] in diameter, stamp cylinders from the remaining cake. To make each cylinder, press the cutter firmly down into the cake and twist it. Then lift the cutter; the cake will remain inside. Push the cylinder of cake gently out with your thumb and set it on the baking sheet.

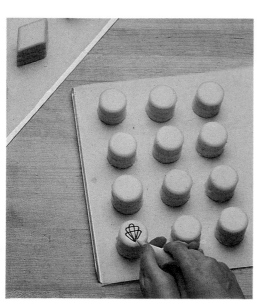

9 **Decorating.** When all of the iced cakes are dry, make a paper pastry bag and fill it with the melted chocolate. Use the bag to pipe free-form designs on the white cakes and the pink cakes. Make another pastry bag, fill it with the reserved white fondant icing, and pipe designs on the chocolate cakes.

10 **Finishing.** For an extra garnish, dip the bases of the white and pink cakes in the remaining chocolate: Dip each cake so that the chocolate comes ¼ inch [6 mm.] up the sides, then hold the cake in the air for a moment (inset) to let the chocolate set. The cakes may be served at once (above) or covered and kept at room temperature for as long as three days.

Colorful Layers of Ice Cream and Cake

Ice cream and cake, perennial birthday favorites, can be combined into splendid assemblies. Any ice cream may serve, and almost any cake: The exceptions are very light egg-foam cakes, such as angel food cake, which lack the strength needed for support. Two basic shaping methods are used, depending on the effect you want and the time you have.

A dome-shaped cake can be made in a relatively short time from two butter-spongecake layers *(recipe, page 94)*, split horizontally. One disk of cake is pressed into a large bowl to form a well; this is filled with layers of soft ice cream, interleaved with the remaining pieces of cake—cut to fit the bowl as necessary. The assembly is frozen, then unmolded and decorated with whipped cream.

When an ice-cream cake is made this way, the cake will absorb some ice cream so that, when the dessert is cut, the cake and filling will not be distinct. To make a cake whose elements are clearly demarcated, you must follow the longer process demonstrated here, combining cake layers with ice cream firmed separately.

Each layer of ice cream is shaped by freezing it in a spring-form pan, which has removable sides that facilitate unmolding. The unmolded layers are stored in the freezer and the pan is next used for baking a cake—here, a devil's food cake *(recipe, page 151)*—the same size as the ice-cream layers. The pan is then used to mold alternate layers of cake and ice cream, producing an assembly with a regular surface.

Any number of variations are possible with either type of cake. The ice cream may be augmented with chopped fruit or nuts. The cake layers can be glazed with sugar syrup *(recipe, page 164)* or thin chocolate icing *(recipe, page 165)*—chosen for this demonstration. The finished cake may be covered with meringue *(recipe, page 167)* and baked for five minutes in a preheated 375° F. [190° C.] oven. Or, as here, it can be covered with sweetened whipped cream, then embellished with chopped nuts *(pages 18-19)*, chocolate curls *(pages 16-17)* or fruit.

1 Shaping ice cream. Spread 1 quart [1 liter] of softened ice cream—in this case, pistachio—in the bottom of a 9-inch [23-cm.] spring-form pan. Press the ice cream down firmly with the back of a spoon to eliminate air pockets, and smooth the surface to make an even layer. Freeze the ice cream for one to two hours, until it is hard.

5 Frosting the cake. Chop nuts—here, blanched pistachios—to make about 1 cup [¼ liter]. Whip 2 cups [½ liter] of heavy cream until stiff, and sweeten it Spread the whipped cream lavishly on the sides of the cake, then transfer it to a decorating wheel and frost the top.

6 Scoring the cake. Smooth the cake surface, removing excess whipped cream. For ease of serving, score the cake with a serrated knife to outline thick wedges. Ice-cream layers tend to soften and slide as they warm during serving, so the cake cannot be cut thin and it must be divided all at once.

7 Decorating the cake. If you like, pipe decorations onto each scored wedge. Here, a large No. 6 closed star tube is used to make rosettes *(page 24)*. Each rosette is crowned with a peeled pistachio half.

2 **Unmolding.** Remove the pan from the freezer and run a knife around the edge to free the ice cream. Remove the pan sides, cover the ice cream with foil, and invert the two together. Loosen the base of the pan with a knife; remove the base. Return the ice cream to the freezer. Repeat Steps 1 and 2 with another quart of ice cream.

3 **Assembly.** Bake a devil's food cake in the pan. Slice the cake into three layers. Make 1½ cups [375 ml.] of chocolate icing. Put a cake layer on the base of the pan and ice it, leaving a ½-inch [1-cm.] border to prevent streaking. Invert an ice-cream layer onto the cake; peel off the foil.

4 **Completing the assembly.** Cover the ice-cream layer with the remaining cake and ice-cream layers, glazing each cake layer with the chocolate icing. Replace the sides of the pan to reshape the edges of the softened ice-cream layers, and freeze the cake for at least three hours, until it has frozen hard.

8 **Finishing the decoration.** Lift the cake on one hand, and pat the chopped nuts into the whipped cream on the sides. Transfer the cake to a serving platter and serve it immediately. Or cover the cake with an inverted bowl to protect the decoration, and store it in the freezer for as long as 10 days.

Ivory Tiers Graced with Garlands

That most spectacular of assemblies, a tiered wedding cake, requires planning, patience and practice, but none of the skills employed in making one will be unknown to the experienced cake baker.

The basic cake must be of a type both light and sturdy so that no sagging occurs when the tiers are stacked; the cake must also be rich enough to stay moist throughout its rather lengthy assembly period. An ideal choice is a creamed cake such as the one used in this demonstration *(recipe, page 106)*. The tiers—which can be baked the day before assembly to ease the work of the cook—should be of graduated sizes: The cake here has 6-, 9- and 12-inch [15-, 23- and 30-cm.] tiers. Each tier is given a firm base by a cardboard cake circle, and each receives additional support from short wooden dowels inserted into the tier beneath. To prevent the assembled tiers from sliding sideways, a longer wooden dowel pins all the tiers together; suitable ¼-inch [6-mm.] dowels are available at hardware and cakemaking-supply stores.

Wedding cakes receive their basic coat of frosting—traditionally, it is an ivory-colored rich butter cream *(recipe, page 166)*—before the tiers are stacked. Decorations piped onto the assembled cake should be of the same ivory butter cream as the basic frosting: A mistake made with frosting of a contrasting color is impossible to erase. Colored decorations, such as the pink roses used for this cake, should be piped separately in advance, then attached with butter cream. Techniques for creating decorative stringwork, shell borders, leaves and flowers are shown on pages 22-27.

The disassembling and cutting of a tiered cake is an art in itself; the basic method is demonstrated on page 84. The cake shown provides about 100 servings.

1 **Trimming a layer top.** Bake and cool six creamed-cake layers—two of them 6 inches [15 cm.] in diameter, two of them 9 inches [23 cm.] and two of them 12 inches [30 cm.]. With a long serrated knife, trim each layer in turn, beginning by removing the brown sugar-bloom crust from the top.

2 **Trimming the layer sides.** With a gentle, downward sawing motion, trim the crust from the sides of each cake layer. Prepare 12 cups [3 liters] of vanilla-flavored butter cream.

5 **Smoothing the frosting.** Hold the spatula blade against the side of the frosted tier and rotate the decorating wheel to scrape away excess frosting. Smooth the top of the tier. Transfer the tier to a serving platter. Repeat Steps 3 through 5 to assemble and frost the 9-inch [23-cm.] and 6-inch [15-cm.] tiers. Set these tiers aside on cake circles.

3 **Steadying the cake.** To help prevent the cake from shifting during decorating, smear butter cream on a 12-inch [30-cm.] cardboard cake circle. Center a trimmed, 12-inch cake layer on the cake circle, pressing it gently into the butter cream.

4 **Assembling the bottom tier.** Spread butter cream ¼ to ½ inch [6 mm. to 1 cm.] thick on top of the cake layer. Set the second 12-inch [30-cm.] layer on top. Balance the assembled tier on one hand and, using a narrow-bladed spatula, apply a thick layer of butter cream all around the sides of the tier. Transfer the tier to a decorating wheel and cover the top with a layer of butter cream.

6 **Preparing to stack.** Measure in 1½ inches [4 cm.] from opposite sides of the rim on the top surface of the bottom tier and mark by pricking the butter cream with a wooden pick. Align the rim of a 9-inch [23-cm.] cake circle with the marks and set it on the tier. With a wooden pick, draw a circle in the frosting around the rim of the cake circle. Remove the circle.

7 **Providing support.** Insert a wooden dowel ¼ inch [6 mm.] in diameter into the tier about 1 inch [2½ cm.] inside the drawn circle; push the dowel all the way through the tier, then lift it to reveal the top mark left by the butter cream. Cut off the dowel at this mark; pruning shears are used here. Withdraw the dowel and cut three more dowels of the same length.

8 **Stacking tiers.** Insert the dowels into the bottom tier about 1 inch [2½ cm.] inside the drawn circle and the same distance from one another. Sprinkle the area with confectioners' sugar. Place the 9-inch [23-cm.] tier—still on its cake circle—on the bottom tier, aligning it with the drawn circle. Repeat Steps 6 through 8—using a 6-inch [15-cm.] cake circle—for the top tier of the cake.▶

9 **Anchoring the tiers.** Cut a ¼-inch [6-mm.] dowel to a length that matches the height of the cake, and sharpen one end in a pencil sharpener. Measure in 3 inches [8 cm.] from the rim of the top tier, and mark the point on the surface. Set the point of the dowel on this center mark; drive the dowel straight down through all three tiers.

10 **Forming teardrops.** Fit a pastry bag with a coupling device and a No. 22 star tube, and half-fill the bag with butter cream. Pipe teardrop shapes at ¼-inch [6-mm.] intervals around the side of the top cake tier just beneath the rim.

11 **Applying stringwork.** Replace the pastry-bag tube with a small No. 4 plain tube. Pipe the butter cream in a thin line of swags over the teardrop shapes on the top tier. Replace the butter cream in the bag as necessary to keep it half-full.

13 **Decorating the central tier.** Pipe a shell border around the base of the top tier. Replace the pastry-bag tube with a small No. 4 plain tube and, using the curving motion employed for making a reversed-shell border, pipe a sprigged vine around the center of the sides of the second tier.

14 **Adding rosebuds.** Pipe dabs of butter cream onto the vine at 2-inch [5-cm.] intervals. Press into each dab a pale pink rosebud, piped the day before with a No. 104 rose petal tube and left to dry overnight.

15 **Finishing the central tier.** Use a small No. 4 plain tube to pipe a tiny calix—three curved strips—below each rosebud. Use a No. 67 leaf tube to pipe leaves on the vine *(above)*. Use a small No. 18 star tube to pipe a shell border around the top surface of the tier next to the rim, and a small No. 22 star tube to pipe a shell border at the base.

12 **Forming a border.** Replace the pastry-bag tube with a small No. 18 star tube. Pipe a shell border around the surface of the top tier next to the rim.

16 **Finishing.** Decorate the bottom tier in the same way as the top one, using a small No. 32 star tube for the teardrops, a small No. 4 plain tube for the stringwork, a small No. 32 star tube for the top border, and a large No. 4B star tube for the bottom one. With butter cream, attach roses to the base of the cake. Pipe rose leaves, using a No. 67 leaf tube.

17 **Adding the final garnish.** Pipe a small mound of butter cream onto the center of the top cake tier, covering the top of the dowel. Into the butter cream, press 1½-inch [4-cm.] and 1-inch [2½-cm.] pale pink roses. Use a No. 67 leaf tube to pipe leaves around the bottom of each rose. ▶

18 **Cutting the first slice.** Make parallel cuts in the bottom cake tier just to the edge of the second tier, spacing the cuts about 1 inch [2½ cm.] apart. Join the cuts with a third cut made parallel to the edge of the tier, then lift out the piece. This ceremonial slice is traditionally shared by the bride and groom.

19 **Removing the top tier.** Slide a broad-bladed spatula under the cake circle that supports the top cake tier (above). Using one hand to hold the spatula and the other to steady the tier, lift the tier off the central dowel. Wrap the tier in foil and freeze it for the bride and groom's first anniversary, or set it aside for serving.

20 **Removing the dowel.** Twist the central dowel, and pull it straight up and out of the remaining tiers. With a sharp knife, make a circular cut through the middle tier to the cake circle beneath, using as a guide the imprint left behind by the top cake tier. Remove the four now-visible supporting dowels.

21 **Cutting the middle tier.** By slicing to the circular cut, divide the middle tier into 1-inch [2½-cm.] pieces. Lift off the center of this tier (Step 19). Divide the edge of the bottom tier into slices the same way.

22 **Making final slices.** If serving the top tier, cut it into 1¼-inch [3-cm.] wedges. Then divide the remains of the first and second tiers into wedges of the same size.

Anthology
of Recipes

Drawing upon the cooking literature of more than 20 countries, the editors and consultants for this volume have selected 200 published recipes for the Anthology that follows. The selections range from the familiar to the elaborate—from simple gingerbreads and upside-down cakes to the festive *bûche de Noël,* a French Christmas cake artfully decorated to resemble a log. Many of the recipes were written by world-renowned exponents of the culinary art, but the Anthology also includes selections from rare and out-of-print books and from works that have never been published in English. Whatever the sources, the emphasis in these recipes is always on techniques that are practical for the home cook.

Since many early recipe writers did not specify amounts of ingredients, sizes of pans, or even cooking times and temperatures, the missing information has been judiciously added. In some cases, clarifying introductory notes have also been supplied; they are printed in italics. Modern recipe terms have been substituted for archaic language but, to preserve the character of the original recipes and to create a true anthology, the authors' texts have been changed as little as possible.

In keeping with the organization of the first half of the book, most of the recipes are categorized according to the technique and the ingredients. Recipes for standard preparations—frostings, icings and almond paste among them—appear at the end of the Anthology. Unfamiliar cooking terms and uncommon ingredients are defined or explained in the combined General Index and Glossary.

All ingredients are listed within each recipe in order of use, with both the customary United States measurements and the metric measurements provided. All quantities reflect the American practice of measuring such solid ingredients as sugar or cocoa powder by volume rather than by weight, as is done in Europe. White granulated sugar is simply referred to as sugar throughout the Anthology unless brown or confectioners' sugar is used in the same recipe. All measures given for nuts, except those for chestnuts, are for shelled nuts.

To make the quantities simpler to measure, many of the figures have been rounded off to correspond to the gradations on U.S. metric spoons and cups. (One cup, for example, equals 237 milliliters; however, wherever practicable in these recipes, the metric equivalent of 1 cup appears as a more readily measured 250 milliliters—¼ liter.) Similarly, the weight, oven-temperature and linear metric equivalents have been rounded off slightly. Thus the American and metric figures do not exactly match, but using one set or the other will produce the same good results.

Angel Food and Meringue Cakes

Angel Cake

To make one 9-inch [23-cm.] tube cake

1¼ cups	sugar	300 ml.
1 cup	sifted cake flour	¼ liter
½ tsp.	salt	2 ml.
1¼ cups	egg whites (about 10)	300 ml.
2 tbsp.	water, or 1 tbsp. [15 ml.] water plus 1 tbsp. strained fresh lemon juice	30 ml.
1 tsp.	cream of tartar	5 ml.
½ tsp.	vanilla extract	2 ml.
½ tsp.	almond extract	2 ml.
2 cups	thin chocolate icing *(recipe, page 165)*	½ liter

Sift the sugar twice. Resift the flour three times with ¼ cup [50 ml.] of the sifted sugar and the salt. Whip the egg whites with the water, or water and lemon juice, until the mixture is foamy, then add the cream of tartar and continue whipping until the whites are stiff but not dry. Fold in the vanilla and almond extracts. Gradually whip in—about 1 tablespoon [15 ml.] at a time—the remaining sifted sugar. Sift the flour-and-sugar mixture, about ¼ cup at a time, over the batter. Fold it in gently and briefly after each addition. Pour the batter into an unbuttered tube cake pan. Bake in a preheated 350° F. [180° C.] oven for about 45 minutes, or until the cake is lightly golden on top. To cool, invert the pan and let the cake hang by resting the pan on its legs for about one and one half hours. When the cake has cooled, turn it right side up and loosen it by running a knife around the outside edge and the center tube. Then invert the cake onto a wire rack and ice it with the thin chocolate icing.

IRMA S. ROMBAUER AND MARION ROMBAUER BECKER
THE JOY OF COOKING

Forgotten Torte

This cake is better two or three days after baking.

To make one 10-inch [25-cm.] cake

5	egg whites	5
¼ tsp.	salt	1 ml.
½ tsp.	cream of tartar	2 ml.
1½ cups	sugar	375 ml.
1 tsp.	vanilla extract	5 ml.

Beat the egg whites until frothy. Add the salt and cream of tartar, and beat until the whites are very stiff. Gradually beat in the sugar, 2 tablespoons [30 ml.] at a time. Then blend in the vanilla extract.

Lightly butter and flour the bottom of a spring-form pan and spread the egg-white mixture in it. Place the pan in a preheated 400° F. [200° C.] oven and immediately turn off the heat. Leave the door of the oven closed and let the torte remain in the oven overnight; remove it from the oven the following morning. Serve the torte with ice cream and fresh berries or other fruit.

HAZEL G. ZENKER
CAKE BAKERY

Almond Cake

Gâteau aux Amandes

To make one 10-inch [25-cm.] cake

20	egg whites	20
	salt	
3 cups plus 2 tbsp.	sugar	780 ml.
4 cups	sifted cake flour	1 liter
½ lb. plus 1½ tbsp.	butter, softened	280 g.
	lemon extract or finely grated lemon peel	
⅓ cup	almonds, blanched, peeled and slivered	75 ml.

Beat the egg whites with a pinch of salt until they are very firm. Gently mix in the sugar, spoonful by spoonful, whisking between additions to keep the mixture creamy but still firm. Add all at once the flour, the butter, and a few drops of lemon extract or a pinch of grated lemon peel. Mix well, but gently, to avoid deflating the whites. Fill a well-buttered spring-form pan with the preparation and sprinkle it lavishly with the almonds. Bake in a preheated 375° F. [190° C.] oven for 45 minutes, or until a tester inserted in the cake comes out moist but clean. Remove the cake from the pan and cool it on a rack before cutting it into serving portions.

LOUISETTE BERTHOLLE
SECRETS OF THE GREAT FRENCH RESTAURANTS

Almond Meringue Cake

Gâteau à la Bennich

To make one 7-inch [18-cm.] cake

1 cup	almonds, blanched, peeled and ground (about ¼ lb. [125 g.])	¼ liter
½ cup	superfine sugar	125 ml.
4	egg whites, stiffly beaten	4
2 cups	rich butter cream *(recipe, page 166)*	½ liter
	toasted slivered almonds	

Add the ground almonds and sugar to the stiffly beaten egg whites. Pour the batter into two buttered and floured layer-cake pans, and bake in a preheated 300° F. [150° C.] oven for 30 minutes, or until a tester inserted in the center comes out clean. Turn the cakes out on racks to cool.

When the layers are cool, stack them, spreading some of the butter cream between them. Spread the rest of the cream on top. Sprinkle with toasted slivered almonds.

INGA NORBERG
GOOD FOOD FROM SWEDEN

Meringue Cake

Le Succès

This cake may also be formed into a heart shape as demonstrated on pages 42-43. The praline-flavored rich butter cream may be replaced by rich white butter cream.

To make one 8-inch [20-cm.] cake

3½ oz.	almonds, blanched, peeled and ground (about 1 cup [¼ liter])	105 g.
¼ cup	sugar	50 ml.
⅔ cup	confectioners' sugar	150 ml.
4	egg whites, stiffly beaten	4
2 cups	rich butter cream *(recipe, page 166)*	½ liter
¼ cup	praline powder *(recipe, page 167)*	50 ml.
	almonds, blanched, peeled and chopped	

In a bowl, mix the ground almonds and sugar with ⅓ cup [75 ml.] of the confectioners' sugar. With a spatula, fold the almond mixture into the beaten egg whites, being careful not to make the whites collapse. Put the mixture into a pastry bag and, using a large No. 4 plain tube, pipe it into two spiral rounds on a buttered and floured baking sheet. Bake in a preheated 325° F. [160° C.] oven for one hour, reducing the oven temperature if the meringue rounds color too rapidly. Allow them to cool completely before removing them from the baking sheet.

Meanwhile, make the butter cream and fold in the praline powder. Spread one of the cooled meringue rounds with a ½-inch [1-cm.] layer of butter cream, cover it with the other round, and spread the top and sides of the cake with butter cream. Sprinkle the cake surface with the remaining confectioners' sugar, and press the chopped almonds into the sides. The cake may be refrigerated overnight.

JEAN KELLER
LES PÂTISSERIES ET LES BONBONS

Chocolate and Meringue Cake

Dacquoise au Chocolat

To make one 9-inch [23-cm.] cake

¾ cup	sugar	175 ml.
1½ tbsp.	cornstarch	22½ ml.
½ cup	hazelnuts	125 ml.
½ cup	almonds	125 ml.
6	egg whites, stiffly beaten	6
1½ cups	rich butter cream *(recipe, page 166)* flavored with 3 oz. [90 g.] semisweet chocolate	375 ml.
3 tbsp.	almonds or hazelnuts, chopped	45 ml.
1 tbsp.	confectioners' sugar	15 ml.

Butter and flour a baking sheet and two flan rings 9 inches [23 cm.] in diameter and 1 inch [2½ cm.] deep. Place the rings on the prepared baking sheet.

Mix the sugar and cornstarch together. Grind the almonds and hazelnuts in a blender and add them to the sugar. Fold the egg whites into the almond mixture. Pour the mixture into the two prepared rings and bake in a preheated 390° to 400° F. [195° to 200° C.] oven for 20 minutes. Let the meringue cool in the rings.

Remove the rings from the two disks of meringue. One side of each (the side that touched the baking sheet) will be very flat. Place one layer, flat side down, on a serving tray. Spoon all but 2 tablespoons [30 ml.] of the butter cream on top. Place the other layer, flat side up, on top of the cream. Using a spatula, smooth the remaining butter cream around the cake. Press the chopped almonds into the cream all around the cake. Put the powdered sugar in a sieve and sprinkle over the cake so that the top is covered with a white blanket. Refrigerate. Serve cold, cut into little wedges.

JACQUES PÉPIN
A FRENCH CHEF COOKS AT HOME

Butter-Cream Layer Cake

Marjolaine

The 5-by-20-inch [12-by-50-cm.] cake pan specified in this recipe is available at kitchen-equipment stores. If the pan is not available, the layer shapes can be traced onto parchment paper, the paper set on a baking sheet, and the mixture spread evenly on the paper. If using this method, trim off the edges of the cakes after baking them. The technique for making chocolate shavings is demonstrated on page 17.

To make one 5-by-20-inch [12-by-50-cm.] cake

1¾ cups	almonds, blanched (about 7 oz. [200 g.])	425 ml.
1¼ cups	hazelnuts (about 5 oz. [150 g.])	300 ml.
1¼ cups	superfine sugar	300 ml.
¼ cup	flour	50 ml.
8	egg whites, stiffly beaten	8
	chocolate shavings	
	confectioners' sugar	

Chocolate cream

1 cup	heavy cream	¼ liter
12 oz.	semisweet baking chocolate, melted	350 g.

White cream

1 cup	heavy cream, whipped and flavored with vanilla sugar, and drained in a strainer for ½ hour to remove excess liquid	¼ liter
4 tbsp.	butter, softened	60 ml.

Praline cream

1 cup	heavy cream, whipped and flavored with vanilla sugar, and drained in a strainer for ½ hour to remove excess liquid	¼ liter
4 tbsp.	butter, softened	60 ml.
6 tbsp.	praline powder (recipe, page 167)	90 ml.

Roast the almonds and the hazelnuts on separate baking sheets in a 400° F. [200° C.] oven for 10 minutes, or until lightly browned. Rub the skins off the hazelnuts in a towel. Grind the nuts together in a mortar or blender, then add the sugar and the flour, and grind everything together very fine. Gently fold the nut mixture into the beaten egg whites, sprinkling it on lightly as you fold. Spread the mixture into four buttered and lightly floured baking pans. Bake in a preheated 400° F. [200° C.] oven for three to four minutes, or until evenly browned and swollen in the center. Cool the layers and remove them from the pans.

To make the chocolate cream, stir the heavy cream into the melted chocolate. Bring the mixture to a boil, stirring constantly, then remove from the heat and cool. To make the white cream, beat the drained whipped cream into the softened butter, little by little, until no more can be absorbed. Make the praline cream in the same way as the white cream, folding in the praline powder at the end.

Spread half of the chocolate cream on the first cake layer, top with the second layer, and spread this layer with all of the white cream. Top with the third layer, and spread this layer with all of the praline cream, then top with the fourth layer. Spread the entire cake with the remaining chocolate cream. Press chocolate shavings into the sides of the cake, and sprinkle the top with confectioners' sugar. Refrigerate for 24 hours before serving.

FERNAND POINT
MA GASTRONOMIE

Hazelnut Torte

To make one 9-inch [23-cm.] cake

1½ cups	hazelnuts (about 6 oz. [175 g.])	375 ml.
1⅓ cups	superfine sugar	325 ml.
4	egg whites, stiffly beaten	4
3 tsp.	vanilla extract	15 ml.
1 tsp.	strained fresh lemon juice	5 ml.
1 cup	heavy cream, whipped	¼ liter
2 tbsp.	granulated sugar	30 ml.
	confectioners' sugar	

Roast the hazelnuts in a preheated 475° F. [240° C.] oven for about 10 minutes, or until the skins crack open and the nuts are toasted. Shake the pan occasionally so the nuts will brown evenly. Empty the nuts onto a clean towel and rub them briskly to remove the skins. Put the skinned nuts through a nut grinder or grind them in a food processor. Sift the ground nuts to eliminate any large pieces.

Beat the superfine sugar gradually into the egg whites and continue to beat for several minutes. Add 2 teaspoons [10 ml.] of the vanilla extract, then the lemon juice, and beat for two or three minutes longer to make sure that all of the sugar has been thoroughly dissolved in the egg whites. Carefully fold in a little more than three quarters of the nuts. Divide the mixture in half and spread it evenly in two buttered and floured layer-cake pans, the bottoms of which have been lined with parchment paper.

Bake in a preheated 300° F. [150° C.] oven for about 30 minutes, or until the cakes are firm but not browned. Turn the layers out onto a wire rack and remove the paper immediately. Let the cakes cool.

When ready to serve, set one layer on a plate. Mix the whipped cream with the granulated sugar and the remaining vanilla extract. Fold in the rest of the nuts, spread the cream on the layer and cover with the second layer. Sprinkle the top of the cake with confectioners' sugar and serve.

ANN SERANNE
THE COMPLETE BOOK OF DESSERTS

Creole Pecan Torte

To make one 9-inch [23-cm.] cake

6	egg whites, stiffly beaten	6
¾ cup	granulated sugar	175 ml.
1 tbsp.	vanilla extract	15 ml.
3 cups	pecans, finely ground (about ¾ lb. [⅓ kg.])	¾ liter
	Rum cream filling	
6	egg yolks	6
3 tbsp.	dark brown sugar	45 ml.
about ¾ cup	praline powder (recipe, page 167), made with ⅔ cup [150 ml.] chopped pecans, ½ cup [125 ml.] granulated sugar, ¼ cup [50 ml.] water and 1 tsp. [5 ml.] strained fresh lemon juice	about 175 ml.
about ½ lb.	unsalted butter, softened	about ¼ kg.
⅓ cup	rum	75 ml.
	confectioners' sugar	

Butter and flour three baking sheets. Trace a circle on each with a 9-inch [23-cm.] pot lid. Beat the egg whites until stiff, adding 3 tablespoons [45 ml.] of the granulated sugar and the vanilla extract toward the end of the beating. Fold in a mixture of the remaining sugar and the ground pecans. Spread the meringue in the circles on the prepared baking sheets and bake in a preheated 325° F. [160° C.] oven for 20 to 25 minutes. If only one oven and one baking sheet are available, make one sheet at a time; keep the batter refrigerated while waiting.

Beat the egg yolks to the ribbon stage, then add the brown sugar and praline powder. Cream in the butter, tablespoon by tablespoon. Add the rum. If the filling separates, add 1 to 2 more tablespoons [15 to 30 ml.] of butter. Trim the edges of the meringue layers neatly, and fill with rum cream. Refrigerate the cake and let it mellow for 24 hours. Sprinkle the top with confectioners' sugar before serving.

MADELEINE KAMMAN
THE MAKING OF A COOK

Macadamia Nut Cake with Rum-flavored Butter Cream

La Hawaiienne

To make one 8-inch [20-cm.] cake

½ cup	sifted flour	125 ml.
½ tsp.	baking powder	2 ml.
4 tbsp.	unsalted butter, softened	60 ml.
1 cup	unsalted macadamia nuts or almonds, blanched and very finely chopped (about ¼ lb. [125 g.])	¼ liter
4	egg whites	4
	salt	
½ cup	sugar	125 ml.
2 tbsp.	rum	30 ml.
2 cups	simple butter cream (recipe, page 166), flavored with 2 tbsp. [30 ml.] of rum and ¾ cup [175 ml.] of ground macadamia nuts or ground almonds	½ liter
7 or 8	pistachio nuts, blanched, peeled and coarsely chopped	7 or 8

Sift the flour with the baking powder. Beat the butter with the chopped nuts until the mixture is very creamy. Add the flour mixture.

Beat the egg whites with a pinch of salt until they form soft peaks. Continue beating, sprinkling in the sugar, until the resulting meringue holds fairly stiff peaks. Stir one quarter of the meringue into the butter-and-nut mixture to lighten it, then delicately fold in the rest of the meringue. Turn the batter into a well-buttered spring-form pan or a buttered cake pan 4 inches [10 cm.] deep lined with buttered parchment paper.

Bake in a preheated 375° F. [190° C.] oven for 20 to 25 minutes, or until the cake has risen nicely, has pulled away from the sides of the pan, and is slightly golden. Remove the pan to a wire rack. After 10 minutes, run a knife around the inside edges of the pan and turn the cake out onto the rack; remove the paper if you have used it.

When the cake has cooled completely, slice it in half horizontally to make two even layers. Sprinkle the rum over the cut surfaces. Spread one layer with about one third of the butter cream. Press the second layer firmly on top. Spread the remaining butter cream smoothly over the top and sides of the cake. Press the chopped pistachios into the sides of the cake. The cake can be stored for a day or two in the refrigerator, but remove it 30 minutes before serving so that the butter cream will be creamy.

SIMONE BECK AND MICHAEL JAMES
NEW MENUS FROM SIMCA'S CUISINE

Hungarian Cake

To make two 9-inch [23-cm.] or three 8-inch [20-cm.] cakes

9	egg whites	9
1½ cups	sifted confectioners' sugar	375 ml.
½ cup	fine cracker crumbs	125 ml.
8 oz.	unsweetened chocolate, grated	¼ kg.
2 tbsp.	flour	30 ml.
1 tsp.	baking powder	5 ml.
½ cup	hazelnuts, almonds, walnuts or pecans, blanched, peeled and ground	125 ml.
¼ cup	sweet white or red wine	50 ml.
2 tsp.	vanilla extract	10 ml.
1 tbsp.	strained fresh lemon juice	15 ml.
2 to 3 cups	rich butter cream (recipe, page 166), flavored with 3 oz. [90 g.] unsweetened chocolate	½ to ¾ liter
	shaved chocolate	
	confectioners' sugar	
	candied cherries (optional)	

Beat the egg whites until they stand in firm peaks, gradually folding in the sifted confectioners' sugar. Combine the cracker crumbs, grated chocolate, flour, baking powder and nuts, and carefully fold the mixture into the beaten egg whites. Fold in the wine, vanilla extract and lemon juice. Turn the batter into two or three layer-cake pans that have been buttered, floured and lined with buttered parchment paper. Bake in a preheated 350° F. [180° C.] oven for 40 to 45 minutes, or until a cake tester inserted in the centers of the layers comes out clean. Unmold the cakes and cool them on a wire rack.

Frost the cakes with butter cream and garnish them with shaved chocolate. Sprinkle the tops with confectioners' sugar and, if desired, put a candied cherry in the center. (These cakes can also be filled and stacked in conventional layer-cake fashion with the top decorated as described.)

HENRI PAUL PELLAPRAT
THE GREAT BOOK OF FRENCH CUISINE

Progress Cake

Gâteau Progrès

Almond flour, also known as almond powder, is obtainable at specialty food stores. Or, to make it at home, grind almonds a few at a time in a food processor operated in short spurts. Then pass the powder through a fine sieve to remove any large bits. About 1 pound [½ kg.] of nuts will yield the 4 cups [1 liter] of flour needed for this recipe.

Praline paste is sold in jars at specialty food stores.

To make one 6-by-9-inch [15-by-23-cm.] cake

10	egg whites	10
2 cups	sugar	½ liter
¼ cup	cornstarch	50 ml.
4 cups	almond flour	1 liter
½ cup	praline paste	125 ml.
2 cups	rich butter cream (recipe, page 166)	½ liter
	kirsch	
2 oz.	unsweetened chocolate, melted and cooled	60 g.
¼ cup	almonds, blanched, peeled, toasted and sliced thin	50 ml.

Beat the egg whites with the sugar. When the mixture is thick, add the cornstarch. Mix in the almond flour gently with your hands. With a pastry bag or spatula, spread the mixture on baking sheets lined with parchment paper to make three thin rectangular layers, each about 6 by 9 inches [15 by 23 cm.]. Bake in a preheated 200° F. [100° C.] oven for 30 minutes. When you take this meringue from the oven it will be soft. Invert the rectangles onto cake racks lined with parchment paper and let them cool and harden. Then remove the paper.

Mix half of the praline paste with the butter cream and a drop of kirsch. Spread one quarter of the mixture on one of the meringue layers. Cover with another layer. Spread it with another quarter of the butter-cream mixture. Cover this with the remaining layer to form the cake. Spread the remaining butter-cream mixture over the whole cake. Mix the remaining praline paste with the melted chocolate and refrigerate for one hour. Remove the mixture from the refrigerator and work it with a wooden spoon. Roll it into a sausage shape. Flatten and use to make a diagonal band across the cake from one corner to another. Sprinkle the almonds over all of the top except the chocolate band.

CHARLOTTE ADAMS
THE FOUR SEASONS COOKBOOK

Cinnamon Apple Cake

Kaneläppelkaka

To make one 10-inch [25-cm.] cake

¼ cup	fine dry bread crumbs	50 ml.
4	eggs	4
1¼ cups	sugar	300 ml.
½ lb.	butter, melted	¼ kg.
1½ cups	sifted flour	375 ml.
1 tsp.	baking powder	5 ml.
3	apples, peeled, cored and cut into wedges	3
2 tsp.	ground cinnamon	10 ml.

Sprinkle a buttered cake pan or cast-iron skillet with the bread crumbs. Beat the eggs with 1 cup [¼ liter] of the sugar until the mixture is thick and pale. Add the melted butter and the flour—sifted with the baking powder—and blend well. Pour this batter into the cake pan or skillet. Dip the apples in the remaining sugar mixed with the cinnamon. Put the apples into the cake batter.

Bake in a preheated 350° F. [180° C.] oven for 30 to 35 minutes, or until the top is golden and an inserted tester comes out clean. Serve the cake hot or at room temperature.

GÖREL KRISTINA NÄSLUND
SWEDISH BAKING

Black-Walnut Chiffon Cake

To make one 9-inch [23-cm.] cake

1 cup	black walnuts, finely ground (about ¼ lb. [125 g.])	¼ liter
2¼ cups	sifted cake flour	550 ml.
¾ cup	granulated sugar	175 ml.
1 tbsp.	baking powder	15 ml.
1 tsp.	salt	5 ml.
¾ cup	brown sugar	175 ml.
½ cup	vegetable oil	125 ml.
5	egg yolks	5
8	egg whites, stiffly beaten with ½ tsp. [2 ml.] cream of tartar	8
¾ cup	cold water	175 ml.
2 tsp.	vanilla extract	10 ml.
2 cups	seven-minute icing (recipe, page 165), flavored with 1 tsp. [5 ml.] maple syrup	2 ml.
	halved black walnuts	

Sift together the ground black walnuts, the flour, granulated sugar, baking powder and salt. Stir in the brown sugar.

Add consecutively the oil, egg yolks, water and vanilla extract. Beat the batter until very smooth. Gradually pour the batter into the stiffly beaten egg whites, folding the batter into the whites until just blended.

Pour the batter into two buttered and floured layer-cake pans that have been lined with parchment paper. Bake the cake for 45 minutes in a preheated 325° F. [160° C.] oven. Then increase the heat to 350° F. [180° C.] and bake the cake for 10 minutes more, or until a tester inserted in the center of each layer comes out clean. Cool the layers on a rack.

Spread the icing between the layers and over the cake, and decorate the top with halved black walnuts.

LANDON SCHOOL
LANDON'S FAVORITE DESSERTS COOKBOOK

Praline Chiffon Cake

To make one 10-inch [25-cm.] tube cake

1 cup plus 2 tbsp.	sifted cake flour	280 ml.
¾ cup	sugar	175 ml.
1½ tsp.	baking powder	7 ml.
½ tsp.	salt	2 ml.
¼ cup	vegetable oil	50 ml.
3	egg yolks	3
6 tbsp.	cold water	90 ml.
½ tsp.	vanilla extract	2 ml.
½ tsp.	almond extract	2 ml.
1 tsp.	grated lemon peel	5 ml.
½ cup	egg whites (about 4)	125 ml.
¼ tsp.	cream of tartar	1 ml.
2 cups	simple butter cream (recipe, page 166)	½ liter
½ cup	praline powder (recipe, page 167)	125 ml.

Sift the flour with the sugar, baking powder and salt into a mixing bowl. Make a well in the center. Place the oil, egg yolks, water, vanilla and almond extracts, and lemon peel in the well, and gradually pull in the dry ingredients while mixing. Beat the batter until smooth. Whip the whites, adding the cream of tartar when they become frothy. Beat until they are very stiff. Fold the batter gently into the egg whites.

Gently turn the batter into an unbuttered tube cake pan. Smooth the top. Bake in a preheated 325° F. [160° C.] oven for approximately one hour, or until a cake tester comes out clean. Remove the cake from the oven and invert the pan, allowing the cake to hang by resting the pan on its center tube, for one hour, or until completely cool. Remove the cake from the pan and frost it with the butter cream. Cover the sides and top of the cake with the praline powder.

HAZEL G. ZENKER
CAKE BAKERY

Lemon Chiffon Cake

Do not use the cream of tartar if you are beating the egg whites in a copper bowl.

Fresh orange juice and peel may be used in place of lemon to make orange chiffon cake. This cake also may be iced with glacé icing flavored with fresh lemon juice.

To make one 10-inch [25-cm.] tube cake

2¼ cups	cake flour	550 ml.
1½ cups	sugar	375 ml.
3 tsp.	baking powder	15 ml.
1 tsp.	salt	5·ml.
½ cup	vegetable oil	125 ml.
½ cup	strained fresh lemon juice	125 ml.
¼ cup	water	50 ml.
6	eggs, yolks separated from the whites, plus 1 extra white	6
1 tsp.	grated lemon peel	5 ml.
½ tsp.	cream of tartar	2 ml.
1 cup	glacé icing *(recipe, page 165)*, made with 2 to 3 tbsp. [30 to 45 ml.] unstrained fresh lemon juice instead of water, and flavored with 1 tsp. [5 ml.] grated lemon peel	¼ liter

Sift the flour, sugar, baking powder and salt into a large mixing bowl and make a well in the center. Add the oil, lemon juice, water, egg yolks and lemon peel. Beat the mixture with a spoon, pulling in the dry ingredients until the batter is smooth.

Beat the egg whites until they are foamy, then add the cream of tartar and beat until very stiff peaks form. Fold the batter gradually and gently into the egg whites.

Pour into an unbuttered tube cake pan and bake in a preheated 325° F. [160° C.] oven for 55 minutes, or until a cake tester inserted in the center comes out clean.

Remove the cake from the oven and invert the pan onto its slightly protruding center tube. Let the cake, which now will be hanging upside down in the pan, cool for one hour. Loosen the cake by running a knife around the inside edges, turn it out of the pan, and pour the glacé icing over it.

HAZEL G. ZENKER
CAKE BAKERY

Spongecakes

Catalan Spongecake
Pa de-Pessic

To make one cake 9 inches [23 cm.] square

1 cup	sugar	¼ liter
8	eggs, yolks separated from whites, whites stiffly beaten	8
1 tsp.	vanilla extract	5 ml.
2 tsp.	grated lemon peel	10 ml.
1 cup	flour	¼ liter
¾ cup	cornstarch	175 ml.
4 tbsp.	butter, melted and cooled	60 ml.

Beat the sugar, egg yolks, vanilla extract and lemon peel together until the mixture is pale and fluffy. Alternately stir in—a tablespoonful [15 ml.] or so at a time—the flour and cornstarch until both are used up. Beat in the butter. Fold in the egg whites.

Put the mixture into a buttered square cake pan, and bake in a preheated 350° F. [180° C.] oven for 30 to 35 minutes, or until the cake springs back when touched lightly in the center.

ÉLIANE THIBAUT COMELADE
LA CUISINE CATALANE

Narcissa Nale's Spongecake

To make one 9-inch [23-cm.] cake

1 cup	sifted superfine sugar	¼ liter
4	eggs, yolks separated from whites, whites stiffly beaten	4
½ cup	sifted potato starch	125 ml.
1 tsp.	baking powder	5 ml.
¼ tsp.	salt	1 ml.

Gradually beat half of the sugar into the egg whites, leaving them stiff but not dry. In another bowl beat the egg yolks until they are thick and lemon-colored, then beat in the remaining sugar. Sift the potato flour with the baking powder and salt. Blend the flour mixture into the egg yolks, then cut and fold the whites into the mixture until the batter is well mixed. Do not beat it.

Pour the batter into an unbuttered cake pan—it should be about two thirds full—and bake in a preheated 350° F. [180° C.] oven for 30 to 40 minutes, or until the sides of the cake begin to shrink from the pan and the top is golden brown. Cool the cake in the pan for 10 minutes before turning it out onto a wire rack.

NARCISSE CHAMBERLAIN AND NARCISSA G. CHAMBERLAIN
THE CHAMBERLAIN SAMPLER OF AMERICAN COOKING

Génoise

To make one 9-inch [23-cm.] cake

6	whole eggs	6
¾ cup	sugar	175 ml.
¾ cup	sifted flour	175 ml.
½ cup	sugar syrup (recipe, page 164), flavored with a few drops of vanilla extract	125 ml.
2 cups	rich butter cream (recipe, page 166)	½ liter

Place the eggs and ¾ cup [75 ml.] of the sugar in the top of a double boiler. Set the mixture over warm, not hot, water and beat with a rotary or electric beater until the mixture forms a ribbon. Remove the top pan from the double boiler and continue beating the mixture until it cools to room temperature. At this point, sift the flour into the mixture a small quantity at a time; fold the flour in thoroughly but gently after each addition. Pour the batter into a buttered and floured cake pan.

Bake in a preheated 400° F. [200° C.] oven for 30 to 35 minutes, or until a tester inserted in the center comes out clean. Turn the cake out immediately onto a wire rack to cool. When it is cold, split it in two horizontally.

Spoon the sugar syrup over the cut surfaces of the *génoise*, then fill and frost it with the rich butter cream.

HELEN MC CULLY, JACQUES PÉPIN AND WILLIAM JAYME
THE OTHER HALF OF THE EGG

Steamed Spongecake

To make one cake 9 inches [23 cm.] square

6	eggs, yolks separated from whites, whites stiffly beaten	6
1 to 1½ cups	sugar	250 to 375 ml.
2½ tbsp.	water	37 ml.
1½ cups	flour	375 ml.
½ tsp.	baking powder	2 ml.
1 tsp.	vanilla extract	5 ml.

Beat the yolks in a large bowl. Add the sugar and water and beat the mixture until it is fluffy. Sift together the flour and the baking powder and gradually add them to the egg yolks,

mixing well. Blend in the vanilla extract. Fold the egg whites into the batter. Pour the batter into a cake pan 3 inches [8 cm.] deep that has been lined with parchment paper or foil. Rap the pan sharply on the table several times to remove large air bubbles.

Place a rack or inverted bowl in a deep pot; add water to the pot to come just below the level of the rack or the upturned base of the bowl, and bring the water to a boil. Place the batter-filled cake pan on the rack or on the base of the bowl; the boiling water should not touch the cake pan. Cover the large pot and steam the cake for about 20 minutes, until a tester inserted in the center of the cake comes out clean. Let the cake cool for a few moments in the pan, then invert the cake onto a large, flat platter. Remove the parchment paper or foil. Turn the cake right side up. Cut it into 2-inch [5-cm.] squares for serving.

GLORIA BLEY MILLER
THE THOUSAND RECIPE CHINESE COOKBOOK

St. George's Cake

Pastel Sant Jordi

This cake is a particular specialty of Barcelona.

To make one 4-by-8-inch [10-by-20-cm.] cake

6	eggs, yolks separated from whites	6
⅔ cup	sugar	150 ml.
1¾ cups	flour	425 ml.
1 cup	simple butter cream (recipe, page 166), flavored with 1 tbsp. [15 ml.] cocoa powder	¼ liter
	confectioners' sugar	

Beat the egg whites with the sugar until stiff. Lightly beat the yolks and add them to the whites. Finally, add the flour, mixing everything gently so that the beaten egg whites do not liquefy. Pour the mixture into a buttered baking pan approximately 8 by 12 inches [20 by 30 cm.]. Bake in a preheated 400° F. [200° C.] oven for 40 minutes, or until the top of the cake is nicely browned. Take it out, remove the cake from the pan, and let it cool on a wire rack.

Cut the cake crosswise into three slices and stack them one on top of the other, spreading a coating of butter cream between each layer. The top layer of cake should not be spread with the cream. Place the cake in the refrigerator. Just before serving, sprinkle it with confectioners' sugar.

MARÍA DEL CARMEN CASCANTE
150 RECETAS DE DULCES DE FÁCIL PREPARACIÓN

Household Savarin

Savarin de Menage

Classic savarin, made with yeast dough, appears on pages 66-67. This version is designed to be made more quickly at home.

To make one 9-inch [23-cm.] ring cake

2	eggs	2
1 cup	sifted flour	¼ liter
½ cup	sugar	125 ml.
1 tsp.	baking powder	5 ml.
	salt	
1 cup	heavy cream, whipped with 2 tsp. [10 ml.] sugar and 1 tsp. [5 ml.] vanilla extract (optional)	¼ liter
Rum syrup		
6 tbsp.	rum	90 ml.
2 tbsp.	hot water	30 ml.
¼ cup	sugar	50 ml.

Heat a mixing bowl by rinsing it with very hot water. Dry the bowl and wrap its base in a hot towel. Beat the eggs in the bowl until they have doubled in size, then combine the flour, sugar, baking powder and a pinch of salt and fold them gradually into the eggs, beating well all the time. Put the batter into a buttered ring mold so that the mixture comes halfway up the sides. Bake the cake in the center of a preheated 325° F. [160° C.] oven for 20 minutes, then increase the heat to 400° F. [200° C.] and cook for 10 minutes longer, until a tester inserted in the cake comes out clean. Remove the cake from the pan, place it on a wire rack, cover it with a towel, and let it cool for five minutes. Then invert the cake onto a serving plate, and prick the cake all over lightly with a fork. Heat the syrup ingredients gently until the sugar dissolves; do not let the syrup boil or the rum will lose its alcoholic content. Spoon the syrup over the cake. Let the cake steep for at least one hour. Serve the cake plain or with the whipped cream.

THEODORA FITZGIBBON
A TASTE OF PARIS

French Spongecake

This batter may be baked in two 9-inch [23-cm.] layer-cake pans, in which case the baking time should be increased to 20 to 25 minutes.

To make approximately two 9-by-13-inch [23-by-38-cm.] cakes

2 cups	sugar	½ liter
	salt	
9	eggs, yolks separated from whites	9
4 tsp.	grated lemon peel	20 ml.
2 cups	cake flour	½ liter

Whip the egg yolks and 1 cup [¼ liter] of the sugar to a thick consistency—about 15 minutes. Fold in the grated lemon peel. Sift in the flour, gently folding it into the yolk mixture. In a separate bowl, whip the egg whites and remaining sugar to a medium peak and fold them gently into the mixture.

Pour the batter lightly into buttered and floured pans. Shake the pans slightly to level the mixture. Be careful to pour the mixture in equal amounts over the entire pan so that a minimum of smearing with the spatula is required to distribute the batter evenly over the pans. Excessive smearing to spread the batter may cause a loss of some of the air. Bake the cake in a preheated 350° F. [180° C.] oven for 15 to 20 minutes. The cakes will feel springy to the touch when properly baked. Cool the cakes in the pan.

WILLIAM J. SULTAN
MODERN PASTRY CHEF

French Butter Spongecake

Génoise

To make one 9-inch [23-cm.] cake, 3 inches [8 cm.] deep, increase the baking time to 35 to 40 minutes. A génoise can be kept for several days if it is stored in an airtight container, or it can be frozen.

To make two 9-inch [23-cm.] cakes

6	eggs	6
1 cup	sugar	¼ liter
1 tsp.	vanilla extract or 4 tsp. [20 ml.] grated lemon peel, or ¼ cup [50 ml.] grated orange peel, or 2 tsp. [10 ml.] orange-flower water, or 2 or 3 drops anise oil	5 ml.
1 cup	flour, sifted three times with a pinch of salt	¼ liter
6 tbsp.	clarified butter (optional)	90 ml.

Put the eggs in a large bowl, preferably copper, and gradually beat in the sugar. Set the bowl over a pan of hot but not boiling water or over very low heat and beat eight to 10 minutes, or until the mixture is light and thick enough to leave a ribbon trail when the whisk is lifted. Take the bowl from the heat, add the chosen flavoring, and continue beating until the mixture is cool.

Sift the flour over the batter in three batches, folding in each batch with a wooden spatula or metal spoon as lightly as possible. Add the butter when you sift in the last batch, and fold in both together.

The batter quickly loses volume after the butter is added, so immediately pour the batter into two buttered and floured layer-cake pans that have been lined with parchment paper. Bake in a preheated 350° F. [180° C.] oven for 25 to 30 minutes, or until the cake shrinks slightly from the sides of the pan and the top springs back when lightly pressed with a finger tip. Run a knife around the sides of the cake to loosen it and turn it out onto a rack to cool.

ANNE WILLAN
LA VARENNE'S PARIS KITCHEN

Moss Rose Cake

To make one 8-inch [20-cm.] cake

4	eggs	4
2 cups	sugar	½ liter
½ tsp.	almond extract	2 ml.
1 cup	milk, scalded	¼ liter
2 cups	sifted cake flour	½ liter
2 tsp.	baking powder	10 ml.
1 cup	boiled icing (recipe, page 164)	¼ liter
2 cups	freshly grated coconut	½ liter
1	large orange, peel grated, juice strained	1
	sugar	

Break the eggs over the sugar and beat for 12 minutes—this must be done. Add the almond extract to the hot milk and let it cool slightly. Sift the flour with the baking powder and add them to the egg-and-sugar mixture.

Add the milk, slowly, and beat for three minutes. Pour the batter into two buttered and floured layer-cake pans and bake in a preheated 350° F. [180° C.] oven for 25 minutes, or until the layers shrink slightly from the sides of the pans. Turn the cakes out onto wire racks to cool completely.

Spread the boiled icing on the two cooled cake layers, but do not put the layers together.

Mix the coconut with the orange peel and juice, and sweeten to taste. When the frosting on the layers has begun to set but is not yet hard, pat the orange-coconut mixture into it and put the layers together.

MARION BROWN
THE SOUTHERN COOK BOOK

Mock Saddle of Venison Cake

Rehrücken

Rehrücken is a German word meaning "saddle of venison." Molds made in the appropriate shape of a stylized saddle of venison are sold in stores that specialize in international cookware. If a *Rehrücken* mold is not available, the cake may be made in a 4-by-12-inch [10-by-30-cm.] pan.

To make one 12-inch [30-cm.] Rehrücken or one 4-by-12-inch [10-by-30-cm.] loaf cake

5	eggs, yolks separated from whites, plus 2 whole eggs	5
½ cup	sugar	125 ml.
½ tsp.	ground cinnamon	2 ml.
2½ tbsp.	finely chopped candied citron	37 ml.
½ lb.	almonds, blanched and peeled, ¼ lb. [125 g.] grated (about 1 cup [¼ liter]) and ¼ lb. left whole	¼ kg.
2¼ oz.	unsweetened chocolate, grated (about ⅓ cup [75 ml.])	67½ g.
2 cups	thin chocolate icing (recipe, page 165)	½ liter

Beat the five egg whites until they foam, then beat in ¼ cup [50 ml.] of the sugar, 1 tablespoon [15 ml.] at a time. Continue beating until the whites form stiff peaks.

Combine the five yolks, the whole eggs and the rest of the sugar, and beat the mixture until it is pale yellow and thick. Beat in the cinnamon and citron. Stir the grated almonds and the chocolate into the egg-yolk mixture. Continue beating until all the ingredients are thoroughly blended.

With a rubber spatula, mix about one quarter of the egg whites into the batter, then reverse the process and pour the batter over the rest of the whites. Fold the ingredients together until no trace of the whites remain.

Pour the batter into a well-buttered loaf pan or *Rehrücken* mold that has been dusted with the dry bread crumbs, and bake in the middle of a preheated 350° F. [180° C.] oven for 25 to 30 minutes, or until the cake shrinks slightly away from the sides of the pan, is golden brown, and is springy to the touch.

Remove the cake from the oven and let it cool for two to three minutes. (In cooling, this very delicate cake may shrink slightly or fall a bit in the center, but in neither event will its final shape be affected.) Turn the cake out onto a wire rack to cool while you make the icing.

Set the rack on a jelly-roll pan and, holding the saucepan containing the icing about 2 inches [5 cm.] above the cake, pour the icing evenly over the cake. Halve the remaining almonds, and press them upright into the icing about 1 inch [2½ cm.] apart in a regular pattern. Let the cake cool completely, about 45 minutes, before serving. Slice the *Rehrücken* so that one of the shorter rows of almond halves decorates each serving.

FOODS OF THE WORLD/THE COOKING OF VIENNA'S EMPIRE

Yule Log
La Bûche de Noël

Rolling and decorating a Yule Log is demonstrated on pages 72-73. This recipe calls for an 8-by-12-inch [20-by-30-cm.] jelly-roll pan. If this pan size is unobtainable, use a 12½-by-15½-inch [31-by-39-cm.] jelly-roll pan and double the amounts of ingredients. Any leftover batter can be used to make cupcakes.

To make one rolled cake 12 inches [30 cm.] long

2 tbsp.	butter	30 ml.
4	eggs, yolks separated from whites, whites stiffly beaten	4
7 tbsp.	superfine sugar	105 ml.
	salt	
⅔ cup	flour	150 ml.
⅓ cup plus 2 tbsp.	sugar syrup (recipe, page 164), flavored with 1 tsp. [5 ml.] vanilla extract or 1 tbsp. [15 ml.] kirsch	105 ml.
2 cups	rich butter cream (recipe, page 166)	½ liter
2½ oz.	semisweet chocolate, melted and cooled	75 g.
	confectioners' sugar	
	almond paste (recipe, page 167), colored with green food coloring (optional)	

In a saucepan, melt the butter over low heat and cool it. Beat the egg yolks with the sugar and a pinch of salt until the mixture is lemon-colored and forms a ribbon. Add the flour and mix thoroughly. Gently fold in the beaten egg whites and then carefully blend the melted butter into the mixture. Pour the batter into a buttered and floured jelly-roll pan that has been lined with buttered parchment paper. The batter should be a little more than ½ inch [1 cm.] deep. Bake the cake in a preheated 450° F. [230° C.] oven for 10 minutes, until the cake is springy to the touch.

Turn the cake out onto a kitchen towel, pull off the paper, then roll the cake up with the towel to make a cylinder; let it cool. Unroll the cake and sprinkle it with the sugar syrup.

Mix 1½ cups [375 ml.] of the rich butter cream with the melted chocolate. Spread the cake with one third of the chocolate cream, and roll it up, starting at the long side. Cut the ends of the roll diagonally to resemble a sawed log. Place two flattened balls of the vanilla butter cream on the log to resemble knots in the wood. Place the remaining chocolate cream in a pastry bag with a large No. 4 open star tube, and pipe the cream in strips the length of the log to resemble bark. Spread the centers of the cut ends with the remaining vanilla butter cream to represent the heart of the log. Refrigerate the log until the cream is firm.

Dip a knife tip in hot water, and make holes in the chocolate cream over the balls of vanilla cream so that the knots show through. Sprinkle the log with confectioners' sugar, and decorate it as desired with ivy or holly formed from green almond paste. The log may be refrigerated overnight before serving.

JEAN KELLER
LES PÂTISSERIES ET LES BONBONS

Chestnut Almond Torte
Kastanien Mandel Torte

The torte is even more delicious when served with lightly sweetened whipped cream.

To make one 10-inch [25-cm.] cake

about ¾ lb.	chestnuts	about 350 g.
2 tbsp.	dark rum	30 ml.
4	eggs, yolks separated from whites, plus 1 white, whites stiffly beaten	4
¾ cup	sugar	175 ml.
1 cup	almonds, blanched, peeled and ground (about ¼ lb. [125 g.])	¼ liter
½ cup	apricot jam glaze (recipe, page 167)	125 ml.
2 cups	thin chocolate icing (recipe, page 165)	½ liter
Chocolate whipped-cream filling		
3 oz.	semisweet chocolate	90 g.
3 to 4 tbsp.	water	45 to 60 ml.
1 cup	heavy cream, whipped	¼ liter

Boil the chestnuts for 15 to 20 minutes. One by one, take the nuts from the water and peel them. Reserve half of one nut, and put the rest through a food mill or strainer to make 2¼ cups [550 ml.] of purée. Sprinkle the purée with the rum.

Beat the egg yolks and sugar until very light and fluffy. Gradually add the chestnut purée. Mix well. Fold in the ground almonds and the egg whites. Mix gently but thoroughly. Pour into a buttered and floured spring-form pan.

Place the cake in a preheated 350° F. [180° C.] oven. After 10 minutes, reduce the heat to 325° F. [160° C.] and bake the cake for 45 to 60 minutes. To test for doneness, insert a cake tester into the center of the cake; it should come out dry. Remove the outer ring of the spring-form pan and let the torte cool in a dry place. To make the filling, melt the chocolate in a double boiler with the water, cool almost to room temperature, and then fold in the whipped cream.

Slice the cooled torte into two layers. Spread chocolate filling over one layer and cover with the second layer. Refrigerate for several hours before spreading apricot glaze over the top of the torte. Pour the chocolate glaze over the top and sides of the cake and refrigerate again to set the icing. Place the reserved chestnut half in the center of the torte.

LILLY JOSS REICH
THE VIENNESE PASTRY COOKBOOK

Lemon Cupcakes

If possible, make the topping the night before you plan to bake the cupcakes.

	To make 12 cupcakes	
6	eggs, yolks separated from whites, whites stiffly beaten	6
2 cups	sugar	½ liter
1½ tbsp.	strained fresh lemon juice	22½ ml.
1 tsp.	grated lemon peel	5 ml.
½ cup	boiling water	125 ml.
2 cups	sifted flour	½ liter
1 cup	glacé icing (recipe, page 165), flavored with 1 tbsp. [15 ml.] fresh strained lemon juice, 1 tbsp. fresh strained orange juice, 1 tsp. [5 ml.] finely grated lemon peel and 1 tsp. finely grated orange peel	¼ liter

Beat the egg yolks well; add the sugar and beat together thoroughly. Add the fresh lemon juice and the grated peel, the boiling water and the sifted flour. Fold in the stiffly beaten egg whites. Half-fill buttered and floured cupcake pans with the batter. Bake in a preheated 450° F. [230° C.] oven about five or six minutes, until a cake tester inserted in the center of a cupcake comes out clean. Remove the cakes from the pans and, while they are still hot, dip the cakes in the glacé icing. After dipping, place the cakes on a cake rack set over wax paper to allow any excess icing to drain off.

ST. STEPHEN'S EPISCOPAL CHURCH
BAYOU CUISINE

Raspberry Roll

Hallonrulltårta

	To make one rolled cake 11 inches [27 cm.] long	
3	eggs	3
about ⅔ cup	sugar	about 150 ml.
⅔ cup	sifted cake flour	150 ml.
1 tsp.	baking powder	5 ml.
	Raspberry filling	
4 cups	raspberries	1 liter
1½ cups	heavy cream, whipped	375 ml.
	sugar	

Beat the eggs with ½ cup [125 ml.] of the sugar until the mixture is thick and pale. Sift together the flour and baking powder and blend them into the egg batter. Spread the bat-ter evenly in a buttered jelly-roll pan lined with buttered parchment paper. Bake in a preheated 425° F. [220° C.] oven for five to six minutes, or until golden. Sprinkle the cake with the remaining sugar and invert it onto a wire rack covered with parchment paper. Let the cake cool before lifting off the pan.

To make the filling, mix half of the whipped cream with the raspberries, reserving a handful of berries for garnish. Add sugar to taste. Spread the raspberry filling over the cooled cake, and roll the cake starting from one short side. Cover the roll with the remaining whipped cream and garnish it with the reserved berries.

GÖREL KRISTINA NÄSLUND
SWEDISH BAKING

Deluxe Chocolate Icebox Cake

	To make two 4½-by-9-inch [11½-by-23-cm.] cakes	
3	eggs, yolks separated from whites, whites stiffly beaten	3
1 cup	sugar	¼ liter
¼ cup	cold water	50 ml.
1 cup	flour	¼ liter
½ tsp.	salt	2 ml.
½ tsp.	baking powder	2 ml.
1 tsp.	vanilla extract	5 ml.
2 cups	rich butter cream (recipe, page 166), flavored with 4 oz. [125 g.] unsweetened chocolate	½ liter
2 cups	heavy cream, whipped, sweetened and lightly flavored with vanilla extract	½ liter

Beat the egg yolks and sugar until the mixture is very light. Slowly add the cold water and beat until the mixture is foamy. Sift together the flour, salt and baking powder, and add them to the egg yolks. Carefully fold in the egg whites and the vanilla extract.

Pour the batter into an unbuttered pan 9 inches [23 cm.] square that has been lined with parchment paper. Bake in a preheated 325° F. [160° C.] oven for 30 minutes, or until the cake shrinks from the sides of the pan. Invert the cake on a wire rack and cool it completely before lifting the pan off.

Cut the cooled spongecake in half vertically. Using a sharp knife, cut one half horizontally into as many thin layers as possible. Reserve 1 cup [¼ liter] of whipped cream for frosting. Spread a thin layer of butter cream on the bottom layer of cake; top it with a second layer. Spread whipped cream on that layer and top with the next layer of cake. Build up the layers, alternating butter cream and whipped cream, and ending with a layer of cake. Treat the other half of the cake similarly; refrigerate the two cakes. When ready to serve, cover the cakes with the reserved whipped cream.

THE JUNIOR CHARITY LEAGUE OF MONROE
THE COTTON COUNTRY COLLECTION

Carrot Cake
Rüblitorte

The marzipan carrots used to decorate this cake are obtainable from candy stores.

To make one 8-inch [20-cm.] cake

5	eggs, yolks separated from whites, whites stiffly beaten	5
1¼ cups	sugar	300 ml.
1 tsp.	grated lemon peel	5 ml.
10 oz.	almonds, blanched, peeled and finely ground (about 2½ cups [625 ml.])	300 g.
5	carrots, peeled and grated (about 1⅓ cups [325 ml.])	5
½ cup	flour	125 ml.
1 tsp.	baking powder	5 ml.
	salt	
2 tbsp.	jam, preferably apricot, thinned with 1 tbsp. [15 ml.] water	30 ml.
1 cup	glacé icing (recipe, page 165), made with fresh lemon juice	¼ liter
8	small marzipan carrots	8

Beat together the egg yolks and sugar until foamy, then add the lemon peel, almonds and grated carrots. Sift together the flour, baking powder and a pinch of salt, and combine them with the egg-yolk mixture. Fold in the egg whites, and turn the cake batter into a well-buttered and floured cake pan. Bake in a preheated 325° F. [160° C.] oven for 50 minutes, or until a tester inserted into the center of the cake comes out clean. Let the cake cool completely on a wire rack and brush it with the thinned jam.

Ice the cake and decorate with the marzipan carrots. Keep the cake in an airtight container for at least a day before serving.

EVA MARIA BORER
TANTE HEIDI'S SWISS KITCHEN

Swedish Almond Cake

This cake may be prepared as much as two days ahead of time; it may also be frozen.

To make one 8-inch [20-cm.] cake

1 cup plus 1 tbsp.	flour	265 ml.
1½ tsp.	baking powder	7 ml.
⅛ tsp.	salt	½ ml.
2	eggs	2
1 cup	sugar	¼ liter
1 tsp.	vanilla extract	5 ml.
¼ cup	cream	50 ml.
8 tbsp.	butter, melted and cooled	120 ml.
Sugared almond topping		
⅓ cup	almonds, blanched, peeled and slivered	75 ml.
4 tbsp.	butter	60 ml.
3 tbsp.	sugar	45 ml.
2 tbsp.	flour	30 ml.
1 tbsp.	cream	15 ml.

After measuring the flour, sift it together with the baking powder and salt.

Beat the eggs with an electric mixer; add the sugar gradually and beat until thick and lemony. Add the vanilla extract, then add the flour alternately with the cream, and beat just to mix. Be careful not to overbeat. Pour in the butter and blend with a spatula. Pour the mixture into a buttered and floured cake pan, and bake on the middle shelf of a preheated 350° F. [180° C.] oven for 30 minutes (or five minutes longer if the cake moves slightly in the center when you give it a little push).

While the cake is baking, mix all of the topping ingredients in a small saucepan and cook over high heat until the sugar dissolves.

Remove the cake from the oven, raise the oven temperature to 375° F. [190° C.], and spread the topping over the cake—the cake will sink when you add the topping. Return the cake to the oven for five to 10 minutes, or until the topping sizzles and browns.

JULIE DANNENBAUM
MENUS FOR ALL OCCASIONS

Walnut Torte

Hazelnuts or almonds may be substituted for walnuts in this recipe and the batter may be baked in a jelly-roll pan, in which case the baking time should be reduced to 15 to 20 minutes. The cake thus formed may be sliced to make three thin layers. It may be filled and topped with 2 to 3 cups [½ to

¾ liter] of rich white butter cream (recipe, page 166) instead of the chocolate icing specified in the recipe.

To make one 10-inch [25-cm.] cake		
6	eggs, yolks separated from whites, whites stiffly beaten	6
½ cup	sugar	125 ml.
2 tsp.	grated lemon peel	10 ml.
¼ cup	dry bread crumbs	50 ml.
1½ tbsp.	strained fresh lemon juice	22½ ml.
2½ cups	walnuts, finely ground (10 oz. [300 g.])	625 ml.
2 cups	thick chocolate icing (recipe, page 165), flavored with 1 tsp. [5 ml.] strong black coffee and ½ tsp. [2 ml.] vanilla extract	½ liter
	confectioners' sugar	

Beat the egg yolks and sugar until the mixture is very light and foamy. Mix the lemon peel and bread crumbs and sprinkle them with the lemon juice, then add the mixture to the sweetened egg yolks. Gently fold in the ground walnuts and egg whites, and pour the batter into a well-buttered and floured spring-form pan.

Bake in a preheated 350° F. [180° C.] oven for 30 to 40 minutes, or until a cake tester inserted into the center of the cake comes out clean and the top feels springy to the touch. Remove the outer ring of the pan and let the cake cool. Slice the cake horizontally into two layers. Spread thick chocolate icing between the layers and sandwich them together. Sprinkle the top of the torte with confectioners' sugar.

LILLY JOSS REICH
THE VIENNESE PASTRY COOKBOOK

New England Walnut Torte

To make one 10-inch [25-cm.] cake		
12	eggs, yolks separated from whites	12
1 cup	sugar	¼ liter
¾ cup	sifted flour	175 ml.
¼ cup	sifted cornstarch	50 ml.
1¼ cups	walnuts (5 oz. [150 g.]), about ¾ cup [175 ml.] finely ground and about ½ cup [125 ml.] chopped	300 ml.
1 tsp.	grated lemon peel	5 ml.
2 cups	rich butter cream (recipe, page 166)	½ liter

Combine the egg yolks with ¾ cup [175 ml.] of the sugar and beat until thick and light-colored.

In a separate bowl, beat six of the egg whites until they stand in soft peaks; reserve the remaining whites for an-

other use. Sprinkle the beaten whites with the rest of the sugar and beat only until the sugar is thoroughly mixed—do not let the whites become stiff. Fold one third of the egg whites into the egg-yolk mixture. Fold in the flour and cornstarch. Fold the ground walnuts into the batter along with the grated lemon peel and the remaining beaten egg whites. Pour the batter into a buttered and floured cake pan lined with parchment paper. Bake in a preheated 400° F. [200° C.] oven for 25 to 30 minutes, or until the cake springs back when touched lightly. Let the cake cool in the pan.

Remove the cake from the pan and cut it horizontally into two layers. Cover the bottom layer with one quarter of the butter cream. Sprinkle half of the chopped walnuts onto the covered layer. Place the second layer on top and spread the remaining butter cream on the top and sides of the cake. Sprinkle the rest of the chopped walnuts over the cake.

ALBERT STOCKLI
SPLENDID FARE: THE ALBERT STOCKLI COOKBOOK

Royal Mazurka

Mazurek Królewski

Mazurkas are traditional Polish Easter cakes. They should be baked in shallow rectangular pans.

To make one 9-by-12-inch [23-by-30-cm.] cake		
6	eggs	6
2⅔ cups	confectioners' sugar	650 ml.
½ cup	boiling water	125 ml.
3 tbsp.	strained fresh lemon juice	45 ml.
3¼ cups	flour	800 ml.
1 cup	almonds, blanched, peeled and ground (about ¼ lb. [125 g.])	¼ liter
¾ lb.	butter, melted	350 g.
1 cup	apricot jam	¼ liter
1 cup	glacé icing (recipe, page 165), made with 2 tsp. [10 ml.] strained fresh lemon juice instead of water	¼ liter

Beat the eggs with the sugar at high speed for 10 minutes. Mix the water with the lemon juice. Add this liquid to the eggs, in a thin stream, beating continuously. Beat for five minutes more. Add the flour, almonds and butter alternately in small portions. Mix lightly.

Divide the batter between two 9-by-12-inch [23-by-30-cm.] baking pans that have been buttered and lined with buttered parchment paper. Bake in a preheated 375° F. [190° C.] oven for 30 minutes, or until golden. Cool the cakes slightly, then turn them out onto a rack to cool. Spread one cake with the jam, cover it with the other cake, and spread the icing over the top. Serve in small squares.

ALINA ŻERAŃSKA
THE ART OF POLISH COOKING

Pistachio Cake

Vert-Vert

For the green coloring used in the pistachio cream, blanch a few leaves of spinach for one minute in boiling water, then force them through a fine sieve. Heat the resulting purée, drain it thoroughly, and use the thick paste that remains.

To make one 9-inch [23-cm.] cake

4	eggs	4
½ cup	sugar	125 ml.
2 oz.	pistachios, blanched, peeled and ground (about ⅓ cup [75 ml.])	60 g.
¼ cup	kirsch	50 ml.
½ cup	flour	125 ml.
⅓ cup	rice flour	75 ml.
1 tsp.	grated lemon peel	5 ml.
4 tbsp.	butter, melted	60 ml.

Pistachio cream

⅔ cup	pistachios, blanched and peeled	150 ml.
½ cup	kirsch	125 ml.
1 tbsp.	green spinach coloring	15 ml.
1	egg, plus 2 egg yolks	1
⅓ cup	sugar	75 ml.
1 tsp.	flour	5 ml.
	salt	
1 cup	milk	¼ liter
4 tbsp.	butter	60 ml.

For the cake, place the eggs and sugar in a bowl set over a pan of hot water. Never letting the mixture become more than warm, whisk it over very low heat for 10 to 15 minutes, until it is very thick and light and forms a ribbon. Mix the ground pistachios with the kirsch to form a paste, and add this paste to the egg mixture. Sift together the flour and rice flour and add them, with the lemon peel, to the egg mixture. Work the ingredients together with a wooden spoon until everything is thoroughly blended. Stir in the butter. Pour this batter into a buttered and floured cake pan, and bake in a preheated 350° F. [180° C.] oven for 25 to 30 minutes, or until the cake shrinks slightly from the sides of the pan. Turn the cake out onto a rack to cool.

For the cream, pound the peeled pistachios in a mortar, gradually adding the kirsch to form a fine paste. Transfer the paste to a bowl and add the spinach coloring. In a separate bowl, beat the egg and yolks with the sugar until the mixture whitens. Add the flour and a pinch of salt, whisk for one minute more, then add the milk. Transfer this custard to a saucepan and place it over low heat. Stir constantly until the mixture comes to a boil. Pour the hot custard into the pistachio paste and stir until the mixture cools slightly. Work in 2 tablespoons [30 ml.] of the butter.

Slice the cooled cake horizontally into three layers. Spread each layer with a quarter of the pistachio cream and stack the layers. Spread a thin layer of pistachio cream around the sides of the cake. Heat the remaining pistachio cream slightly to soften it and incorporate the remaining butter. Decorate the top of the cake with this mixture, using a pastry bag. The cake is just as good the next day.

MME. JEANNE SAVARIN (EDITOR)
LA CUISINE DES FAMILLES

———————————◆———————————

Ginger Roll

To make one rolled cake 15 inches [38 cm.] long

3	eggs	3
½ cup	sugar	125 ml.
¼ tsp.	salt	1 ml.
⅔ cup	cake flour	150 ml.
2 tsp.	baking powder	10 ml.
1 tsp.	ground ginger	5 ml.
1 tsp.	ground cinnamon	5 ml.
1 tsp.	ground allspice	5 ml.
¼ cup	dark molasses	50 ml.

Applesauce filling

1 ½ cups	applesauce	375 ml.
½ cup	apricot jam	125 ml.
1 tsp.	grated lemon peel	5 ml.
2 tbsp.	brandy	30 ml.

Beat the eggs in a mixing bowl with the sugar and salt until the mixture is very thick and holds its shape (this will take about five minutes). Sift together the flour, baking powder, and spices; add this to the egg mixture, and fold in very gently. Fold in the molasses. Spread the mixture in a jelly-roll pan that has been buttered and lined with buttered parchment paper. Bake in a preheated 375° F. [190° C.] oven for 12 to 14 minutes, until the cake springs back when lightly pressed in the center.

Remove the cake from the oven, dust the surface with granulated sugar, and turn out the cake upside down onto two overlapping sheets of parchment paper. Peel off the lining paper and roll up the cake like a jelly roll. Chill the roll for at least one hour, then unroll it carefully.

Mix the filling ingredients together and spread the filling over the roll; roll it up again and chill before serving.

JULIE DANNENBAUM
MENUS FOR ALL OCCASIONS

Brandy Cake

To make one 8-inch [20-cm.] cake

3	eggs	3
1 cup	sugar	¼ liter
1 tsp.	ground mace	5 ml.
4 tsp.	grated lemon peel	20 ml.
1 cup	fine dry bread crumbs	¼ liter
¾ cup	brandy	175 ml.
1⅔ cups	almonds, blanched, peeled and ground (about 6½ oz. [185 g.])	400 ml.
1 cup	glacé icing (recipe, page 165), made with 2 tbsp. [30 ml.] lemon juice instead of water	¼ liter
	toasted almond halves (optional)	

Beat the eggs and the sugar until light. Beat in the mace and the lemon peel. Stir in alternately the bread crumbs and the brandy. Beat in the almonds. Turn the batter into a buttered and floured spring-form pan. Bake in a preheated 350° F. [180° C.] oven for 30 to 35 minutes, or until the cake shrinks from the sides of the pan. Remove the sides of the spring-form pan and cool the cake. When cool, remove the pan bottom. Ice the cake with the lemon-flavored glacé icing. If you will, decorate the cake with toasted almond halves.

NIKA HAZELTON
I COOK AS I PLEASE

Spongecake with Rum

Pantespani me Romion

To make one 8-by-12-inch [20-by-30-cm.] cake or one 10-inch [25-cm.] cake

10	eggs, yolks separated from whites, whites stiffly beaten	10
½ cup plus 1 tsp.	sugar	130 ml.
1½ cups	almonds, blanched, peeled, toasted and chopped (about 6 oz. [175 g.])	375 ml.
½ cup	cake flour	125 ml.
1 tbsp.	baking powder	15 ml.
3 tbsp.	rum	45 ml.
2 cups	sugar syrup (recipe, page 164), flavored with 1 tbsp. [15 ml.] strained fresh lemon juice and 1 tbsp. rum	½ liter
2 cups	heavy cream, whipped	½ liter
	candied cherries	

Beat the egg yolks with ½ cup [125 ml.] of the sugar until thick and pale in color. Fold in 1 cup [¼ liter] of the chopped

almonds. Fold in the flour mixed with the baking powder, then stir in the rum. Carefully fold the egg whites into the batter. Turn the batter into a buttered and floured pan, and bake in a preheated 400° F. [200° C.] oven for about 30 minutes, or until a tester inserted in the cake comes out clean.

Remove the cake from the oven and prick the entire surface with a toothpick. Pour the hot syrup over the cake before the cake cools. When the cake has cooled, fold the remaining teaspoon of sugar into the whipped cream and frost the cake lavishly with the sweetened cream. Cut the cake into squares and sprinkle with the remaining almonds. Decorate with the cherries.

ST. PAUL'S GREEK ORTHODOX CHURCH
THE ART OF GREEK COOKERY

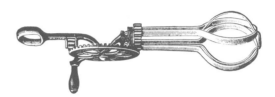

Spongecake with Rum and Almond

Turinos

To make one cake 8 inches [20 cm.] square

4	eggs, yolks separated from whites	4
½ cup plus 2 tbsp.	sugar	155 ml.
2 cups	sifted cake flour	½ liter
	salt	
	dark rum	
3 cups	pastry cream (recipe, page 166), flavored with ¼ cup [50 ml.] dark rum	¾ liter
1¼ cups	almond paste (recipe, page 167), flavored with 2 tbsp. [30 ml.] dark rum	300 ml.

In a bowl, beat the yolks and sugar until they form a ribbon. Add the sifted flour and blend well. Separately beat the whites with a pinch of salt until stiff peaks are formed. Carefully fold the whites into the batter. Bake in a buttered and floured pan in a preheated 350° F. [180° C.] oven for 30 to 35 minutes, until a tester inserted in the center comes out clean. Remove the cake from the oven and let it stand for five minutes before inverting it onto a cake rack to cool. Let the cake cool for one hour.

Cut the cake into three horizontal slices. Sprinkle each slice with a little rum. Spread half of the pastry cream on one of the slices. Cover with a second slice and spread the remaining cream on top. Cover with the last slice. Cover the entire surface with a smooth layer of the almond-paste coating. Let the coating harden before cutting the cake.

LOUISETTE BERTHOLLE
SECRETS OF THE GREAT FRENCH RESTAURANTS

Alwine's Kirsch Wedding Cake

Gâteau au Kirsch du Mariage D'Alwine

To make one 10-inch [25-cm.] cake

4	eggs	4
¾ cup	sugar	175 ml.
¼ tsp.	salt	1 ml.
¾ cup	kirsch	175 ml.
1 cup	sifted flour	¼ liter
3 cups	raspberry jam, warmed and strained	¾ liter
⅔ cup	water	150 ml.

Berry filling

6 cups	strawberries	1½ liters
¾ cup	granulated sugar	175 ml.
4½ tbsp.	strained fresh lemon juice	67 ml.
	pinch of salt	
⅓ cup	kirsch	75 ml.
2½ tbsp.	unflavored powdered gelatin	37 ml.
3 cups	heavy cream	¾ liter
	confectioners' sugar	
2 cups	fresh raspberries	½ liter

Place the eggs in a large mixing bowl. Add ½ cup [125 ml.] sugar and the salt, and whip at very high speed until the mixture foams heavily and falls from the beaters in one heavy ribbon. Add 2 tablespoons [30 ml.] kirsch. Beat another moment; then fold in the flour. Spread the mixture in a lightly buttered and floured jelly-roll pan, and bake the cake in a preheated 325° F. [160° C.] oven for about 15 minutes, until the cake springs back when pressed lightly.

Immediately remove the cake from the pan. Trim the edges of the cake, brush with the warm raspberry jam, and roll as tightly as you can. Cool completely on a rack.

Cut the cake into vertical slices ⅓ inch [1 cm.] thick. Mix the water with the remaining kirsch and ¼ cup [50 ml.] sugar, and stir until the sugar has dissolved. Dip one side only of each cake slice into this syrup. Line a 10-inch [25-cm.] cake pan with the slices of cake so as to leave no spaces between the pieces of cake and to form a casing. Drizzle what is left of the syrup inside the casing and pack well with the back of your hand. Cover with plastic wrap and refrigerate while you make the filling.

To make the berry filling, first purée the strawberries. Add the sugar and cook until the mixture is reduced to 1¾ cups [425 ml.]. Add the lemon juice, salt and 3 tablespoons [45 ml.] of the kirsch. Dissolve the gelatin with ½ cup of water in a double boiler and stir it into the warm purée.

Whip 2 cups [½ liter] of cream with 2 tablespoons of kirsch and 2 tablespoons of confectioners' sugar until it barely mounds. Refrigerate the cream. Place the strawberry pu-

rée over ice and stir until the purée starts to thicken. Immediately fold in the whipped cream and turn this mixture into the cake casing.

Cover the cake again with plastic wrap and refrigerate. When ready to serve or about one hour before, invert the cake onto a round cake platter. Whip the last cup [¼ liter] of heavy cream, lightly sugared with 2 tablespoons confectioners' sugar, to the stiff stage. Pipe tiny rosettes of this cream all around the base and the top of the cake, and crown each rosette with a raspberry. Keep the cake chilled until you are ready to serve it.

MADELEINE KAMMAN
WHEN FRENCH WOMEN COOK

Passover Wine Cake

You can substitute 2½ tablespoons [37 ml.] of cornstarch for the potato starch. Matzo cake meal is unbleached wheat flour baked into a flat bread and then very finely ground. It can be bought packaged at Passover in stores that sell Jewish foods.

To make one 10-inch [25-cm.] tube cake

9	eggs, yolks separated from whites, whites stiffly beaten	9
1½ cups	sugar	375 ml.
⅔ cup	matzo cake meal	150 ml.
⅓ cup	potato starch	75 ml.
1 tsp.	ground cinnamon	5 ml.
½ tsp.	ground ginger	2 ml.
	salt	
¾ cup	walnuts, ground	175 ml.
about ¼ cup	sweet red wine	about 50 ml.

Beat the egg yolks until they are foamy, gradually adding the sugar. Sift together the matzo meal, potato starch, cinnamon, ginger and a pinch of salt. Add this mixture gradually to the egg yolks. Place the ground walnuts in a cup and add enough sweet wine to fill the cup. Fold the wine and nuts into the batter; fold in the egg whites. Pour the batter into a buttered and floured tube cake pan. Bake in a preheated 350° F. [180° C.] oven for 50 to 60 minutes, or until the cake shrinks from the sides of the pan.

JOAN NATHAN
THE JEWISH HOLIDAY KITCHEN

Madeleines

Madeleines are small cakes baked in shell-shaped molds—obtainable at kitchen-supply stores.

To make about 20 small cakes

1 cup	superfine sugar	¼ liter
2 cups	sifted cake flour	½ liter
	salt	
4	eggs, plus 1 lightly beaten white	4
2 tsp.	grated lemon peel	10 ml.
½ lb.	butter, melted and cooled	¼ kg.
	confectioners' sugar	

Mix together the sugar, flour and a pinch of salt in a bowl. Add the whole eggs one by one, beating very thoroughly. (Use an electric mixer if possible, as this makes the cake very light.) Fold in the grated lemon peel and finally the butter, seeing that the batter is very well mixed. Fill about 20 buttered molds two thirds full and bake in a preheated 375° F. [190° C.] oven for about 25 minutes, or until the madeleines have risen and are well browned. Brush them with the egg white, dust with confectioners' sugar, and put them back in a very low oven for five minutes to dry out.

Cool the cakes on a wire rack.

THEODORA FITZGIBBON
A TASTE OF PARIS

Pound and Butter Cakes

Poundcake

This cake batter may be enriched with 1 pound [½ kg.] of almond paste (recipe, page 167): Mix the broken-up paste with the sugar before creaming it with the butter. The batter may be baked in two 4-by-9-inch [10-by-23-cm.] loaf pans for one and one half hours. Or it may be baked in four 9-inch [23-cm.] cake pans for 30 to 35 minutes.

To make three 3-by-8-inch [8-by-20-cm.] loaf cakes

1 lb.	butter, softened	½ kg.
2 cups	sugar	½ liter
10	eggs	10
2 tbsp.	vanilla extract or brandy	30 ml.
4 cups	cake flour	1 liter

Cream the butter well, add the sugar gradually, and cream the mixture until it is light and fluffy. Add the eggs, two at a time, beating well after each addition. Add the flavoring. Sift the flour twice and add it gradually to the batter, beat-

ing until smooth. Pour the mixture into three loaf pans that have been buttered, floured and lined with parchment paper. Bake in a preheated 300° F. [150° C.] oven for about one hour and 15 minutes, or until a tester inserted in the middle comes out clean.

THE SETTLEMENT COOK BOOK

Four Quarters (Poundcake)

Quatre-Quarts

To make one 7-inch [18-cm.] cake

3	eggs, yolks separated from whites, whites stiffly beaten	3
¾ cup	sugar	175 ml.
12 tbsp.	butter, softened	180 ml.
1½ cups	flour	375 ml.
2 tsp.	grated lemon peel, or ½ tsp. [2 ml.] vanilla extract	10 ml.

Beat the egg yolks with the sugar until they are pale in color. Gradually beat in the softened butter in small amounts alternately with the flour. Add the lemon peel or vanilla extract. Finally, fold the stiffly beaten egg whites into the mixture. Pour into a buttered and floured cake pan and bake in a preheated 350° F. [180° C.] oven for 40 to 50 minutes, or until the edges of the cake shrink slightly from the sides of the pan. Cool the cake in the pan for 10 minutes before turning it out onto a wire rack.

GINETTE MATHIOT
JE SAIS FAIRE LA PÂTISSERIE

Whole-wheat Poundcake

To make one 4-by-9-inch [10-by-23-cm.] loaf cake

1½ cups	oil	375 ml.
1½ cups	honey	375 ml.
¼ tsp.	salt	1 ml.
6	eggs, yolks separated from whites	6
6 tbsp.	grated orange peel	90 ml.
¾ cup	strained fresh orange juice	175 ml.
2 cups	whole-wheat flour	½ liter
¼ tsp.	ground mace	1 ml.

Blend the oil, honey and salt, and beat in the egg yolks one at a time until the mixture is well blended. Stir in all of the remaining ingredients except the egg whites. Beat these until stiff and gently fold them into the batter. Pour the batter into a buttered and floured loaf pan. Bake in a preheated 300° F. [150° C.] oven for about one hour, or until the cake springs back when touched gently in the center.

BEATRICE TRUM HUNTER
THE NATURAL FOODS COOKBOOK

Quick Poundcake

True poundcakes are made without baking powder. The leavening agents are the air included by creaming and the egg-white foam. Traditional poundcakes owe their name to their composition, which is always 1 pound [½ kg.] each of flour, sugar, eggs and butter. In French, they are called *quatre-quarts,* or "four quarters," because they include ¼ pound [125 g.] of each main ingredient.

To make one 5-by-9-inch [13-by-23-cm.] loaf cake

8 tbsp.	butter, softened	120 ml.
½ cup	sugar	125 ml.
1 cup	flour, sifted	¼ liter
2	eggs, yolks separated from whites, whites stiffly beaten	2

Cream the butter, add the sugar, and cream well together. Add the egg yolks, one at a time, beating after each addition. Beat in the flour. Fold in the beaten egg whites. Pour the mixture into a buttered loaf pan that has been lined with parchment paper. Bake in a preheated 350° F. [180° C.] oven for about 45 minutes, or until the cake shrinks slightly from the sides of the pan. The top of the cake will crack due to internal steam pressure. Allow the cake to cool completely in the pan, and keep it for 24 hours before slicing it.

MADELEINE KAMMAN
THE MAKING OF A COOK

Almond-Lemon Poundcake

To make this cake into loaves, divide the batter evenly between two buttered and floured loaf pans. Bake in a preheated 325° F. [160° C.] oven for 45 to 50 minutes, or until a cake tester inserted in the center comes out dry and the cakes begin to shrink slightly from the sides of the pan. Poundcake keeps well if stored in a securely covered tin, or wrapped thoroughly in foil or plastic wrap.

To make one 10-inch [25-cm.] tube cake

3 cups	sifted flour	¾ liter
	salt	
1 tsp.	baking powder	5 ml.
1 lb.	butter, softened	½ kg.
2 cups	sugar	½ liter
9	eggs, yolks separated from whites, whites stiffly beaten	9
½ tsp.	almond extract	2 ml.
½ tsp.	lemon extract	2 ml.
½ tsp.	rose water	2 ml.

Sift the flour, a pinch of salt and the baking powder together twice. Cream or work the butter with an electric mixer or

with your hands until it is light and fluffy. Gradually work in the sugar until the mixture is very creamy. Beat the egg yolks very hard with a rotary beater or, better, an electric beater until very thick, pale and fluffy. Stir in the flavorings. Stir the beaten yolks into the creamed mixture. Add the flour mixture a few tablespoons at a time, stirring only until the batter is smooth. Stir about one third of the egg whites into the batter with a wire whisk, then fold in the remaining whites gently but thoroughly with a rubber spatula.

Pour the batter into a buttered and floured tube pan, and bake in a preheated 350° F. [180° C.] oven for 35 minutes. Reduce the heat to 325° F. [160° C.] and continue baking for 25 minutes longer, or until a tester inserted in the center comes out dry, without any batter clinging to it.

HELEN MC CULLY, JACQUES PÉPIN AND WILLIAM JAYME
THE OTHER HALF OF THE EGG

Lemon and Orange Poundcake

To make one 10-inch [25-cm.] tube cake

½ lb.	butter, softened	¼ kg.
2 cups	sugar	½ liter
6	eggs	6
2 cups	flour	½ liter
2 tbsp.	strained fresh orange juice	30 ml.
1 tsp.	almond extract	5 ml.
1 tsp.	pure lemon extract	5 ml.
⅓ cup	orange-flavored liqueur	75 ml.
2 cups	glacé icing (recipe, page 165), flavored with 1 tsp. [5 ml.] grated lemon peel, 2 tbsp. [30 ml.] strained fresh lemon juice and 2 tbsp. strained fresh orange juice	½ liter

In an electric mixer, cream the butter, add the sugar, and cream again. Using an electric mixer, beat in the eggs, one at a time, mixing well after each addition. At the mixer's lowest speed, gradually beat in the flour. When all of the flour is incorporated, turn the mixer to medium speed and beat the batter for 10 minutes. Add the orange juice and the almond and lemon extracts. Pour the batter into a buttered and floured tube cake pan. Bake in a preheated 350° F. [180° C.] oven for about one hour. For the first 30 minutes of cooking, put a pan of water on the shelf under the cake. Remove the water for the remainder of the cooking time.

Turn the cake out onto a cake rack placed over foil. Sprinkle the warm cake with the orange-flavored liqueur, then immediately spread the icing over the cake. Cover the cake with a large bowl and wait a few hours before serving.

THE JUNIOR LEAGUE OF DALLAS
THE DALLAS JUNIOR LEAGUE COOKBOOK

Spiced Poundcake

Ladyfingers are small, finger-shaped pieces of spongecake. They can be bought packaged in specialty food stores. Bread crumbs may be substituted for them.

To make one 12-inch [30-cm.] cake

1 lb.	butter, softened	½ kg.
2 cups	superfine sugar	½ liter
12	eggs, yolks separated from whites, yolks well beaten, whites stiffly beaten	12
4 cups	flour	1 liter
½ tsp.	finely grated tangerine peel	2 ml.
½ tsp.	ground cinnamon	2 ml.
½ tsp.	grated nutmeg	2 ml.
½ cup	finely ground ladyfingers	125 ml.

Stir the butter to a cream; beat in the sugar, then the beaten egg yolks, followed by the flour and spices, previously well mixed. Lastly, fold in the beaten egg whites. Pour the cake mixture into a pan that has been buttered and dusted with ladyfinger crumbs. Place a piece of buttered parchment paper on top of the pan and bake in a preheated 350° F. [180° C.] oven for one and one half to two hours, or until the cake shrinks slightly from the sides of the pan. Allow the cake to cool in the pan.

HILDAGONDA J. DUCKITT
HILDA'S "WHERE IS IT?" OF RECIPES

Cream Cheese Poundcake

To make one 10-inch [25-cm.] cake

½ lb.	cream cheese	¼ kg.
¾ lb.	butter, softened	350 g.
3 cups	sugar	¾ liter
	salt	
1½ tsp.	vanilla extract	7 ml.
6	eggs	6
3 cups	sifted flour	¾ liter

Cream the cream cheese, butter, and sugar together until light and fluffy. Add a pinch of salt and the vanilla extract, and beat the mixture well. Add the eggs, one at a time, beating thoroughly after each addition. Stir in the flour.

Pour the batter into a buttered and floured cake pan, and bake the cake in a preheated 325° F. [160° C.] oven for one and one half hours, until the cake begins to shrink from the sides of the pan. Cool the cake in the pan for five minutes before turning it out onto a wire rack.

LANDON SCHOOL
LANDON'S FAVORITE DESSERTS COOKBOOK

Sour-Cream Poundcake

To make two 4-by-9-inch [10-by-23-cm.] loaf cakes

½ lb.	butter, softened	¼ kg.
3 cups	sugar	¾ liter
6	eggs, yolks separated from whites, whites stiffly beaten	6
3 cups	flour	¾ liter
¼ tsp.	baking soda	1 ml.
1 cup	sour cream	¼ liter
1 tsp.	vanilla extract	5 ml.

Cream the butter with the sugar, then, one at a time, beat in the egg yolks. Sift the baking soda with the flour, then, alternating with the sour cream, add it to the creamed mixture. Stir in the vanilla extract. Carefully fold the egg whites into the batter. Pour the batter into two buttered and floured loaf pans and bake in a preheated 325° F. [160° C.] oven for one hour and 15 minutes, or until the tops are lightly browned and feel springy when pressed.

SOUTHERN RAILWAY LADIES CLUB COOKBOOK

Princess Cake

To make one 10-inch [25-cm.] tube cake

½ lb.	butter, softened	¼ kg.
2⅔ cups	sifted flour	650 ml.
1 tsp.	vanilla extract	5 ml.
8	egg whites	8
	salt	
¼ tsp.	cream of tartar	1 ml.
1⅔ cups	sugar	400 ml.

Cream the butter with half of the flour until the mixture is light and fluffy. Add the vanilla extract.

Beat the egg whites with the salt and cream of tartar until they hold soft peaks. Add the sugar, 1 tablespoon [15 ml.] at a time, beating well after each addition. Beat the whites for at least five minutes, or until they are very stiff.

Fold a quarter of the stiffly beaten egg whites thoroughly into the creamed mixture, then pour the mixture back over the remaining egg whites. Fold the ingredients together while sprinkling in the remaining flour. Do not overmix.

Pour the mixture into a buttered and floured pan. Bake about one hour in a preheated 350° F. [180° C.] oven, or until the cake is golden brown and pulls away from the pan.

PAULA PECK
PAULA PECK'S ART OF GOOD COOKING

Victoria Sandwich

Traditionally, this cake is sandwiched together with jam and the top sprinkled with confectioners' sugar.

To make one 8-inch [20-cm.] cake

8 tbsp.	butter, softened	120 ml.
½ cup	superfine sugar	125 ml.
2	eggs, beaten	2
1 tbsp.	warm water	15 ml.
1 cup	flour	¼ liter
1 tsp.	baking powder	5 ml.

Cream the butter and sugar together until fluffy. Add the eggs gradually, then add the warm water and beat well. Sift the flour with the baking powder, and stir them in thoroughly until the mixture will spread easily.

Put into two well-buttered and floured layer-cake pans. (Do not forget to put a small piece of parchment paper on the bottom of the pans to ease turning out.) Bake in a preheated 350° F. [180° C.] oven for about 20 minutes, or until the cakes are springy to the touch. Allow the layers to cool before sandwiching them together.

MISS READ'S COUNTRY COOKING

Paradise Cake

To make one 12-inch [30-cm.] cake

1 lb.	butter, softened	½ kg.
2 cups	superfine sugar	½ liter
1 tsp.	grated lemon peel	5 ml.
1½ cups plus 1½ tbsp.	potato starch	400 ml.
8	eggs, plus 10 yolks	8
2 cups	flour	½ liter
1 tbsp.	baking powder	15 ml.
	vanilla sugar	

Put the softened butter in a warm, dry earthenware pan; beat the butter with a wire whisk until it is creamed. Add the sugar and continue beating until combined. Add the lemon peel and 1½ tablespoons [22½ ml.] of the potato starch, and mix well until a smooth paste is obtained.

Beat the 10 egg yolks in a bowl; then add the eight whole eggs, beating constantly and energetically for 10 minutes or more. Sift the flour twice with the remaining 1½ cups [375 ml.] of potato starch and the baking powder.

Returning to the butter-and-sugar paste, start beating this, adding a little at a time the beaten eggs and the sifted flour, making sure that no lumps form. Pour the mixture into a buttered baking pan. Bake in a preheated 350° F. [180°

C.] oven for about 50 minutes, or until the cake is well browned. Let it cool before removing it from the pan; sprinkle with vanilla sugar and serve.

LUIGI CARNACINA
LUIGI CARNACINA PRESENTS ITALIAN HOME COOKING

Wedding Cake

The technique for making a tiered wedding cake is shown on pages 80-84. The making of decorations is demonstrated on pages 22-27.

For a tiered cake, make the batter and the rich ivory butter cream specified in this recipe two additional times. Divide the cake batter among two 6-inch [15-cm.] cake pans, two 9-inch [23-cm.] cake pans and two 12-inch [30-cm.] cake pans. Bake the 6-inch layers for 20 to 25 minutes, the 9-inch layers for about 50 minutes, and the 12-inch layers for one hour to one hour and 15 minutes, or until a tester inserted in the layers comes out clean.

To make one 12-inch [30-cm.] cake

½ lb.	butter, softened	¼ kg.
2 cups	sugar	½ liter
½ tsp.	almond extract	2 ml.
1 tsp.	vanilla extract	5 ml.
3 cups	cake flour	¾ liter
½ tsp.	salt	2 ml.
3 tsp.	baking powder	15 ml.
1 cup	milk	¼ liter
6	egg whites	6
4 cups	rich ivory butter cream (recipe, page 166)	1 liter

Cream the butter, gradually adding 1¼ cups [300 ml.] of the sugar, and beat until light and fluffy. Blend in the almond and vanilla extracts. Sift together all of the dry ingredients. Add the milk, alternately with the sifted dry ingredients, to the creamed butter and sugar.

Beat the egg whites until they form peaks; gradually add the remaining sugar and beat until stiff. Gently fold the egg whites into the batter.

Turn the batter into a cake pan that has been buttered and floured. Bake in a preheated 350° F. [180° C.] oven for 50 to 55 minutes, or until a cake tester inserted into the center of the cake comes out clean.

Let the cake cool in the pan a few minutes, and then turn it out onto a wire rack to cool completely. Remove the paper, then ice and decorate the cake.

HAZEL G. ZENKER
CAKE BAKERY

Yogurt and Nut Cake

To make one 9-by-13-inch [23-by-32½-cm.] cake

1 cup	sugar	¼ liter
½ lb.	butter, melted and cooled	¼ kg.
5	eggs, beaten	5
1 cup	plain yogurt	¼ liter
½ tsp.	baking soda	2 ml.
½ cup	milk	125 ml.
3 cups	sifted cake flour	¾ liter
1 tbsp.	baking powder	15 ml.
¼ lb.	walnuts, chopped (about 1 cup [¼ liter])	125 g.
2 cups	sugar syrup (recipe, page 164)	½ liter

Add the sugar a little at a time to the melted butter, and cream together thoroughly. Add the beaten eggs and mix well. Stir in the yogurt.

Combine the baking soda and milk and add them to the yogurt mixture. Combine the sifted flour and baking powder and blend them into the yogurt mixture, 1 cup [¼ liter] at a time. Beat the batter vigorously until thoroughly blended. If you use an electric mixer, be careful not to overbeat or the finished cake will have air holes.

Pour the batter into a buttered and floured pan, and bake in a preheated 350° F. [180° C.] oven for one hour, or until the cake is medium brown on top. While the cake is still hot, cut it into serving pieces. Sprinkle the nuts over the top and spoon the cool sugar syrup over each piece.

LANDON SCHOOL
LANDON'S FAVORITE DESSERTS COOKBOOK

Yogurt Cake

Yaourtopita

This is an extremely moist but light cake. Some people like to add to the ingredients either grated lemon peel or just a whiff of vanilla extract.

To make one cake 10 inches [25 cm.] square

½ lb.	butter, softened	¼ kg.
¾ cup	superfine sugar	175 ml.
5	eggs, yolks separated from whites, whites stiffly beaten	5
1¼ cups	yogurt	300 ml.
3 cups	flour, sifted with 2 tsp. [10 ml.] baking powder and a pinch of salt	¾ liter
	confectioners' sugar	

Cream the butter and sugar until light and fluffy. Add the egg yolks, one by one, beating vigorously after each addition.

Then, when this mixture is well blended, add the yogurt, beating all the while to a fairly liquid consistency. Mix the sifted flour into the creamed mixture and beat again until the flour is thoroughly blended. Fold in the egg whites and pour the cake batter into a buttered and floured cake pan 3 inches [8 cm.] deep. Bake in a preheated 350° F. [180° C.] oven for about one hour, or until the cake shrinks slightly from the sides of the pan. Take the cake from the oven, remove it from the pan and allow it to cool on a cake rack. Then dust it generously with confectioners' sugar.

ROBIN HOWE
GREEK COOKING

Old-fashioned Caramel Cake

To make one 8-inch [20-cm.] cake

8 tbsp.	butter, softened	120 ml.
1½ cups	sugar	375 ml.
2	eggs	2
2 cups	sifted flour	½ liter
1 cup	buttermilk	¼ liter
1 tsp.	baking soda	5 ml.
1 tbsp.	vinegar	15 ml.
3 cups	caramel fudge frosting (recipe, page 166), made with 1 cup [¼ liter] granulated sugar and 1 cup dark brown sugar	¾ liter

Cream the butter and the sugar together until light and fluffy. Add the eggs one at a time, and continue beating. Add the flour alternately with the buttermilk. Blend well. Dissolve the baking soda in the vinegar and stir the solution into the batter. Pour the batter into two buttered and floured layer-cake pans. Bake in a preheated 350° F. [180° C.] oven for 35 minutes, or until a tester inserted in the middle of the cake comes out dry. Let the layers cool completely before filling and frosting.

THE JUNIOR LEAGUE OF FAYETTEVILLE
THE CAROLINA COLLECTION

Sunday Night Cake

To make one cake 9 inches [23 cm.] square

8 tbsp.	butter, softened	120 ml.
1½ cups	superfine sugar	375 ml.
3	eggs	3
2 cups minus 2 tbsp.	flour, sifted twice before measuring	470 ml.
3 tsp.	baking powder	15 ml.
¼ tsp.	salt	1 ml.
⅔ cup	milk	150 ml.
1 tbsp.	vanilla extract	15 ml.

Brown-sugar glaze

1 cup	brown sugar	¼ liter
3 tbsp.	cold water	45 ml.

Remove the milk, eggs and butter from the refrigerator in time for them to be at room temperature before you begin to mix the cake batter.

Cream the butter until it has a satiny appearance (if you are using an electric mixer, beat at medium-low speed). Add the sugar gradually until it is well blended, then add the eggs one at a time, mixing in well.

Sift the flour with the baking powder and salt. Then add the flour to the creamed mixture in three parts alternately with the milk, beginning and ending with the flour. Mix well after each addition, but only until the batter is blended. Add the vanilla extract and give a quick beat by hand, or beat for one or two seconds with a mixer at high speed.

Spoon the batter into a cake pan that has been buttered and floured on the bottom only. Bake in the center of the middle shelf of a preheated 375° F. [190° C.] oven for 35 minutes, or until a tester inserted in the center of the cake comes out clean.

When you remove the cake from the oven, slide a thin knife around the edges, place a cake rack over the pan and invert the pan and rack together. After the cake has cooled for 15 minutes, cover it with a clean cloth to prevent hardening of the surface and drying of the cake. Wait an hour before adding the glaze.

To make the glaze, place the sugar and water in a saucepan over medium heat, and boil the mixture until it reaches 230° F. [112° C.] on a candy thermometer. Do not stir at any point during the cooking, but remove any scum that comes to the surface. As soon as the exact temperature is reached, remove the pan from the heat and place it in a pan of ice water to stop cooking and cool the glaze enough to thicken it.

When the glaze sets thick enough to spread, smooth it over the cake with a narrow-bladed spatula or dinner knife.

EDNA LEWIS AND EVANGELINE PETERSON
THE EDNA LEWIS COOKBOOK

Frankfurt Crown

To make one 9-inch [23-cm.] tube cake

8 tbsp.	butter, softened	120 ml.
¾ cup	sugar	175 ml.
1 tsp.	grated lemon peel	5 ml.
4	eggs	4
¾ cup	sifted flour	175 ml.
½ cup	sifted cornstarch	125 ml.
2 tsp.	baking powder	10 ml.
	rum, kirsch or orange-flavored liqueur	
about 4 cups	rich butter cream (recipe, page 166)	about 1 liter
	praline powder (recipe, page 167)	
	candied cherries	
	pistachios	

Place the butter, sugar and lemon peel in a mixing bowl. Mix until fluffy and well blended. Beat in the eggs one at a time.

Sift together the flour, cornstarch and baking powder, and gradually add them to the creamed mixture. Turn the batter into a well-buttered and lightly floured ring mold or tube cake pan. Bake in a preheated 325° F. [160° C.] oven for 40 minutes, or until a tester inserted in the center of the cake comes out clean. Cool the cake in the pan for 10 minutes, then turn it out of the pan onto a wire rack.

When the cake is cold, split it into three or four layers and sprinkle each with kirsch, rum or orange-flavored liqueur.

Put the layers together in layer-cake fashion with the butter cream, then frost the top and sides. Sprinkle the cake with praline powder.

Put additional frosting into a pastry bag fitted with a large No. 8 open star tube and decorate the top of the cake with rosettes. Garnish each rosette with a candied cherry and two pistachios. This cake is best the day after it is made.

HENRI PAUL PELLAPRAT
THE GREAT BOOK OF FRENCH CUISINE

Minnehaha Cake

To make one 7-inch [18-cm.] cake

1½ cups	sugar	375 ml.
8 tbsp.	butter, softened	120 ml.
6	egg whites or 3 whole eggs, lightly beaten	6
2½ cups	flour, sifted with 2 tsp. [10 ml.] cream of tartar and 1 tsp. [5 ml.] baking soda	625 ml.
½ cup	milk	125 ml.
2 cups	boiled icing (recipe, page 164)	½ liter
1¼ cups	raisins, finely chopped, or ¼ lb. [125 g.] chopped hickory nuts (about ½ cup [125 ml.])	300 ml.

Beat together the sugar and butter until light and creamy. Then beat in the egg whites or whole eggs alternately with the flour. Beat in the milk. Pour into three buttered and floured layer-cake pans and bake in a preheated 350° F. [180° C.] oven for 20 minutes, or until the cakes shrink slightly from the sides of the pans. Turn them out onto wire racks to cool completely.

Stir the raisins or hickory nuts into the boiled icing, and spread it between the cooled layers of the cake.

MARGARET TAYLOR AND FRANCES MC NAUGHT
THE EARLY CANADIAN GALT COOK BOOK

Lady Baltimore Cake

To make one 9-inch [23-cm.] cake

½ lb.	butter, softened	¼ kg.
2 cups	sugar	½ liter
3 cups	flour	¾ liter
3 tsp.	baking powder	15 ml.
½ tsp.	salt	2 ml.
4	eggs, yolks separated from whites, yolks beaten, whites stiffly beaten	4
1 cup	milk	¼ liter
1 tsp.	vanilla or almond extract	5 ml.
2 cups	boiled icing (recipe, page 164), flavored with 1 tsp. [5 ml.] vanilla or almond extract	½ liter
1 cup	raisins, chopped	¼ liter
1 cup	walnuts, chopped (¼ lb. [125 g.])	¼ liter
12	dried figs, chopped	12

Cream the butter and sugar until light and fluffy. Sift the flour, baking powder and salt together. Add the egg yolks to the creamed butter, then add the milk, alternately with the sifted dry ingredients. Finally, stir in the vanilla or almond extract and fold in the egg whites. Pour the batter into two buttered and floured layer-cake pans, and bake in a preheated 350° F. [180° C.] oven for 35 to 40 minutes, or until a cake tester inserted in the middle of the cake comes out clean.

Cool the layers on a rack. Add the raisins, nuts, and figs to the icing, and spread it on the layers as filling and icing.

HOPE ANDREWS AND FRANCES KELLY
MARYLAND'S WAY

Eggnog Cake

To make one 9-inch [23-cm.] cake

½ lb.	butter	¼ kg.
2 cups	sugar	½ liter
3¼ cups	flour	800 ml.
1 tbsp.	baking powder	15 ml.
1 cup	milk	¼ liter
1 tsp.	vanilla extract	5 ml.
8	egg whites, stiffly beaten	8
2 cups	boiled icing (recipe, page 164)	½ liter

Bourbon and nut filling

1 cup	sugar	¼ liter
8 tbsp.	butter	120 ml.
1 tbsp.	flour	15 ml.
8	egg yolks, beaten	8
½ cup	bourbon	125 ml.
1 cup	pecans, chopped (¼ lb. [125 g.])	¼ liter
1 cup	raisins	¼ liter
1 cup	grated fresh coconut	¼ liter

Cream the butter and sugar until smooth. Sift the flour and baking powder together and beat them into the butter-sugar mixture alternately with the milk. Add the vanilla extract and fold in the egg whites.

Pour the mixture evenly into two buttered and floured layer-cake pans, and bake in a preheated 350° F. [180° C.] oven for 30 minutes, or until a tester inserted in the middle of the cake comes out clean. Cool the layers on a wire rack.

To make the filling, cream the butter, sugar and flour together. Add the egg yolks, and cook the mixture gently in the top of a double boiler over simmering water until it is thick enough to cut. Cool the mixture completely and stir in the bourbon, pecans, raisins and coconut.

Spread the filling over one cake layer. Place the second layer on top and frost the sides and top of the cake.

THE JUNIOR LEAGUE OF DALLAS
THE DALLAS JUNIOR LEAGUE COOKBOOK

Lane Cake

To make on 9-inch [23-cm.] cake

½ lb.	butter, softened	¼ kg.
2 cups	sugar	½ liter
2 tsp.	vanilla extract	10 ml.
3¼ cups	sifted cake flour	800 ml.
3½ tsp.	baking powder	17 ml.
½ tsp.	salt	2 ml.
¼ tsp.	ground mace	1 ml.
1 cup	milk	¼ liter
8	egg whites, stiffly beaten	8

Lane filling

8	egg yolks	8
1¼ cups	sugar	300 ml.
8 tbsp.	butter	120 ml.
1 tsp.	grated orange peel	5 ml.
¼ tsp.	ground mace	1 ml.
⅛ tsp.	ground cardamom	½ ml.
¼ tsp.	salt	1 ml.
1 cup	pecans, chopped (¼ lb. [125 g.])	¼ liter
1 cup	finely chopped candied pineapple	¼ liter
1 cup	finely chopped candied cherries	¼ liter
1 cup	shredded coconut	¼ liter
⅓ cup	bourbon	75 ml.

Cream the butter and sugar together until light and fluffy; add the vanilla extract. Sift together the flour, baking powder, salt and mace. Add the flour mixture and the milk alternately to the butter mixture. Fold in the egg whites. Pour the batter into three buttered and floured layer-cake pans. Bake in a preheated 375° F. [190° C.] oven for 20 minutes, or until a tester inserted into the center comes out clean. Turn out onto wire racks to cool.

To make Lane filling, beat the egg yolks lightly; add the sugar, butter, orange peel, mace, cardamom and salt. Cook the mixture, stirring constantly, for about five minutes, until the sugar melts and the mixture thickens slightly. Remove the mixture from the heat and add the remaining ingredients. Let the mixture cool, then spread it between the layers and on top of the cooled cake. Store the cake in a covered container in a cool place for about three days, letting the cake ripen. Each day spoon the filling that has run off back onto the cake.

MC CORMICK'S SPICES OF THE WORLD COOKBOOK

Boston Cream Pie

A simpler, but equally traditional, version of Boston cream pie is filled with raspberry jam and topped with confectioners' sugar. Melt ½ cup [125 ml.] of jam over low heat, force it through a fine sieve, then spread it smoothly over the bottom cake layer. Set the top layer in place and sprinkle it lightly with ¼ cup [50 ml.] of sifted confectioners' sugar.

To make one 9-inch [23-cm.] cake

1½ cups	cake flour	375 ml.
2 tsp.	baking powder	10 ml.
¼ tsp.	salt	1 ml.
6 tbsp.	butter, softened	90 ml.
¾ cup	sugar	175 ml.
2	eggs	2
1 tsp.	vanilla extract	5 ml.
½ cup	milk	125 ml.
1 cup	thin chocolate icing (recipe, page 165)	¼ liter

Custard filling

½ cup	light cream	125 ml.
½ cup	milk	125 ml.
¼ cup	sugar	50 ml.
	salt	
4 tsp.	cornstarch	20 ml.
2	eggs, lightly beaten	2
½ tsp.	vanilla extract	2 ml.

Combine the cake flour, baking powder and salt, and sift them onto a plate or wax paper.

In a deep bowl, cream the butter and the sugar together, beating them against the sides of the bowl with the back of a large spoon until they are light and fluffy. Beat in the eggs, one at a time, and the vanilla extract. Then, beating constantly, sprinkle in about ½ cup [125 ml.] of the cake-flour mixture and, when it is incorporated, add 2 to 3 tablespoonfuls [30 to 45 ml.] of the milk. Repeat two more times, adding the remaining flour alternately with the milk, and continue to beat until the batter is smooth.

Pour the batter into two buttered and floured layer-cake pans, dividing it equally and smoothing the surfaces with a spatula. Bake in the middle of a preheated 375° F. [190° C.] oven for 15 minutes, or until the cake layers shrink away from the sides of the pans and the centers spring back immediately when prodded gently with a finger. Turn the cake layers out onto wire racks to cool to room temperature.

To make the filling, warm the cream and half of the milk over moderate heat in a heavy 2- to 3-quart [2- to 3-liter] saucepan. When bubbles begin to form around the edges of the liquid, add the sugar and a pinch of salt, and stir until the sugar has dissolved. Remove the pan from the heat and cover it to keep the filling warm.

Combine the remaining milk and the cornstarch in a bowl and stir them with a wire whisk until smooth. Whisk in the eggs and then, stirring the mixture continuously, pour in the cream and milk in a slow, thin stream. Return the contents of the bowl to the saucepan and, stirring all the while, cook over low heat until the custard thickens and is smooth. Once it thickens, remove it from the heat; overcooking will make it lumpy. Add the vanilla extract and let the custard cool to room temperature.

Place one cake layer, upside down, on a serving plate. With a metal spatula, spread the top evenly with the cooled custard. Carefully set the second layer, also upside down, on top of the custard. Pour the icing evenly over the cake, allowing it to flow down the sides of the layers.

FOODS OF THE WORLD/AMERICAN COOKING: NEW ENGLAND

Fresh-Fruit Cakes

Apple Raisin Cake

Ciasto z Jablkiem i Rodzynkami

To make one 9-inch [23-cm.] cake

½ lb.	butter, softened	¼ kg.
2 cups	sugar	½ liter
4	eggs	4
2 cups	sifted flour	½ liter
2 tsp.	ground cinnamon	10 ml.
1 tsp.	baking soda	5 ml.
4 cups	apples, peeled, cored and coarsely shredded	1 liter
¾ cup	raisins	175 ml.
1 cup	walnuts, finely chopped (¼ lb. [125 g.])	¼ liter

Beat the butter with the sugar until creamy; add the eggs and beat for five minutes more. Add the flour, cinnamon and baking soda, and beat for three more minutes. Fold in the fruits and nuts. Place in a buttered and floured spring-form pan. Bake in a preheated 350° F. [180° C.] oven for one and one half hours.

ALINA ŻERAŃSKA
THE ART OF POLISH COOKING

Apple-Orange Coffeecake

To make one 9-inch [23-cm.] tube cake

6	apples, peeled, cored and sliced (about 3 cups [¾ liter])	6
2⅓ cups	sugar	575 ml.
5 tsp.	ground cinnamon	25 ml.
3 cups	flour	¾ liter
3 tsp.	baking powder	15 ml.
1 tsp.	salt	5 ml.
1 cup	vegetable oil	¼ liter
4	eggs	4
¼ cup	strained fresh orange juice	50 ml.
1 tbsp.	vanilla extract	15 ml.
1 cup	heavy cream, whipped	¼ liter

Combine the apples, ⅓ cup [75 ml.] of the sugar, and the cinnamon, and set aside. Sift the flour, baking powder, salt and remaining sugar into a bowl. Make a well in the center and pour in the oil, eggs, orange juice and vanilla extract. Beat with a wooden spoon until the batter is well blended. Drain the apple mixture of excess moisture. Spoon one third of the batter into a buttered and floured tube-cake pan. Make a ring of half of the drained apple mixture on top of the batter, taking care not to have any apple touching the sides of the pan.

Spoon another third of the batter over, make a ring of the remaining apples and top with the remaining batter. Bake in a preheated 375° F. [190° C.] oven for one and one quarter hours, or until the cake shrinks from the sides of the pan. Cover the top of the pan with aluminum foil if the cake begins to overbrown.

Let the cake cool in the pan until lukewarm before turning it out onto a serving plate. Serve immediately, garnished with whipped cream.

JEAN HEWITT
THE NEW YORK TIMES NEW ENGLAND HERITAGE COOKBOOK

Apple Upside-down Cake

Nectarines, peaches, pears or pitted cherries may be substituted for the apples specified in this recipe.

To make one cake 8 inches [20 cm.] square

4 tbsp.	butter	60 ml.
½ cup	light brown sugar	125 ml.
¼ tsp.	grated nutmeg	1 ml.
2	large apples, peeled, cored and sliced thin (about 2 cups [½ liter])	2
1 tsp.	strained fresh lemon juice	5 ml.
1⅓ cups	cake flour	325 ml.
¾ cup	sugar	175 ml.
1¾ tsp.	baking powder	9 ml.
¼ tsp.	salt	1 ml.
3 tbsp.	vegetable shortening or butter, at room temperature	45 ml.
½ cup	milk	125 ml.
1 tsp.	vanilla extract	5 ml.
1	egg	1

Melt the butter in an 8-inch [20-cm.] square pan. Add the brown sugar and nutmeg and blend well. Remove the pan from the heat and arrange the apple slices, slightly overlapping them, on the brown-sugar mixture. Sprinkle the apples with the lemon juice.

Sift the flour with the sugar, baking powder and salt. Stir the vegetable shortening or butter just to soften it, then stir in the flour mixture, milk and vanilla extract. Mix until the flour is dampened.

Beat the batter for two minutes with an electric mixer at medium speed or beat 300 strokes by hand. Add the egg, and beat for one minute longer with the mixer or 150 strokes by hand. Pour the batter over the apples.

Bake in a preheated 375° F. [190° C.] oven for 35 minutes. Cool the cake in the pan for five minutes and then invert it onto a serving plate; let it stand for one minute more before removing the pan. Serve warm.

JEAN HEWITT
THE NEW YORK TIMES NEW ENGLAND HERITAGE COOKBOOK

Apple Cake Mousse

To make the applesauce specified in this recipe, wash, quarter and core 1 pound [½ kg.] of apples, and put them in a saucepan with about ¼ cup [50 ml.] of water. Simmer the apples until tender, then purée them through a vegetable mill.

This cake can be made a day ahead but not before.

To make one 8- to 10-inch [20- to 25-cm.] cake

2 cups	graham cracker crumbs	½ liter
1 tsp.	ground cinnamon	5 ml.
3 tbsp.	butter, melted	45 ml.
3	eggs, yolks separated from whites, whites stiffly beaten	3
1 tbsp.	cornstarch	15 ml.
1¾ cups	sweetened condensed milk	425 ml.
3 tbsp.	strained fresh lemon juice	45 ml.
2 cups	applesauce	½ liter

Pour the graham cracker crumbs into a mixing bowl and stir in the cinnamon. Pour the butter over the crumbs and stir until all of the butter has been absorbed. Pat half of the crumbs into a deep, well-buttered spring-form or cake pan.

Beat the cornstarch into the egg yolks, then stir in the condensed milk and lemon juice. Beat the batter until smooth. Finally, beat in the applesauce.

Fold half of the beaten whites into the batter, then fold in the remaining half. Pour the batter carefully into the pan, so as not to disturb the layer of crumbs. Smooth the top of the batter. Sprinkle the remaining crumbs over the top in a smooth layer; pat gently.

Bake in a preheated 350° F. [180° C.] oven for 45 to 50 minutes, or until a crack begins developing on the top of the cake. Cool the cake in its pan.

If a spring-form pan was used, remove the ring that forms the sides and place the cake on a platter. If the cake was baked in a regular cake pan, cut and serve directly from the pan. Use a serrated cake or bread knife and cut in a gentle sawing motion.

CAROL CUTLER
THE SIX-MINUTE SOUFFLÉ AND OTHER CULINARY DELIGHTS

Apple Coffeecake

Nuts may be added to the batter to make a richer loaf.

To make one 4-by-8-inch [10-by-20-cm.]
loaf cake

8 tbsp.	butter	120 ml.
2	tart apples, peeled, cored and grated	2
2	eggs	2
1 cup	sugar	¼ liter
2 tbsp.	buttermilk	30 ml.
1 tsp.	vanilla extract	5 ml.
½ tsp.	ground cinnamon	2 ml.
¼ tsp.	grated nutmeg	1 ml.
¼ tsp.	salt	1 ml.
2 tsp.	baking powder	10 ml.
½ tsp.	baking soda	2 ml.
2 cups	flour	½ liter

In a heavy skillet, melt the butter and add the apples, turning them over and over to coat them thoroughly with the butter. Simmer the apples for 30 seconds, remove them from the heat and set them aside.

Beat together the eggs and sugar; then add the milk, vanilla extract, cinnamon, nutmeg, salt, baking powder and baking soda, and mix well. Add the flour slowly and beat thoroughly. Fold in the apples and melted butter.

Pour into a buttered and floured loaf pan. Bake in a preheated 350° F. [180° C.] oven for 50 to 55 minutes, or until the surface cracks and a tester plunged into the center comes out clean. Remove the cake from the pan while it is still slightly warm.

THE GREAT COOKS' GUIDE TO CAKES

Blueberry Cake

To make one 10-inch [25-cm.] cake

4 tbsp.	butter, softened	60 ml.
2 cups	sugar	½ liter
2	eggs	2
2 cups	flour	½ liter
1 cup	sour milk	¼ liter
1 tsp.	baking soda	5 ml.
2 cups	blueberries	½ liter

Cream the butter and sugar until the mixture is light and fluffy. Beat in the eggs one at a time, then add the flour, milk

and baking soda. Mix the batter until well blended, then stir in the blueberries. Pour the batter into a buttered and floured cake pan and bake in a preheated 350° F. [180° C.] oven for one and one half hours, or until the center of the cake is firm to the touch.

THE LADIES AUXILIARY OF THE LUNENBURG HOSPITAL SOCIETY
DUTCH OVEN

Capp's Blackberry-Jam Cake

To make one 9-inch [23-cm.] tube cake

1 cup	raisins	¼ liter
1 cup	red wine or grape juice	¼ liter
1 cup	finely chopped citron	¼ liter
1 cup	pecans, finely chopped (¼ lb. [125 g.])	¼ liter
3½ cups	sifted flour	875 ml.
2 tsp.	baking powder	10 ml.
1 tsp.	baking soda	5 ml.
1 tsp.	salt	5 ml.
½ lb.	butter, softened	¼ kg.
1 cup	sugar	¼ liter
5	eggs	5
1 cup	strained blackberry jam	¼ liter
¾ cup	buttermilk	175 ml.
1 tbsp.	confectioners' sugar	15 ml.

Soak the raisins overnight in the wine or grape juice. Strain the raisins and reserve the liquid.

Sift together the flour, baking powder, baking soda and salt. Dredge the raisins, citron and pecans in ½ cup [125 ml.] of the flour mixture.

Cream the butter and the sugar, beating until fluffy. Beat in the eggs, one at a time. Add the jam and beat until the batter is smooth. Add the flour mixture alternately with the buttermilk, beating the batter until smooth after each addition, then blend in the reserved liquid. Add the dredged fruit to the batter and mix thoroughly.

Pour the batter into a buttered and floured tube cake pan, and bake in a preheated 350° F. [180° C.] oven for one and one quarter hours, or until the cake shrinks from the sides of the pan. Cool the cake on a wire rack and dust confectioners' sugar over the top before serving.

CLEMENTINE PADDLEFORD
THE BEST IN AMERICAN COOKING

Lemon-Cherry Cake

To make one 8-inch [20-cm.] cake

½ lb.	butter, softened	¼ kg.
1 cup	superfine sugar	¼ liter
4	eggs, lightly beaten	4
2 cups	flour	½ liter
½ tsp.	baking powder	2 ml.
1½ cups	candied cherries, quartered	375 ml.
⅓ cup	candied citron, chopped	75 ml.
1 cup	almonds, blanched, peeled and ground (¼ lb. [125 g.])	¼ liter
1	lemon, peel grated, juice strained	1

Cream the butter and sugar thoroughly, then beat in the eggs. Add the flour and baking powder. Stir the cherries and candied citron into the ground almonds and add the mixture to the cake batter; add the fresh lemon peel and juice. Turn the batter into a buttered and floured cake pan and bake in a preheated 350° F. [180° C.] oven for approximately two hours, or until the cake has shrunk slightly from the sides of the pan.

MARGARET BATES
TALKING ABOUT CAKES

Bread Cherry Cake

Housková Bublanina

To make one 12-by-16-inch [30-by-40-cm.] cake

8 tbsp.	butter, softened	120 ml.
½ cup	sugar	125 ml.
4	eggs, yolks separated from whites, whites stiffly beaten	4
2⅓ cups	fresh fine bread crumbs	575 ml.
2 tsp.	baking powder	10 ml.
¼ tsp.	ground cinnamon	1 ml.
1 to 1½ lb.	cherries, pitted	½ to ¾ kg.
	confectioners' sugar	

Cream the butter thoroughly with the sugar and egg yolks. Blend in the bread crumbs mixed with the baking powder and cinnamon. Fold in the egg whites.

Spread the mixture 1 to 1½ inches [2½ to 4 cm.] deep in a buttered and floured jelly-roll pan. Arrange the cherries on top of the cake and bake in a preheated 325° F. [160° C.] oven for 20 to 30 minutes. Cool the cake in the pan. To serve, cut it into squares and sprinkle them with confectioners' sugar.

JOZA BŘÍZOVÁ
THE CZECHOSLOVAK COOKBOOK

Cherry Cake

Kirschenkuchen

To make one 9-inch [23-cm.] cake

½ lb.	butter, softened	¼ kg.
1½ cups	sugar	375 ml.
5	eggs, yolks separated from whites	5
	salt	
2 tsp.	grated lemon peel	10 ml.
1 tsp.	vanilla extract	5 ml.
2⅓ cups	cake flour	575 ml.
3 cups	Bing cherries, stemmed but not pitted	¾ liter
	confectioners' sugar	

Cream the butter with half of the sugar. Beat in the egg yolks, one by one, until the mixture is foamy. Add a pinch of salt, the lemon peel and vanilla extract. Beat the egg whites until just stiff, then add the remaining sugar gradually while continuing to beat until very stiff. Fold the egg whites into the yolk mixture while adding the flour, little by little. Pour the batter into a buttered spring-form or deep cake pan and cover the entire surface with the cherries. Bake in a preheated 375° F. [190° C.] oven for about 50 minutes, or until the cake is brown and has risen around the cherries. Sprinkle the top of the cake with confectioners' sugar. Cool the cake, turn it out, and sprinkle on confectioners' sugar again just before serving.

LILLIAN LANGSETH-CHRISTENSEN
VOYAGE GASTRONOMIQUE

Lemon-Yogurt Cake

To make one 10-inch [25-cm.] tube cake

3 cups	cake flour or 2¾ cups [675 ml.] all-purpose flour	¾ liter
1 tsp.	baking soda	5 ml.
¼ tsp.	salt	1 ml.
2 cups	sugar	½ liter
½ lb.	butter, softened	¼ kg.
6	eggs, yolks separated from whites	6
2 tsp.	grated lemon peel	10 ml.
2 tbsp.	strained fresh lemon juice	30 ml.
1 cup	plain yogurt	¼ liter

Sift the flour, baking soda and salt together. Beat egg whites until soft peaks form. Gradually add ½ cup [125 ml.] of the sugar, beating until stiff but not dry. Beat the butter with the remaining sugar and the egg yolks, lemon peel and lemon juice until fluffy. Stir the flour mixture, alternately with the yogurt, into the creamed-butter mixture. Gently fold the mixture into the egg whites. Pour the batter into a buttered and floured tube cake pan. Bake in a preheated 350° F. [180° C.] oven for 50 to 60 minutes, or until a tester inserted in the cake comes out clean. Cool the cake in the pan for 10 minutes before turning it out onto a cake rack to finish cooling.

THE JUNIOR LEAGUE OF FAYETTEVILLE
THE CAROLINA COLLECTION

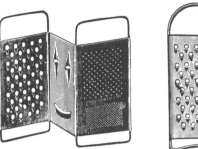

Lemon Cake

Zitronenkuchen

To make one 8-inch [20-cm.] cake

12 tbsp.	butter, softened	180 ml.
¾ cup	sugar	175 ml.
3	eggs	3
2	lemons, peel grated and juice of 1 strained	2
1¾ cups	flour	425 ml.
2 tsp.	baking powder	10 ml.
1 cup	cornstarch	¼ liter
½ cup	milk	125 ml.
1 cup	glacé icing *(recipe, page 165)*, made with 2 tbsp. [30 ml.] fresh lemon juice instead of water	¼ liter

Cream the butter in a bowl and beat in the sugar, then add the eggs and lemon juice. Beat for 10 minutes, or until the mixture is creamy.

Sift the flour with the baking powder, and beat it and the cornstarch into the batter. Add the lemon peel and finally the milk, a little at a time. Pour the batter into a buttered and floured cake pan, and bake in a preheated 350° F. [180° C.] oven for 45 minutes, or until the top is light brown. Turn the cake out onto a wire rack placed over a piece of foil. Spread the icing over the cake while the cake is still warm.

HERMINE KIEHNLE AND MARIA HÄDECKE
DAS NEUE KIEHNLE-KOCHBUCH

Holiday Carrot Cake

To make one 10-inch [25-cm.] tube cake

3 cups	sifted flour	¾ liter
2 tsp.	baking powder	10 ml.
2 tsp.	baking soda	10 ml.
½ tsp.	salt	2 ml.
2 tsp.	ground cinnamon	10 ml.
2 cups	sugar	½ liter
1½ cups	vegetable oil	375 ml.
3 cups	grated raw carrots	¾ liter
4	eggs	4
½ cup	walnuts, chopped	125 ml.
Cream cheese frosting		
3 oz.	cream cheese	85 g.
4 tbsp.	butter	60 ml.
2 cups	confectioners' sugar	½ liter
1 tsp.	strained fresh lemon juice	5 ml.

Sift the flour, baking powder, baking soda, salt and cinnamon together into a large bowl. In another bowl, combine the sugar and oil, and mix thoroughly. Add the carrots and blend well. Add the eggs, one at a time, to the carrot mixture, beating well after each addition. Fold in the nuts, and then gradually add the flour mixture, blending well. Pour the batter into a buttered and floured 10-inch [25-cm.] fluted tube pan, and bake in a preheated 350° F. [180° C.] oven for one hour. Turn the cake out onto a wire rack to cool.

When the cake is cool, blend together the frosting ingredients and frost.

JOAN NATHAN
THE JEWISH HOLIDAY KITCHEN

Lémania Cake

To make one 8-inch [20-cm.] cake

8 tbsp.	butter, softened	120 ml.
1 cup	superfine sugar	¼ liter
¾ tsp.	baking soda	4 ml.
¼ tsp.	salt	1 ml.
1 tsp.	grated lemon peel	5 ml.
3	eggs, yolks separated from whites, whites stiffly beaten	3
1¾ cups	sifted flour	425 ml.
¼ cup	sifted cornstarch	50 ml.
2½ tbsp.	strained fresh lemon juice	37 ml.
½ cup	milk	125 ml.
2 cups	simple butter cream *(recipe, page 166)*, flavored with 1 tbsp. [15 ml.] strained fresh lemon juice	½ liter
	confectioners' sugar	
about ¼ cup	candied cherries	about 50 ml.

Beat the butter until it is fluffy and lemon-colored. Gradually blend in the sugar, baking soda, salt and lemon peel. Beat until the mixture is smooth and creamy. Add the egg yolks, one at a time, beating vigorously after each addition. Sift the flour with the cornstarch; combine the lemon juice and milk; add the flour mixture to the butter-and-egg mixture alternately with the milk and lemon juice. Carefully fold the egg whites into the batter.

Divide the batter between two well-buttered, lightly floured layer-cake pans. Bake in a preheated 375° F. [190° C.] oven for 25 to 30 minutes, or until a tester inserted in the center comes out clean. Cool the layers in the pans for 10 minutes, then turn them out onto a wire rack to finish cooling. Put the layers together with some of the butter cream; use the remainder to frost the sides and top. Decorate the top with alternating rows of sifted confectioners' sugar and candied cherries.

HENRI PAUL PELLAPRAT
THE GREAT BOOK OF FRENCH CUISINE

Cranberry Cake

To make one 9-inch [23-cm.] tube cake

2¼ cups	flour	550 ml.
¼ tsp.	salt	1 ml.
1 tsp.	baking powder	5 ml.
1 tsp.	baking soda	5 ml.
2 cups	sugar	½ liter
2	eggs, lightly beaten	2
1 cup	buttermilk	¼ liter
¾ cup	vegetable oil	175 ml.
1 cup	cranberries	¼ liter
1 cup	nuts, chopped (¼ lb. [125 g.])	¼ liter
1 cup	chopped dates	¼ liter
4 tbsp.	grated orange peel	60 ml.
1 cup	strained fresh orange juice	¼ liter
	heavy cream, whipped and lightly flavored with sherry (optional)	

Sift together the flour, salt, baking powder, baking soda and 1 cup [¼ liter] of the sugar. In a separate bowl, mix the eggs with the buttermilk and the oil. Combine the two mixtures and beat until they form a smooth batter. Stir in the cranberries, nuts, dates and orange peel.

Pour the batter into a buttered but unfloured fluted tube pan. Bake in a preheated 325° F. [160° C.] oven for one hour to one and one quarter hours, or until a cake tester inserted in the middle comes out clean.

Turn the cake out onto a wire rack placed over foil. Heat the remaining 1 cup [¼ liter] of sugar with the orange juice until the sugar dissolves, and then pour the mixture over the hot cake.

Let the cake stand overnight. Serve the cake with the whipped cream, if desired.

ST. STEPHEN'S EPISCOPAL CHURCH
BAYOU CUISINE

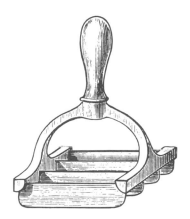

Basque Cake
Gâteau Basque
To make one 9-inch [23-cm.] cake

2 cups	flour	½ liter
1½ tsp.	baking powder	7 ml.
4	eggs, 1 lightly beaten	4
1 cup	granulated sugar	¼ liter
12 tbsp.	butter, melted and cooled	180 ml.
4 tbsp.	strained fresh orange juice	60 ml.
	vanilla extract	
2 tsp.	rum	10 ml.
⅔ cup	pastry cream *(recipe, page 166)*	150 ml.

Sift the flour and the baking powder together onto wax paper. In a bowl, lightly beat the three unbeaten eggs with the sugar, then slowly add the butter. Beat in the flour mixture, a third at a time; add the orange juice, two or three drops of vanilla extract and the rum. Let the batter rest for 15 minutes.

Fit a pastry bag with a large No. 6 open star tube, fill the bag with the batter, and pipe the batter in a spiral shape into an oiled spring-form pan, starting around the outer edge and finishing at the center. Spread the pastry cream on the batter, leaving ½ inch [1 cm.] of the batter uncovered around the edge of the pan. Do not let the pastry cream touch the edge of the pan, lest the cake become difficult to turn out after it is baked. Cover the pastry cream with a spiral of batter, making sure the top and bottom layers of batter enclose the pastry cream around the edge. Brush the top with the beaten egg. Bake the cake in a preheated 400° F. [200° C.] oven for 40 minutes, or until it feels dry. Cool in the pan for 10 minutes. Turn the cake out and serve it cold.

GASTON LENÔTRE
LENÔTRE'S DESSERTS AND PASTRIES

Portugal Cakes
To make one 5-by-9-inch [13-by-23-cm.] cake

½ cup	sugar	125 ml.
4	egg yolks	4
1 tbsp.	rum	15 ml.
½ cup	almonds, blanched, peeled and coarsely chopped	125 ml.
5	egg whites, 4 stiffly beaten	5
⅔ cup	strained fresh orange juice	150 ml.
1 tbsp.	grated orange peel	15 ml.
	confectioners' sugar	

Place the sugar, egg yolks and rum in a bowl, and beat them with a whisk for 10 minutes.

Pound the chopped almonds in a mortar with the unbeaten egg white until they become a smooth pulp, then rub the almond pulp through a sieve into a bowl; add the orange juice and peel and mix thoroughly. Fold the stiffly beaten egg whites into the egg-yolk mixture; add the almond-and-orange mixture and blend well.

Spread the batter in a pan that has been buttered and lined with buttered parchment paper. Sprinkle a little confectioners' sugar over the batter, and bake in a preheated 350° F. [180° C.] oven for 25 minutes, or until lightly browned. Allow the cake to cool in the pan for 10 minutes, then turn it out and remove the paper. Cut the cake into 12 equal parts, and dredge a little confectioners' sugar over the pieces while they are still warm. Serve immediately.

MAY BYRON
MAY BYRON'S CAKE BOOK

Dr. Mally's Orange Cake
To make one 9-inch [23-cm.] tube cake

½ lb.	unsalted butter, at room temperature	¼ kg.
1½ cups	sugar	375 ml.
3	eggs, yolks separated from whites, whites stiffly beaten	3
2 cups	flour	½ liter
1 tsp.	baking powder	5 ml.
1 tsp.	baking soda	5 ml.
1 cup	sour cream	¼ liter
2 tbsp.	grated orange peel	30 ml.
½ cup	walnuts or pecans, chopped	125 ml.
¼ cup	strained fresh orange juice	50 ml.
⅓ cup	orange-flavored liqueur	75 ml.
1 oz.	almonds, blanched, peeled and slivered (about 2 tbsp. [30 ml.])	30 g.

Cream together the butter and 1 cup [¼ liter] of the sugar until light and fluffy. Beat in the egg yolks. Sift together the dry ingredients and add them alternately with the sour cream, stirring until smooth. Stir in the orange peel and the chopped nuts. Fold in the egg whites.

Pour the batter into a buttered and floured tube cake pan and bake in a preheated 350° F. [180° C.] oven for 50 minutes, or until a tester inserted in the center comes out clean.

Combine the remaining ½ cup [125 ml.] of sugar, the orange juice and the liqueur, stirring the mixture until the sugar has dissolved. Spoon this mixture over the hot cake. Let the cake cool, then remove it from the pan and decorate the top with the slivered almonds.

LANDON SCHOOL
LANDON'S FAVORITE DESSERTS COOKBOOK

Orange Kiss-Me Cake

To make one 9-by-13-inch [23-by-32-cm.] cake

1	orange, juice strained, peel sliced	1
1 cup	raisins	¼ liter
½ cup	walnuts, chopped	125 ml.
2 cups	sifted flour	½ liter
1⅓ cups	sugar	325 ml.
1 tsp.	baking soda	5 ml.
1 tsp.	salt	5 ml.
½ cup	shortening	125 ml.
1 cup	milk	¼ liter
2	eggs	2
1 tsp.	ground cinnamon	5 ml.

Grind together the orange peel, raisins and about ⅓ cup [75 ml.] of the walnuts, using the coarse blade of a food chopper.

Sift the flour with 1 cup [¼ liter] of the sugar, the baking soda and the salt into a large mixing bowl. Add the shortening and the milk. Blend well. Add the eggs and blend well again. Add the fruit-and-nut mixture. Pour the batter into a buttered and floured baking pan. Bake in a preheated 350° F. [180° C.] oven for 40 to 50 minutes, or until the cake springs back when it is lightly touched in the center.

Drizzle the reserved orange juice over the warm cake. Combine the remaining sugar and walnuts and the cinnamon; sprinkle the cake with this mixture.

THE PILLSBURY FAMILY COOK BOOK

Orange Mazurka

Mazurek Pomarańczowy

Mazurkas are traditional Polish Easter cakes. They should be baked in shallow rectangular pans.

To make one 8-by-10-inch [20-by-25-cm.] cake

4	oranges	4
2 cups	confectioners' sugar	½ liter
4 cups	flour	1 liter
1 tsp.	baking powder	5 ml.
⅔ cup	sugar	150 ml.
10 tbsp.	butter	150 ml.
2	egg yolks	2
4 to 6 tbsp.	sour cream	60 to 90 ml.
1 cup	almonds, blanched, peeled and chopped (¼ lb. [125 g.])	¼ liter

Prick the oranges in several places with a fork or skewer, cover them with water, bring the water to a boil, and cook the fruit gently for about five minutes, or until it begins to soften. Drain the oranges, reserving the cooking liquid, and let them cool. Slice the oranges. Remove the seeds. Dissolve the confectioners' sugar in the reserved cooking water and boil this mixture for about 10 minutes to make a syrup. Poach the orange slices in the syrup for about 10 minutes, or until the peel is tender. Cool the slices in the syrup.

Sift together the flour, baking powder and sugar, and rub in the butter to make a crumbly mixture. Add the egg yolks and enough of the sour cream to make a soft and workable dough. Roll out the dough, put it in a buttered and floured pan, and bake in a preheated 350° F. [180° C.] oven for about one hour, or until lightly colored.

Turn the cake out of the pan and place it right side up on a floured baking sheet. Arrange a layer of poached orange slices over the top, draining them of excess syrup if necessary. Sprinkle on the almonds. Put the cake back into the oven for a few minutes to dry the orange slices. Serve cold.

J. DMOCHOWSKA-GORSKA
DOMOWE CIASTA I DESERY

Williamsburg Orange Cake

To make one cake 8 inches [20 cm.] square

8 tbsp.	butter, softened	120 ml.
1 cup	sugar	¼ liter
2	eggs	2
1 tsp.	vanilla extract	5 ml.
1⅔ cups	flour	400 ml.
1 tsp.	baking soda	5 ml.
½ tsp.	salt	2 ml.
1 cup	sour milk or buttermilk	¼ liter
1 cup	raisins, chopped	¼ liter
½ cup	walnuts, coarsely chopped	125 ml.
1 tbsp.	grated orange peel	15 ml.
1 cup	glacé icing (recipe, page 165), made with 2 tbsp. [30 ml.] sweet sherry instead of water, and flavored with 1 tbsp. [15 ml.] grated orange peel	¼ liter

Cream together the butter and sugar until light and fluffy. Beat in the eggs and the vanilla extract. In a small bowl, blend the flour, baking soda and salt. Add the flour mixture to the butter mixture alternately with the sour milk or buttermilk, beginning and ending with the flour mixture. Blend well after each addition. Stir in the raisins, walnuts and orange peel. Pour the mixture into a buttered and floured pan, and bake in a preheated 350° F. [180° C.] oven for 45 to 50 minutes, or until a cake tester comes out clean when inserted into the center of the cake. Leave the cake in the pan on a wire rack for 10 minutes before removing it from the pan and cooling it thoroughly on the rack. Cover the cooled cake with the glacé icing.

HYLA O'CONNOR
THE EARLY AMERICAN COOKBOOK

Orange Cake

To make one 8-inch [20-cm.] cake

½ lb.	unsalted butter, softened	¼ kg.
1 cup	sugar	250 ml.
3	large eggs, yolks separated from whites, whites stiffly beaten	3
2 cups	flour	½ liter
1 tsp.	baking powder	5 ml.
1 tsp.	baking soda	5 ml.
1 cup	sour cream	¼ liter
2 tbsp.	grated orange peel	30 ml.
½ cup	walnuts, pecans or hazelnuts, chopped	125 ml.
¼ cup	strained fresh orange juice, pulp strained out	50 ml.
⅓ cup	orange-flavored liqueur	75 ml.
	confectioners' sugar	

Cream together the butter and sugar until light and pale yellow. Beat in the egg yolks. Sift the flour, baking powder and baking soda together, and add them to the butter, sugar and egg mixture alternately with the sour cream, stirring until smooth. Stir in the orange peel and the chopped nuts. Fold the egg whites into the batter. Spoon the mixture into a spring-form or tube pan that has been buttered inside and dusted with sugar. Bake in a preheated 350° F. [180° C.] oven for 45 to 50 minutes, or until the blade of a knife, when inserted, comes out clean.

Mix the orange juice and liqueur, and spoon the mixture over the cake while it is still hot. Cool the cake before removing it from the pan. Dust the top with confectioners' sugar. If the cake is not used right away, store it in an airtight tin or in a plastic bag; if you do this, spoon a little more orange-juice mixture over the cake just before serving it.

MAURICE MOORE-BETTY
THE MAURICE MOORE-BETTY COOKING SCHOOL BOOK OF FINE COOKING

Orange Pecan Crown Cake

You can garnish this cake with fresh strawberries, and serve a small mound of confectioners' sugar for dipping them.

To make one 8-inch [20-cm.] tube cake

6 tbsp.	butter, softened	90 ml.
½ cup	sugar	125 ml.
1	egg	1
½ tsp.	vanilla extract	2 ml.
1 cup	sifted flour	¼ liter
½ tsp.	baking powder	2 ml.
½ tsp.	baking soda	2 ml.
⅛ tsp.	salt	½ ml.
½ cup	buttermilk	125 ml.
2 tbsp.	grated orange peel	30 ml.
½ cup	pecans, finely chopped	125 ml.
6 tbsp.	finely cut pitted dates, tossed in 2 tbsp. [30 ml.] flour	90 ml.
	confectioners' sugar, sifted	

Rum-orange syrup

6 tbsp.	strained fresh orange juice	90 ml.
¼ cup	sugar	50 ml.
2 tbsp.	rum	30 ml.

In a mixing bowl, cream together the butter and sugar thoroughly. Add the egg and vanilla extract, and beat until the mixture is light and fluffy. Sift together the flour, baking powder, baking soda and salt; beat them into the creamed mixture alternately with the buttermilk. Stir in the orange peel. Mix together the pecans and the dates; add them to the batter and mix well.

Turn the mixture into a buttered and floured fluted tube cake pan. Bake in a preheated 350° F. [180° C.] oven for 50 minutes, or until the cake springs back when it is lightly touched. With a fine skewer, poke holes at ½-inch [1-cm.] intervals down through the cake to the bottom of the pan.

Stir together the syrup ingredients, then slowly spoon the syrup over the warm cake, letting the syrup soak in. Cool the cake in its pan on a rack. When cool, cover or wrap tightly and allow to stand for two to three days. With a thin knife, loosen the cake at the edges and turn it out. Dust it with sifted confectioners' sugar.

VICTOR J. BERGERON
TRADER VIC'S RUM COOKERY AND DRINKERY

Meringue Cake with Peaches

To make one 8-inch [20-cm.] cake

8 tbsp.	butter, softened	120 ml.
1½ cups	sugar	375 ml.
4	eggs, yolks separated from whites	4
¼ cup	milk	50 ml.
½ tsp.	vanilla extract	2 ml.
1 cup	sifted flour	¼ liter
1¼ tsp.	baking powder	6 ml.
⅛ tsp.	salt	½ ml.
¼ cup	walnuts or pecans, chopped	50 ml.
1 cup	heavy cream	¼ liter
2 tbsp.	confectioners' sugar	30 ml.
2	peaches, peeled and diced	2

In the bowl of an electric mixer, cream the butter; slowly add ½ cup [125 ml.] of the sugar and beat until light and fluffy. Beat in the egg yolks, one at a time, then add the milk and vanilla extract. Sift the flour with the baking powder and add it to the creamed ingredients, beating slowly until mixed. The mixture will be thick. Scrape the sides of the bowl, and continue beating for at least two minutes. Divide the batter between two buttered and floured cake pans lined with parchment paper. Smooth the batter with a spatula.

Beat the egg whites with the salt until stiff. Add the remaining sugar, a tablespoonful at a time, beating constantly. Continue to beat the meringue until the mixture is like marshmallow and feels smooth when you pinch it. Spread the meringue over the cake batter in the pans, then sprinkle only one layer with the chopped nuts. Bake the layers in a preheated 350° F. [180° C.] oven for 30 minutes. Cool the layers and remove them from the pans.

To assemble the cake, whip the cream and sweeten it with the confectioners' sugar. Fold in the peaches. Place the plain layer, meringue side down, on a serving plate. Spread with all of the peaches and cream. Place the second layer, nut side up, on top. Chill in the refrigerator before serving.

JULIE DANNENBAUM
MENUS FOR ALL OCCASIONS

Pineapple Upside-down Cake

To poach pineapple, simmer fresh pineapple slices in sugar syrup (recipe, page 164) for five minutes.

To make one 9-inch [23-cm.] cake

5	fresh pineapple slices, poached and drained	5
1 cup	granulated sugar	¼ liter
6 tbsp.	hot milk	90 ml.
2	eggs, yolks separated from whites, whites stiffly beaten	2
1 cup	flour, sifted	¼ liter
1 tsp.	vanilla extract	5 ml.
8 tbsp.	butter	120 ml.
1 cup	brown sugar	¼ liter
¼ cup	pecans, chopped	50 ml.

Beating steadily, gradually add half of the granulated sugar and the milk to the egg yolks. Thoroughly mix in the remaining sugar, the flour and the vanilla extract. Then fold in the beaten egg whites.

Melt the butter in a large skillet over medium heat. Add the brown sugar and blend well. Remove the skillet from the heat and arrange the pineapple slices and the nuts in a symmetrical pattern on the butter and sugar. Cover these ingredients with the batter and place the skillet in a preheated 350° F. [180° C.] oven for 25 to 30 minutes, or until a tester inserted in the center comes out clean. Invert the cake immediately onto a serving dish.

THE JUNIOR LEAGUE OF DALLAS
THE DALLAS JUNIOR LEAGUE COOKBOOK

Hard Jelly Cake

To make two 7-inch [18-cm.] cakes

1 cup	shortening	¼ liter
1 cup	sugar	¼ liter
1	egg	1
3½ cups	flour	875 ml.
2½ tsp.	baking powder	12 ml.
½ tsp.	salt	2 ml.
½ tsp.	grated nutmeg	2 ml.
½ cup	milk	125 ml.
1½ cups	red currant jelly	375 ml.
	colored sugar crystals (optional)	
	confectioners' sugar (optional)	

Cream together the shortening, sugar and egg. Sift together the flour, baking powder, salt and nutmeg, and add them, alternately with the milk, to the creamed mixture. Chill the resulting dough.

Take a small piece of chilled dough and roll it out into a sheet about ¼ inch [6 mm.] thick. Select the lid of a cooking pot or a small plate the size of the desired cake, and place it on top of the sheet of dough. Using a knife, cut around the lid or plate to make a circle of dough. Using two spatulas, carefully lift the circle onto a buttered and floured baking sheet. Make two more dough circles the same way and place them on the sheet. Bake in a preheated 350° F. [180° C.] oven for eight to 10 minutes, or until the dough turns light brown.

Remove the baking sheet from the oven and cool the circles on a wire rack. Place one cooled circle on a cake plate, spread it with jelly, put another circle on top, and spread it with jelly. Continue making dough circles and layering them in this way until you have a jelly layer cake with 10 to 12 layers. Use the remaining dough to make a second cake.

For a pretty cake, sprinkle the last uncooked dough circle with red colored sugar crystals before baking. After baking, you may sprinkle the top with confectioners' sugar.

HOPE ANDREWS AND FRANCES KELLY
MARYLAND'S WAY

Prune and Nut Cake

To poach prunes, simmer them in water for about 25 minutes, or until they are soft.

To make one 9-inch [23-cm.] cake or one 9-by-12-inch [23-by-30-cm.] cake

½ cup	shortening	125 ml.
1 cup	sugar	¼ liter
2	eggs	2
1 tsp.	baking powder	5 ml.
2 cups	sifted flour	½ liter
½ tsp.	baking soda	2 ml.
½ tsp.	salt	2 ml.
½ tsp.	grated nutmeg	2 ml.
½ tsp.	ground cinnamon	2 ml.
½ cup	buttermilk or prune juice	125 ml.
1 tsp.	vanilla extract	5 ml.
1 cup	prunes, poached, drained, pitted and chopped	¼ liter
½ cup	walnuts or hazelnuts, chopped	125 ml.

Cream the shortening with the sugar until light and fluffy. Add the eggs, one at a time, and beat thoroughly. Sift the flour, baking soda, salt and spices together. Add the butter-

milk or prune juice alternately with the sifted dry ingredients. Stir in the vanilla extract, prunes and nuts.

Pour the batter into two buttered and floured layer-cake pans or into one jelly-roll pan. Bake in a preheated 350° F. [180° C.] oven for 25 to 30 minutes, or until the cake begins to shrink from the sides of the pan.

MARIAN TRACY (EDITOR)
FAVORITE AMERICAN REGIONAL RECIPES BY LEADING FOOD EDITORS

Prune Cake

To poach prunes, simmer them in enough water to cover for about 25 minutes, or until they are soft.

To make one cake 10 inches [25 cm.] square

2¼ cups	sifted flour	550 ml.
1 tsp.	baking soda	5 ml.
1 tsp.	ground allspice	5 ml.
1 tsp.	ground cinnamon	5 ml.
½ tsp.	ground cloves	2 ml.
¼ tsp.	salt	1 ml.
8 tbsp.	butter, softened	120 ml.
1½ cups	sugar	375 ml.
2	eggs, beaten	2
1 cup	prunes, poached, drained, pitted and puréed	¼ liter
1 cup	sour milk or buttermilk	¼ liter
1½ cups	simple butter cream (recipe, page 166)	375 ml.

Sift the flour, baking soda, spices and salt together. Beat the butter and sugar together until creamy. Blend in the eggs, then the puréed prunes, and mix well.

Add the flour mixture to the batter alternately with the milk, adding a small amount at a time and beating until smooth after each addition. Pour the batter into a buttered and floured pan. Bake in a preheated 350° F. [180° C.] oven for 40 to 45 minutes, or until a cake tester inserted in the middle of the cake comes out clean. Cool the cake for 10 minutes in the pan before turning it out onto a wire rack to cool completely, then frost it with the butter cream.

CLEMENTINE PADDLEFORD
THE BEST IN AMERICAN COOKING

Plum Torte

This torte freezes beautifully. If frozen, defrost and then warm slightly at 350° F. [180° C.] for about 10 minutes.

To make one 9-inch [23-cm.] cake

1¼ cups	sugar	300 ml.
8 tbsp.	butter, softened	120 ml.
1 cup	flour	¼ liter
1 tsp.	baking soda	5 ml.
	salt	
2	eggs	2
24	Italian plums, halved and pitted	24
1½ tsp.	ground cinnamon	7 ml.
1 tsp.	strained fresh lemon juice	5 ml.

Using either an electric mixer or a food processor, cream well together 1 cup [250 ml.] of the sugar and the butter. Then add and blend well the flour, the baking soda, a pinch of salt and the eggs. Spread the batter over the bottom of a buttered and floured spring-form pan. Cover the top of the batter with the plums, pushing them down into the batter slightly. Then sprinkle the plums with the remaining sugar, the ground cinnamon and the lemon juice. Bake in a preheated 350° F. [180° C.] oven for one hour, or until the cake is golden brown. This torte should be served warm.

RONA COHEN (EDITOR)
RECIPES TO RONA

Pumpkin Cake

Le Milla Sarladais

You may omit the baking powder in this recipe. Instead, separate the egg yolks and mix them into the paste. Then beat the whites until stiff, folding them into the mixture, which will swell like a soufflé and can be eaten while hot with a spoon.

To make one 9-inch [22-cm.] cake

1 lb.	pumpkin, peeled and sliced	½ kg.
1¾ cups	cornstarch	425 ml.
1 tsp.	baking powder (optional)	5 ml.
10 tbsp.	superfine sugar	150 ml.
	salt	
5 tbsp.	butter, melted, or 2 tbsp. [30 ml.] oil	75 ml.
5	eggs	5
2 cups	milk	½ liter
2 tbsp.	rum or 2 tbsp. [30 ml.] vanilla sugar or 2 tsp. [10 ml.] grated lemon peel	30 ml.

Simmer the pumpkin for 10 to 15 minutes in ⅔ cup [150 ml.] of lightly salted water. Drain it and pass the pumpkin through a fine-meshed sieve to make a rather dry purée. Beat in the cornstarch, baking powder, sugar, salt and butter. Add the eggs one at a time and the milk, which should be poured gradually. The paste should be thick but runny. Finally, add your chosen flavoring. Then pour the mixture into a generously buttered and floured cake pan that is 3 inches [8 cm.] deep.

Bake the cake in a preheated 350° F. [180° C.] oven for 45 minutes, or until a cake tester inserted in the middle comes out clean. The cake will turn a lovely copper color. Serve the cake cold, sprinkled with vanilla sugar.

ZETTE GUINAUDEAU-FRANC
LES SECRETS DES FERMES EN PÉRIGORD NOIR

Spiced Pumpkin Cake

To make the puréed pumpkin specified in this recipe, slice, peel and remove the seeds and fibers from a 1-pound [½-kg.] pumpkin. Simmer the slices until they are just tender—about 15 minutes—then push them through a sieve to make a purée.

To make one 9-inch [23-cm.] cake

8 tbsp.	butter, softened	120 ml.
1 cup	brown sugar	¼ liter
2	eggs	2
2½ cups	sifted cake flour	625 ml.
2½ tsp.	baking powder	12 ml.
⅓ tsp.	baking soda	1½ ml.
½ tsp.	salt	2 ml.
1 tsp.	ground cinnamon	5 ml.
⅓ tsp.	ground allspice	1½ ml.
⅓ tsp.	ground ginger	1½ ml.
¾ cup	buttermilk	175 ml.
¾ cup	puréed pumpkin	175 ml.
⅔ cup	pecans, finely chopped	150 ml.
1 cup	heavy cream, whipped	¼ liter

Cream the butter and sugar together until light and fluffy. Add the eggs, one at a time, blending well after each addition. Sift the flour, baking powder, baking soda, salt, cinnamon, allspice and ginger together twice. Add the sifted flour and spices to the egg mixture, then add the buttermilk and mix well. Add the puréed pumpkin and the chopped pecans and blend thoroughly, scraping the sides and bottom of the bowl to ensure proper mixing.

Divide the batter equally between two buttered and floured layer-cake pans and bake in a preheated 350° F. [180° C.] oven for approximately 25 minutes, or until a tester inserted through the center comes out clean. Cool the layers for 10 minutes. Remove them from the pan and place them in the refrigerator for 45 minutes, or until cold. Fill and frost the layers with the whipped cream before serving.

DOMINIQUE D'ERMO
THE CHEF'S DESSERT COOKBOOK

Strawberries and Cream Spectacular

To make one 9-inch [23-cm.] cake

2½ cups	sifted cake flour	625 ml.
1⅔ cups	sugar	400 ml.
4 tsp.	baking powder	20 ml.
1 tsp.	salt	5 ml.
½ cup	shortening	125 ml.
1¼ cup	milk	300 ml.
1 tsp.	lemon extract	5 ml.
½ tsp.	vanilla extract	2 ml.
5	egg yolks	5
4 cups	strawberries	1 liter
2 cups	heavy cream, whipped with ¼ cup [50 ml.] sugar and 1 tsp. [5 ml.] vanilla extract	½ liter
¾ cup	red currant jelly	175 ml.

Sift together the cake flour, sugar, baking powder and salt into a mixing bowl. Add the shortening and half of the milk. Beat with an electric mixer at medium speed for two minutes, scraping the bowl occasionally. Add the remaining milk, the lemon extract, the vanilla extract and the egg yolks. Beat with the electric mixer for another two minutes.

Pour the batter into two buttered layer-cake pans that have been lined with parchment paper. Bake in a preheated 350° F. [180° C.] oven for 30 minutes, or until a cake tester inserted into the centers of the layers comes out clean.

Cool the layers in their pans for 10 minutes, then turn them out onto wire racks.

While the cake is cooling, wash and hull the strawberries. Chop enough strawberries to make one cup [¼ liter]; reserve the remaining berries. Fold the chopped strawberries into one cup [¼ liter] of the whipped cream. Place one cake layer, top side down, on a serving plate. Spread it with the strawberry-cream filling. Top with the second cake layer, top side up.

Slice the reserved strawberries lengthwise. Arrange the sliced strawberries on top of the cake, starting at the outer edge and placing the slices with their pointed ends toward the edge of the cake. After the first circle of berries is completed, continue placing the strawberries in this manner until the top is covered. Refrigerate the cake for 10 minutes.

Melt the red currant jelly in a small saucepan over low heat, stirring constantly. Carefully spoon or brush the hot jelly over the strawberries. Spread some of the remaining whipped cream around the sides of the cake.

Spoon the rest of the whipped cream into a pastry bag fitted with a No. 190 drop flower tube. Pipe rosettes between the strawberry points around the rim of the cake. Then change to a No. 24 star tube and fill in the spaces. Finally, change to a No. 71 leaf tube, and pipe a border around the bottom edge of the cake.

If you do not wish to decorate the cake with decorating tips, spoon the remaining cream in small puffs on the top of the cake between the strawberries. Refrigerate the cake until time to serve it.

ELISE W. MANNING
FARM JOURNAL'S COMPLETE HOME BAKING BOOK

Rhubarb Cake

Rhabarberkuchen

To make one 10-inch [25-cm.] cake

10 tbsp.	butter, softened	150 ml.
1½ cups	granulated sugar	375 ml.
2 cups	flour	½ liter
2 tsp.	baking powder	10 ml.
	salt	
3	eggs, lightly beaten	3
1	lemon, peel grated, juice strained	1
¼ cup	milk	50 ml.
1¼ lb.	rhubarb, cut into ¾-inch [2-cm.] pieces (about 5 cups [1¼ liters])	600 g.
1 tsp.	ground cinnamon	5 ml.
	confectioners' sugar	

Cream the butter with ⅔ cup [150 ml.] of the granulated sugar until the mixture is light and fluffy. Sift together the flour, baking powder and a pinch of salt. Alternately beat the flour mixture and the eggs into the butter. Beat in the lemon peel and juice, and lastly the milk. Spoon the batter into a buttered and floured spring-form pan.

Toss the rhubarb with the cinnamon and the remaining granulated sugar, and spread the mixture on top of the batter. Bake the cake in a preheated 375° F. [190° C.] oven for 40 to 45 minutes, or until the rhubarb is soft and the cake has shrunk slightly from the sides of the pan. Let the cake cool completely in the pan. Remove the cake from the pan and sprinkle the top with confectioners' sugar.

HANS KARL ADAM
DAS KOCHBUCH AUS SCHWABEN

Dried-Fruit and Nut Cakes

Traditional Christmas Cake

The original version of this recipe calls for treacle, which is rarely available in the United States. Dark molasses makes a suitable substitute. The recipe specifies that the batter be baked in a 9-inch [23-cm.] pan 5 inches [13 cm.] deep. If such a pan is not available, divide the batter between two 9-inch [23-cm.] spring-form pans and reduce the final baking period at 275° F. [140° C.] to one hour.

To make one 9-inch [23-cm.] cake

1½ cups	diced mixed candied fruit peel	375 ml.
1½ cups	quartered candied cherries	375 ml.
4 cups	raisins	1 liter
4 cups	dried currants	1 liter
3 cups	golden raisins	¾ liter
1 cup	almonds, blanched, peeled and coarsely chopped (¼ lb. [125 g.])	¼ liter
2½ cups	flour	625 ml.
½ lb. plus 4 tbsp.	butter, softened	310 ml.
1½ cups plus 2 tbsp.	brown sugar	405 ml.
2 tbsp.	grated orange peel	30 ml.
2 tsp.	grated lemon peel	10 ml.
1 tbsp.	dark molasses	15 ml.
6	eggs, lightly beaten	6
½ tsp.	salt	2 ml.
½ tsp.	mixed spices	2 ml.
½ tsp.	grated nutmeg	2 ml.
4 to 6 tbsp.	rum, brandy, whiskey or sherry	60 to 90 ml.

In a large bowl, coat the fruits and nuts with ½ cup [125 ml.] of the flour. In a separate bowl, cream the butter and sugar, and beat in the orange and lemon peels and the molasses. Beating with a wooden spoon, gradually add the eggs, with a sprinkling of flour to prevent curdling. Then stir in the rest of the flour—sifted with the salt and spices—and enough of the spirits to make a batter that will drop easily from the spoon. Lastly, stir in the fruits and the nuts.

Turn the mixture into a cake pan 5 inches [13 cm.] deep that has been buttered well and lined with two thicknesses of parchment paper. Tie a band of brown paper around the outside of the pan for extra protection. Hollow out the center of the batter quite deeply; the cake will rise in the middle, thus ensuring a flat top for icing. Cover the top with parchment paper to prevent the cake from browning too much.

Put the cake into a preheated 325° F. [160° C.] oven and, after 20 minutes, reduce the heat to 300° F. [150° C.]. Bake for 40 minutes more, then reduce the heat to 275° F. [140° C.]. Bake for about four hours more, or until a tester inserted in the center comes out clean. Let the cake cool for one hour before turning it out.

MARGARET COSTA
MARGARET COSTA'S FOUR SEASONS COOKERY BOOK

Christmas Cake

To make one 9-inch [23-cm.] tube cake

½ cup	vegetable shortening	125 ml.
8 tbsp.	butter, softened	120 ml.
1 cup	granulated sugar	¼ liter
1 cup	light brown sugar	¼ liter
3	eggs	3
1 tsp.	vanilla extract	5 ml.
1 tsp.	lemon extract	5 ml.
1 tsp.	almond extract	5 ml.
3 cups	flour	¾ liter
1½ tsp.	baking powder	7 ml.
½ tsp.	salt	2 ml.
1 cup	milk	¼ liter
1 cup	golden raisins	¼ liter
½ cup	green candied cherries, chopped	125 ml.
¾ cup	red candied cherries, chopped	175 ml.
1 cup	chopped mixed candied fruit	¼ liter
½ cup	walnuts, chopped	125 ml.

Beat the shortening, butter, granulated sugar and brown sugar together until light and fluffy. Beat in the eggs, one at a time. Beat in the vanilla, lemon and almond extracts.

Sift together the flour, baking powder and salt. Reserve ½ cup [125 ml.] of the flour mixture, and stir the remainder into the batter alternately with the milk. Mix together the raisins, candied cherries, mixed fruit and nuts. Toss the fruits with the reserved flour mixture and stir them into the batter. Spoon the batter into a spring-form tube cake pan that has been buttered and lined with buttered parchment paper. Bake the cake in a preheated 250° F. [120° C.] oven for three hours, or until a tester inserted into the cake comes out clean. Cool the cake for 30 minutes in the pan, then turn it out to finish cooling on a rack.

JEAN HEWITT
THE NEW YORK TIMES NEW ENGLAND HERITAGE COOKBOOK

Iris Morey's Wedding Cake

This cake may be eaten right after baking, but its flavor will improve if it is allowed to mellow in a cool place, in an air-tight container, for six weeks.

To make one 12-inch [30-cm.] cake

2 lb.	mixed candied fruit, chopped	1 kg.
3 lb.	raisins, chopped	1½ kg.
2 lb.	golden raisins	1 kg.
1 lb.	dried currants	½ kg.
4¼ cups	sifted flour	1,050 ml.
1 lb.	butter, softened	½ kg.
2 cups	brown sugar	½ liter
1 cup	molasses	¼ liter
12	eggs, yolks separated from whites, yolks beaten, whites stiffly beaten	12
4 tsp.	ground cinnamon	20 ml.
4 tsp.	ground allspice	20 ml.
1 tsp.	ground mace	5 ml.
1 tsp.	grated nutmeg	5 ml.
1 cup	grape juice	¼ liter
2 cups	strawberry jam	½ liter
¼ lb.	semisweet chocolate, melted	125 g.
½ tsp.	baking soda, dissolved in a little hot water	2 ml.
about ½ cup	brandy	about 125 ml.

Dredge the chopped candied fruit, the raisins, the golden raisins and the currants in ¾ cup [175 ml.] of the flour.

In a large bowl, cream together the butter and brown sugar. One by one, mixing thoroughly after each addition, add the molasses, egg yolks and the remaining flour sifted with the spices; similarly, add and mix in the fruits. Blend in the grape juice, strawberry jam and melted chocolate. Carefully fold in the egg whites and, finally, the baking soda.

Line the bottom of a buttered cake pan 3 inches [8 cm.] deep with three layers of brown paper, cut carefully to fit.

Butter the top layer of paper and pour in the batter—the pan should be about three quarters full. Cover the batter with another buttered circle of paper. Set the pan in a larger pan of water, and steam the cake for three hours in a preheated 300° F. [150° C.] oven; then remove the pan of water and bake the cake three more hours. Turn the cake out onto a rack to cool, then pour the brandy over it.

NARCISSE CHAMBERLAIN AND NARCISSA G. CHAMBERLAIN
THE CHAMBERLAIN SAMPLER OF AMERICAN COOKING

White Fruitcake

To make one 9-inch [23-cm.] tube cake

¾ cup	chopped red candied cherries	175 ml.
½ cup	raisins	125 ml.
⅔ cup	chopped green candied pineapple	150 ml.
⅓ cup	diced candied lemon peel	75 ml.
⅓ cup	unsalted nuts, chopped	75 ml.
1 tsp.	grated lemon peel	5 ml.
⅓ cup	brandy	75 ml.
⅓ cup	yellow cornmeal	75 ml.
2 cups	sifted flour	½ liter
⅓ tsp.	baking soda	1½ ml.
12 tbsp.	butter, softened	180 ml.
1¼ cups	sugar	300 ml.
6	egg whites	6

Soak the fruits and nuts in the brandy, and let them stand in a cool place overnight. Thoroughly drain the soaked fruits and nuts for at least one hour. Spread them out on a large piece of foil, and dust them with the cornmeal mixed with ½ cup [125 ml.] flour.

Sift the remaining flour together with the baking soda. Cream the butter and ¼ cup [50 ml.] sugar until the mixture is light. Stir in the flour and the prepared fruits.

Beat the egg whites stiff, adding the remaining cup [¼ liter] of sugar gradually while beating. Fold the whites into the fruit mixture. Blend well. Pour the mixture into a tube cake pan that has been buttered and lined with parchment paper. Bake in a preheated 325° F. [160° C.] oven for approximately one hour and 30 minutes, or until the point of a knife, when inserted into the cake, comes out clean. Cool in the pan for at least one hour. Remove the cake from the pan and peel off the paper. Store the cake in a tightly sealed container or well wrapped in foil.

DOMINIQUE D'ERMO
THE CHEF'S DESSERT COOKBOOK

Tennessee White Fruitcake

To make one 12-inch [30-cm.] cake

1	large coconut, grated	1
4 cups	candied pineapple, chopped	1 liter
4 cups	golden raisins, chopped	1 liter
4 cups	white or red candied cherries, chopped	1 liter
2 cups	green candied cherries, chopped	½ liter
about 1½ cups	candied citron, chopped	about 375 ml.
1 lb.	almonds, blanched, peeled and ground (about 4 cups [1 liter])	½ kg.
1 lb.	pecans, ground (about 4 cups [1 liter])	½ kg.
3 cups	flour	¾ liter
2 cups	sugar	½ liter
¾ lb.	butter, softened	350 g.
7	eggs	7
½ cup	buttermilk	125 ml.
½ tsp.	baking soda	2 ml.
	salt	
1 tbsp.	grated nutmeg	15 ml.
¾ cup	bourbon	175 ml.
½ cup	strained fresh orange juice	125 ml.
	sweet white wine (optional)	

Mix the coconut, fruits and nuts, and toss them with 2 cups [½ liter] of the flour, reserving some cherries and whole almonds for garnish. Cream the sugar and butter together until the mixture is pale and fluffy, and beat in the eggs one at a time. Mix well after each addition. Beat in the buttermilk, baking soda, a pinch of salt and the remaining flour, and mix well. Stir the nutmeg into the bourbon and add this to the batter along with the orange juice. Fold in the fruits and nuts last.

Pour the cake mixture into a cake pan that has been buttered and lined with parchment paper. The batter should come to within 2 inches [5 cm.] of the top of the pan. Place a layer of parchment paper over the top. Bake in a preheated 275° F. [140° C.] oven for about three hours. The last hour of baking, remove the paper from the cake and decorate the top with the reserved fruit and nuts. When a cake tester inserted into the center of the cake comes out clean, the cake is done. If it needs more than three hours of cooking, cover the top with parchment paper and continue cooking until the tester comes out clean. Remove the cake from the oven and let it cool in the pan, then remove it. If desired, pierce the cake in several places through the top with a long, thin skewer and spoon in a little wine.

MARION BROWN
THE SOUTHERN COOK BOOK

Fig Cake

To prepare the figs for this recipe, wash and stem them, place them in a saucepan, and cover them with water. Stir in ½ cup [125 ml.] of sugar and 2 teaspoons [10 ml.] of strained fresh lemon juice. Cover the pan and simmer the figs until they are soft, about 20 to 30 minutes.

To make one 9-inch [23-cm.] tube cake

3	eggs	3
2 cups	sugar	½ liter
1 cup	vegetable oil	¼ liter
2 cups	flour	½ liter
1 cup	buttermilk	¼ liter
½ lb.	dried figs, poached, drained and chopped (about 1 cup [¼ liter])	¼ kg.
1 tsp.	baking soda	5 ml.
1 tsp.	ground cinnamon	5 ml.
1 tsp.	ground cloves	5 ml.
1 tsp.	salt	5 ml.

Beat the eggs until they are foamy. Add the sugar, and continue to beat until the mixture is light and fluffy. Add the oil.

Stir the baking soda into the buttermilk. Alternately beat the flour and the buttermilk mixture into the eggs.

Add the remaining ingredients to the batter; pour it into a buttered and floured tube cake pan. Bake in a preheated 350° F. [180° C.] oven for one hour and 10 minutes, or until a tester inserted in the middle of the cake comes out clean.

THE JUNIOR CHARITY LEAGUE OF MONROE
THE COTTON COUNTRY COLLECTION

Rum and Fig Cake

Pastel de Higos

To make one 10-inch [25-cm.] cake

2 cups	milk	½ liter
5 tbsp.	butter, cut into small pieces	75 ml.
3¾ cups	flour, sifted with 2 tsp. [10 ml.] baking powder	925 ml.
½ cup	sugar	125 ml.
½ cup	dark rum	125 ml.
½ cup	dried figs, stems removed, cut into small pieces	125 ml.
2	egg whites, stiffly beaten	2

Heat the milk almost to the boiling point. Remove it from the heat and add the butter. When the butter melts, gradually stir in the flour. Then add the sugar, rum and figs. Fold in the egg whites. Pour the mixture into a buttered and floured cake pan, smooth the top, and bake it in a preheated 350° F. [180° C.] oven for about 50 minutes, or until an inserted tester comes out clean.

CANDIDO LÓPEZ
EL LIBRO DE ORO DE LA GASTRONOMÍA

Liberation Fruitcake

This cake may be iced with 2½ cups [625 ml.] of royal icing (recipe, page 165).

A fruitcake should have a layer of almond paste 1 inch [2½ cm.] thick spread over the top before the cake is iced. This is not gilding the lily, it is only bringing its perfume more pronouncedly to your attention.

To make one 12-inch [30-cm.] cake or two 5-by-9-inch [13-by-23-cm.] loaf cakes

1 lb.	butter, softened	½ kg.
2 cups	sugar	½ liter
12	eggs, yolks separated from whites, whites stiffly beaten	12
1½ lb.	candied citron, slivered	¾ kg.
1 lb.	candied cherries, slivered	½ kg.
2 lb.	golden raisins, soaked overnight in brandy and drained	1 kg.
4 cups	flour	1 liter
2 tsp.	ground cinnamon	10 ml.
1 tsp.	ground mace	5 ml.
1 tsp.	grated nutmeg	5 ml.
½ tsp.	ground cloves	2 ml.
1½ lb.	almonds, blanched, peeled and finely chopped (about 6 cups [1½ liters])	¾ kg.
1 cup	brandy	¼ liter
¼ cup	rose or orange-flower water	50 ml.
about 4 cups	almond paste (recipe, page 167)	about 1 liter

Thoroughly cream the butter. Slowly add the sugar, stirring until very light. Beat in the egg yolks, one by one. Mix the citron, cherries and drained raisins together. Sift the flour and sprinkle some of it on the fruits to prevent sticking. Shake the fruits in a sieve to remove all the excess flour and reserve them. Return the excess flour to the remaining flour, along with the cinnamon, mace, nutmeg and cloves.

Slowly sift the seasoned flour into the butter mixture, stirring thoroughly after each addition. Add the almonds, 1 cup [¼ liter] brandy, and the rose or orange-flower water.

Fold the egg whites lightly but thoroughly into the dough. Then fold in the floured fruits. Put the mixture into a cake pan or loaf pans, buttered and lined with buttered parchment paper. Bake in a preheated 350° F. [180° C.] oven—four hours for a cake pan or two and a half hours for loaf pans. Cool the cake in its pan for 15 minutes, then turn it out onto a wire rack. With a moist knife, spread the almond paste over the top of the cake.

ALICE B. TOKLAS
THE ALICE B. TOKLAS COOK BOOK

Vermont Scripture Cake

This old New England recipe originally specified only measurements and Biblical references for the ingredients used in the cake. To find butter, the cook consulted Judges 5:25; to find sugar, Jeremiah 6:20; to find flour, I Kings 4:22; to find raisins and figs, I Samuel 30:12; to find almonds, Genesis 43:11; to find water, Genesis 24:20; to find eggs, Isaiah 10:14; to find salt, Leviticus 2:13; to find honey, Exodus 16:31; and to find spices, I Kings 10:2.

To make this cake, follow Solomon's advice for making good boys (Proverbs 23:14).

To make one 9-inch [23-cm.] cake

2 cups	raisins	½ liter
2 cups	dried figs, chopped	½ liter
1 cup	almonds, blanched, peeled and chopped (¼ lb. [125 g.])	¼ liter
½ lb.	butter, softened	¼ kg.
2 cups	sugar	½ liter
6	eggs	6
3½ cups	flour	875 ml.
	salt	
1½ tsp.	mixed spices	7 ml.
1 cup	water	¼ liter
1 tbsp.	honey	15 ml.

Toss the fruits and nuts in ¼ cup [50 ml.] of the flour. Cream the butter with the sugar, then beat in the eggs, one at a time. Continue to beat until the mixture is light and fluffy.

Sift the spices and a pinch of salt with the flour, and add the sifted flour mixture, alternately with the water, to the butter, sugar and eggs. Add the tossed fruits and nuts and then the honey. Stir the mixture well.

Pour the mixture into a buttered and floured cake pan three inches [8 cm.] deep, and bake in a preheated 375° F. [190° C.] oven for one hour, until a cake tester inserted in the center of the cake comes out clean. Carefully turn the cake out onto a wire rack to cool.

IMOGENE WOLCOTT
THE YANKEE COOK BOOK

Milkless, Eggless, Butterless Cake

To make one cake 8 inches [20 cm.] square

1 cup	dark brown sugar	¼ liter
5 tbsp.	lard	75 ml.
1½ cups	raisins	375 ml.
1 tsp.	ground cinnamon	5 ml.
⅓ tsp.	ground cloves	1½ ml.
¼ tsp.	salt	1 ml.
¼ tsp.	grated nutmeg	1 ml.
1 cup	water	¼ liter
1 tsp.	baking soda	5 ml.
2 cups	sifted flour	½ liter
½ tsp.	baking powder	2 ml.

Place the sugar, lard, raisins, cinnamon, cloves, salt and nutmeg in a saucepan with the water. Bring to a boil and continue to boil for three minutes. Set the mixture aside to cool. Dissolve the baking soda in a little warm water. Sift together the flour and the baking powder. When the boiled mixture has cooled, stir in the baking soda and the flour mixture. When the batter is completely blended, turn it into a buttered and floured pan, and bake in a 350° F. [180° C.] oven for 35 minutes, or until the cake begins to shrink from the sides of the pan. Cool the cake in the pan for 10 minutes before turning it out onto a wire rack.

EDNA EBY HELLER
THE ART OF PENNSYLVANIA DUTCH COOKING

Kate's Boiled Cake

To make two 6-by-12-inch [15-by-30-cm.] loaf cakes

2 cups	sugar	½ liter
1 cup	vegetable shortening	¼ liter
1 cup	dates, raisins or currants	¼ liter
½ cup	nuts, chopped	125 ml.
2 cups	water	½ liter
1 tsp.	grated nutmeg	5 ml.
1 tsp.	ground allspice	5 ml.
1 tsp.	ground cinnamon	5 ml.
1 tsp.	salt	5 ml.
2¼ cups	flour	550 ml.
2 tsp.	baking soda	10 ml.
1	egg	1

In a large saucepan, combine the sugar, shortening, fruits and nuts. Add the water, spices and salt. Bring the mixture

to a boil over medium heat and boil for 10 minutes. Take the saucepan off the heat and let the mixture cool.

Sift the flour and the baking soda gradually into the boiled mixture, stirring after each addition. Add the egg and mix thoroughly.

Pour the mixture evenly into two buttered and floured loaf pans. Bake in a preheated 325° F. [160° C.] oven for one hour, or until the cake shrinks from the sides. This cake needs no frosting and will keep moist for weeks.

ST. STEPHEN'S EPISCOPAL CHURCH
BAYOU CUISINE

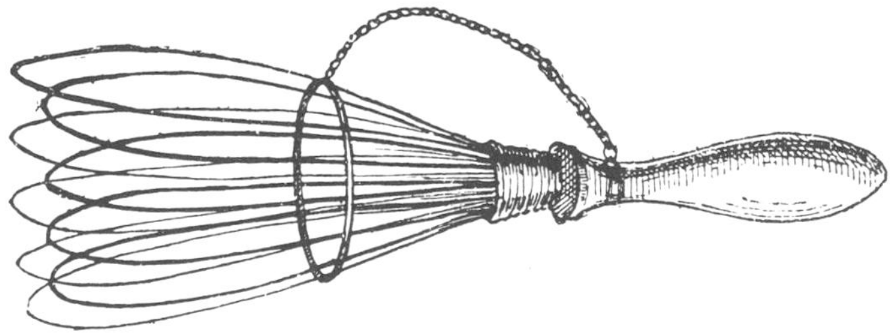

Lawn Tennis Cake

Noyau liqueur is a strong, almond-flavored liqueur made from the kernels of peaches and apricots.

To make one 9-inch [23-cm.] cake

8 tbsp.	butter, softened	120 ml.
6 tbsp.	superfine sugar	90 ml.
2 tbsp.	candied orange peel, very finely chopped	30 ml.
4 or 5 drops	vanilla extract	4 or 5 drops
⅛ tsp.	ground cinnamon	½ ml.
1 cup	flour	¼ liter
¼ cup	rice flour	50 ml.
1 cup	golden raisins, finely chopped	¼ liter
1 cup	candied cherries, finely chopped	¼ liter
2	eggs, yolks separated from whites, whites stiffly beaten	2
7 tbsp.	maraschino or noyau liqueur	105 ml.
1 tsp.	baking powder	5 ml.
	salt	
½ cup	almond paste (recipe, page 167)	125 ml.
1½ cups	glacé icing (recipe, page 165)	375 ml.
	candied cherries and angelica (optional)	

Cream the butter with the sugar, then add the candied peel, vanilla extract and cinnamon. Gradually and lightly stir in the flour, rice flour, raisins, cherries, egg yolks, liqueur, baking powder and salt. Last of all, fold in the whites. Pour the batter into a cake pan 3 inches [8 cm.] deep that has been lined with buttered parchment paper. Bake in a preheated 350° F. [180° C.] oven for about one and one half hours, or until a tester inserted in the center comes out clean. Cool the cake completely, roll out the almond paste, and cover the top of the cake with it. When the paste has set, ice the cake with the glacé icing and decorate it, if you wish, with candied cherries and angelica.

MAY BYRON
MAY BYRON'S CAKE BOOK

Twelfth Night Cake

To make one 8-inch [20-cm.] cake

2 cups	flour	½ liter
1 tbsp.	baking powder	15 ml.
	salt	
	grated nutmeg	
½ lb.	butter, softened	¼ kg.
1 cup	superfine sugar	¼ liter
4	eggs	4
4 cups	dried currants, tossed with flour	1 liter
4 oz.	mixed candied peel, sliced and tossed with flour (about ¾ cup [175 ml.])	125 g.
½ cup	almonds, blanched, peeled and chopped	125 ml.
⅓ cup	brandy	75 ml.
1 cup	glacé icing *(recipe, page 165)*, made with 2 tbsp. [30 ml.] strained fresh lemon juice instead of water	¼ liter
	assorted candied fruits	

Sift the flour with the baking powder and a pinch each of salt and nutmeg. Cream the butter with the sugar until the mixture is light and fluffy, and beat in the whole eggs with a little of the flour mixture. Then stir in the rest of the flour and add the dried currants, candied peel and almonds; last of all, add the brandy.

Pour the batter into a cake pan 3 inches [8 cm.] deep that has been buttered and lined with buttered parchment paper. Make a depression in the center of the batter. Bake the cake in a preheated 325° F. [160° C.] oven for two to three hours, or until an inserted tester comes out clean. When the cake is cooked, keep it in the oven with the heat off for a short while, then lift the cake out and turn it onto a rack to cool.

Cover the cooled cake with the lemon-flavored glacé icing. Before the icing has time to set, decorate it with the candied fruits, pressing them in slightly. Let the icing harden before serving the cake.

GERTRUDE MANN
A BOOK OF CAKES

Grandmother's Wonder Cake

Grossmutters Wunderkuchen

To make two 9-inch [22-cm.] cakes

3½ cups	flour	875 ml.
2½ cups	light rye flour	625 ml.
½ tsp.	pepper	2 ml.
½ tsp.	ground cloves	2 ml.
½ tsp.	ground ginger	2 ml.
½ tsp.	ground cardamom	2 ml.
2 tsp.	ground cinnamon	10 ml.
	salt	
1¾ cups	sugar	425 ml.
1¼ cups	honey	300 ml.
4 tbsp.	butter	60 ml.
1 tbsp.	baking powder, dissolved in 3 to 4 tbsp. [45 to 60 ml.] warm milk	15 ml.
10	eggs, lightly beaten	10
1¾ cups	raisins	425 ml.
⅔ cup	prunes, quartered	150 ml.
⅔ cup	dried figs, seeds removed and flesh cut into quarters	150 ml.
¾ cup	mixed candied fruit peel, chopped	175 ml.
¾ cup	almonds, blanched, peeled and slivered	175 ml.

Sift the flour, rye flour, spices and a pinch of salt together. Put half of the sugar into a saucepan and stir it over low heat until it browns and begins to melt. Add the honey and let it melt with the sugar. When both are liquid, stir in the rest of the sugar and two thirds of the butter. Transfer the mixture to a large bowl and let cool, then stir in the baking powder dissolved in milk, the eggs and the flour mixture. Beat the ingredients well. Lastly fold in the fruit and almonds, mix well and pour into two buttered and floured cake pans 3 inches [8 cm.] deep, filling them no more than halfway to allow room for the cakes to rise. Bake in a preheated 325° F. [160° C.] oven for one and one half hours, or until a tester inserted into the center of the cakes comes out clean. Let the cakes cool completely in the pans before turning them out. They will keep for months in an airtight container.

GRETE WILLINSKY
KULINARISCHE WELTREISE

Simnel Cake

Simnel cake is a rich English fruitcake often coated with almond paste. The title is derived from the French seminel, meaning "fine wheat flour."

To make one 8-inch [20-cm.] cake

2 cups	flour	½ liter
¼ cup	rice flour	50 ml.
1 tsp.	baking powder	5 ml.
	salt	
½ lb.	butter, softened	¼ kg.
1 cup	superfine sugar	¼ liter
5	eggs, plus 1 lightly beaten egg yolk	5
2½ cups	dried currants, tossed with flour	625 ml.
1 cup	mixed candied fruit peel, finely chopped and tossed with flour	¼ liter
4 cups	almond paste (recipe, page 167), flavored with 1 tbsp. [15 ml.] brandy and 2 or 3 drops of almond extract	1 liter

Sift together the flour, rice flour, baking powder and a pinch of salt. Cream the butter and the sugar together until the mixture is very pale, and then beat in the five whole eggs one at a time, adding about 1 tablespoon [15 ml.] of the flour mixture. Add the rest of the flour mixture and stir in the dried currants and the candied peel.

Pour half of the batter into a buttered spring-form pan that has been lined with parchment paper. Cover it evenly and lightly with half of the almond paste. Now add the rest of the cake batter and bake in a preheated 350° F. [180° C.] oven for one and one half hours, or until the cake shrinks slightly from the sides of the pan.

Form the remaining almond paste into a roll about 26 inches [65 cm.] long and join the ends to form a ring the size of the cake. Lay this around the edge on top of the cake, mark a pattern on the paste with the tines of a fork and brush the top of the paste with the egg yolk.

Reduce the heat of the oven to 300° F. [150° C.] and bake the cake again just until the almond paste has colored lightly—about 15 minutes. Let the cake cool for a while before removing it from the pan and serving it.

GERTRUDE MANN
A BOOK OF CAKES

Cornmeal Fruitcake

Torta Detta "La Putana"

To make one 9-inch [23-cm.] cake

4 cups	milk	1 liter
2½ cups	cornmeal	625 ml.
1¾ cups	flour	425 ml.
2	pears, peeled, cored and diced	2
2	apples, peeled, cored and diced	2
1¾ cups	golden raisins	425 ml.
about 1 cup	dried figs, chopped	about ¼ liter
14 tbsp.	butter, cut into pieces	210 ml.
¾ cup plus 2 tbsp.	sugar	205 ml.
½ tsp.	salt	2 ml.
2 tsp.	baking powder	10 ml.

Bring the milk to a boil and gradually stir in the flour and cornmeal to make a thick cream. When the mixture returns to a boil, add all of the fruit, the butter, sugar, salt and baking powder. Cook for about 30 minutes, stirring often.

Pour the cooked mixture into a cake pan that has been buttered and sprinkled with dry bread crumbs and bake in a preheated 350° F. [180° C.] oven for one and one half hours, checking often to see that the top of the cake does not burn. The cake is done when an inserted tester comes out clean.

LUIGI VOLPICELLI AND SECONDINO FREDA
L'ANTIARTUSI: 1000 RICETTE

Cornmeal Cheesecake

Torta Dolce di Polenta e Ricotta

To make one 12-inch [30-cm.] cake

6 to 7 cups	water	1½ to 1¾ liters
2 cups	cornmeal	½ liter
1½ cups	ricotta or farmer cheese	375 ml.
¾ cup	superfine sugar	175 ml.
	salt	
½ cup	golden raisins	125 ml.
¼ cup	pine nuts	50 ml.
1 tsp.	ground cinnamon	5 ml.
	lard	

Bring the water to a boil and gradually pour in the cornmeal. Cook over medium heat, stirring continuously, for 30 minutes, or until the resulting polenta acquires an elastic texture and comes away from the sides of the saucepan.

In a large bowl, mash the ricotta in a little warm water and add the sugar, cinnamon and a pinch of salt. Gradually blend in the cooked polenta, moistening with additional warm water if necessary to make a firm but workable dough. Stir in the raisins.

Pour the mixture into a buttered and floured cake pan, smooth the surface and scatter the pine nuts over the top. Dot the surface with lard. Bake in a preheated 350° F. [180° C.] oven for about 45 minutes, or until the top turns golden brown. Turn the cake out of the pan while still warm and let it cool completely before serving.

LUIGI CARNACINA AND VINCENZO BUONASSISI
IL LIBRO DELLA POLENTA

Catalan Cake

"Cake" a la Catalana

To make one 10-inch [25-cm.] cake

11 tbsp.	butter, softened	165 ml.
11 tbsp.	sugar	165 ml.
3	eggs	3
1¾ cups	flour	425 ml.
1½ tsp.	baking powder	7 ml.
5 oz.	pine nuts, toasted (about ¾ cup [175 ml.])	150 g.
5½ oz.	candied orange slices, cut into small pieces (about 1⅓ cups [325 ml.])	165 g.
½ cup	dark rum	125 ml.

Beat the butter and sugar together until the mixture is very creamy; add the eggs, one by one, beating well until completely blended. Sift the flour with the baking powder and add it to the creamed ingredients, along with the pine nuts and the orange pieces. Then stir in the rum.

Pour the mixture into a buttered and floured cake pan, smoothing the top with a spatula. Bake the mixture in a preheated 350° F. [180° C.] oven for 45 minutes, or until an inserted tester comes out clean. Cool the cake in the pan.

CANDIDO LÓPEZ
EL LIBRO DE ORO DE LA GASTRONOMÍA

Potato Cake

Poten Dato

The quantities of ingredients used in this recipe may be varied according to taste. For a richer flavor, you can use up to 4 tablespoons [60 ml.] of extra butter.

Poten dato was baked regularly in the Welsh counties of Cardiganshire and Pembrokeshire, where potatoes were plentiful in the autumn. Prepared in large quantities, it was baked in the brick wall-oven. This oven was heated at least

once a week for baking bread, and as the bricks retained some heat for several hours it was the custom to bake cakes and puddings in this "after heat" overnight.

To make one 9-inch [23-cm.] cake

2½ cups	mashed boiled potatoes	625 ml.
8 tbsp.	butter, cut into small pieces	120 ml.
¼ cup	sugar	50 ml.
½ cup	dried currants	125 ml.
1 cup	flour	¼ liter
2 tsp.	ground mixed spices	10 ml.
	salt	
1	egg, beaten	1
about ½ cup	milk	about 125 ml.

Put the potatoes into a large bowl. Add a few lumps of butter and blend thoroughly. Mix in the flour, sugar, dried currants, spices and a pinch of salt. Beat in the egg and a little milk to give the mixture a soft consistency. Put the mixture into a buttered and floured shallow pan and bake in a preheated 350° F. [180° C.] oven for 45 minutes, or until golden brown on top. Serve the cake hot.

S. MINWEL TIBBOTT
WELSH FARE

Betsy Cake

A Betsy cake is an English harvest cake.

To make one 8-inch [20-cm.] cake

8 tbsp.	butter, softened	120 ml.
½ cup	sugar	125 ml.
1 tbsp.	English golden syrup	15 ml.
about 3 cups	barley flour	about ¾ liter
2 cups	flour	½ liter
1 cup	milk	¼ liter
2 cups	golden raisins	½ liter
1½ tsp.	baking powder	7 ml.
½ tsp.	salt	2 ml.

Beat the butter and sugar to a cream. Add the English golden syrup, then the flour and milk alternately, the raisins, baking powder and salt last. Mix into a dough, put into a buttered and floured pan, and bake in a preheated 325° F. [160° C.] oven for one and one half to two hours, until the cake shrinks from the sides of the pan. Cool the cake for 10 minutes in the pan before turning it out onto a wire rack to cool completely.

MRS. C. F. LEYEL
CAKES OF ENGLAND

Pork-Sausage Cake

If this cake is not to be served immediately, it should be stored in the refrigerator. The cake also freezes well.

To make one 9-inch [23-cm.] cake

1 cup	raisins, chopped	¼ liter
2 cups	water	½ liter
2½ cups	flour	625 ml.
2 cups	light brown sugar	½ liter
1 tsp.	baking soda	5 ml.
1 tsp.	baking powder	5 ml.
1 tsp.	ground cinnamon	5 ml.
½ lb.	fresh pork sausage	¼ kg.
1 cup	nuts, finely chopped (¼ lb. [125 g.])	¼ liter
3 cups	caramel fudge frosting (recipe, page 166)	¾ liter

Cover the raisins with the water; bring the water to a boil and simmer the raisins for 20 minutes. Drain the raisins, reserving 1 cup [¼ liter] of the cooking water. Sift the flour, brown sugar, baking soda, baking powder and cinnamon into a bowl and, using your hands, work the sausage meat into the mixture until it is evenly distributed.

Add the raisins and the reserved cooking liquid, then stir in the nuts. Pour the mixture into two lightly buttered and floured layer-cake pans and bake in a preheated 350° F. [180° C.] oven for 45 minutes. Cool the layers on racks. When the cake is cool, fill it and frost it with the caramel fudge frosting.

JUNIOR CHARITY LEAGUE OF MONROE
THE COTTON COUNTRY COLLECTION

Almond and Lemon Cake

Gâteau d'Amandes

For this recipe, the almonds may be ground in an electric food processor operated in short spurts, then combined by hand or machine with the other ingredients.

To make one 8-inch [20-cm.] cake

1½ cups	almonds, blanched (about 6 oz. [175 g.])	375 ml.
2 tsp.	grated lemon peel	10 ml.
3	eggs, lightly beaten	3
1½ cups	flour	375 ml.
12 tbsp.	butter, softened	180 ml.
¾ cup	sugar	175 ml.

Pound the almonds in a mortar with the lemon peel. Add the remaining ingredients gradually, pounding them together

to obtain a thick paste. Spread the paste evenly in a buttered cake pan. Bake in a preheated 325° F. [160° C.] oven for about one hour, or until the cake is golden on top.

NOUVEAU MANUEL DE LA CUISINIÈRE BOURGEOISE ET ÉCONOMIQUE

Brittany Cake

Gâteau Breton
To make one 9-inch [23-cm.] cake

½ lb.	salted butter, softened	¼ kg.
1	egg, plus 2 yolks	1
½ cup	sugar	125 ml.
2 tsp.	orange-flower water	10 ml.
¼ tsp.	almond extract	1 ml.
1½ cups	sifted flour	375 ml.
2 tbsp.	cornstarch	30 ml.
⅓ tsp.	baking powder	1½ ml.
⅓ cup	almonds, blanched, peeled and ground	75 ml.

Cream the butter until white. Add the whole egg, one egg yolk and the sugar and beat for 10 minutes. Add the orange-flower water and almond extract and blend well. Mix all of the dry ingredients and the almonds, and blend the mixture slowly into the batter. Turn into a buttered and lightly floured cake pan. Lightly beat the remaining yolk, and brush it generously onto the top of the cake. Trace a decorative crisscross pattern on top of the cake with the tines of a fork. Bake in a preheated 350° F. [180° C.] oven for 30 to 35 minutes, or until a tester inserted into the center comes out clean. Let the cake cool in the pan.

MADELEINE KAMMAN
THE MAKING OF A COOK

Lightning Cake

Kossuth Blitztorte
To make one 10-by-17-inch [25-by-33-cm.] cake

1 cup plus 2 tbsp.	sifted flour	280 ml.
9 tbsp.	butter, softened	135 ml.
⅔ cup	sugar	150 ml.
3	eggs	3
2 tsp.	grated lemon peel	10 ml.
1 cup	almonds, blanched, peeled and slivered (¼ lb. [125 g.])	¼ liter

Cream the butter with the sugar. Beat in the eggs, alternating with the flour mixed with the grated lemon peel. Spread the batter ⅓ inch [1 cm.] thick on a buttered jelly-roll pan lined with buttered parchment paper. Sprinkle on the slivered almonds and bake in a preheated 375° F. [190° C.] oven for about 10 minutes or until golden. Cool a few minutes and cut into diamond shapes with a sharp knife. Loosen the pieces immediately from the paper with a spatula and serve while still warm.

LILLIAN LANGSETH-CHRISTENSEN
VOYAGE GASTRONOMIQUE

Easter Halvah Cake

Halvas

To make one cake 9 inches [23 cm.] square

¾ cup	sugar	175 ml.
12 tbsp.	butter, softened	180 ml.
4	eggs	4
2 cups	coarse semolina	½ liter
1 cup	almonds, blanched, peeled and chopped (¼ lb. [125 g.])	¼ liter
1 tsp.	ground cinnamon	5 ml.
Lemon syrup		
1 tsp.	strained fresh lemon juice	5 ml.
2 cups	sugar	½ liter
5 cups	water	1¼ liters
one 1-inch	cinnamon stick	one 2½-cm.

Cream the sugar with the butter until the mixture is pale and fluffy. Then add the eggs, one by one, and beat until the mixture is very smooth. Still beating, add the semolina and, lastly, the almonds and the ground cinnamon.

Pour the batter into a buttered and floured cake pan 3 inches [8 cm.] deep and bake the halvah in a preheated 350° F. [180° C.] oven for about 40 minutes, or until it shrinks slightly from the sides of the pan.

Meanwhile, boil the syrup ingredients together to a thick syrup. Remove the cinnamon stick, and as soon as you take the halvah out of the oven pour the syrup over it. Cool the cake in its pan before cutting it into squares to serve.

ROBIN HOWE
GREEK COOKING

Coconut Cake

The techniques for making coconut milk appear on page 56.

To make one 9-inch [23-cm.] cake

8 tbsp.	butter, softened	120 ml.
1 cup	sugar	¼ liter
5	eggs, lightly beaten	5
2 cups	flour	½ liter
½ tbsp.	baking powder	7 ml.
¼ tsp.	salt	1 ml.
1 cup	fresh coconut milk	¼ liter
1 tsp.	vanilla extract	5 ml.
½ tsp.	finely grated lime peel	2 ml.
2 cups	boiled icing (recipe, page 164), flavored with 2 tsp. [10 ml.] strained fresh lime juice	½ liter
1 cup	freshly grated coconut	¼ liter

In a deep bowl, cream the butter with the sugar, beating and mashing the mixture against the sides of the bowl with a large spoon until it is light and fluffy. Beating constantly, slowly pour in the eggs in a thin stream, and continue to beat until the eggs are completely absorbed.

Sift together the flour, baking powder and salt, and add them to the batter ½ cup [125 ml.] at a time, beating well after each addition; add the coconut milk, ¼ cup [50 ml.] at a time, alternately with the flour. Beat in the vanilla extract and the lime peel.

Divide the batter between two well-buttered and floured layer-cake pans, and bake in the middle of a preheated 350° F. [180° C.] oven for one half hour, or until a tester inserted in the center comes out clean. Cool the cakes in the pans for about five minutes, then turn them out onto wire cake racks to cool completely.

Place one layer of the cooled cake on a serving plate and, with a spatula or knife, spread it evenly with about ½ cup [125 ml.] of the icing. Sprinkle about ¼ cup [50 ml.] of the grated coconut over the icing, then set the second cake layer on top. Spread the top and sides with the remaining icing and sprinkle them with the rest of the coconut.

FOODS OF THE WORLD
PACIFIC AND SOUTHEAST ASIAN COOKING

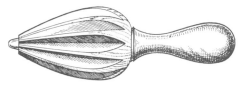

Spiced Coconut Cake

The technique of making coconut milk is shown on page 56.

To make four 7-inch [18-cm.] cakes

2 cups	superfine sugar	½ liter
1 lb.	butter, softened	½ kg.
8	eggs, yolks separated from whites, whites stiffly beaten	8
1½ cups	semolina	375 ml.
1 cup	sifted flour	¼ liter
1 tsp.	baking powder	5 ml.
2	small nutmegs, grated	2
½ tsp.	caraway seeds	2 ml.
½ tsp.	ground cinnamon	2 ml.
½ tsp.	ground ginger	2 ml.
1½	coconuts, flesh removed and grated	1½
½ cup	coconut milk	125 ml.

Cream the sugar and butter together. Add the egg yolks, one by one, beating the mixture constantly. Stir in the egg whites and the semolina; mix well, then add—a little at a time—the flour sifted with the baking powder, nutmeg, cinnamon and ginger. Stir in the caraway seeds. When the batter is thoroughly mixed, stir in the grated coconut. Lastly pour in the coconut milk and stir briefly. Pour the batter into buttered pans and bake in a preheated 350° F. [180° C.] oven for 20 minutes, or until the cakes shrink slightly from the sides of the pans.

MRS. J. BARTLEY
INDIAN COOKERY GENERAL FOR YOUNG HOUSEKEEPERS

Almond-Chestnut Cake

Dort Kaŝtanový

To make one 10-inch [25-cm.] cake

1 lb.	chestnuts	½ kg.
2 cups	milk	½ liter
6 tbsp.	butter, softened	90 ml.
1 cup	sugar	¼ liter
6	eggs, yolks separated from whites, whites stiffly beaten	6
¾ cup	almonds, blanched, peeled and ground	175 ml.
2 cups	heavy cream, whipped	½ liter

To prepare the chestnuts, wash them and, with a sharp knife, make incisions on the rounded sides. Roast the chest-nuts in a preheated 350° F. [180° C.] oven for about 15 minutes to loosen the shells and skins. Peel the nuts and cook them in the milk for about 30 minutes.

Reserve ¼ cup [50 ml.] of the nuts; purée the rest through a strainer while they are still hot, adding whatever liquid has not been absorbed in cooking.

To prepare the cake, cream the butter thoroughly with the sugar and the egg yolks. Add the almonds and puréed chestnuts. Fold in the egg whites. Pour the batter into a buttered spring-form pan that has been dusted with bread crumbs. Bake in a preheated 300° F. [150° C.] oven for 45 minutes to one hour.

Cool the cake in its pan for 10 minutes; then remove the rim of the pan, run a spatula underneath the cake to loosen it, and turn it out onto a wire rack. When it is cold, split the cake into two layers. Fill and cover the cake with the whipped cream. Shred the reserved chestnuts and use them to decorate the frosting.

JOZA BŘÍZOVÁ
THE CZECHOSLOVAK COOKBOOK

Chestnut Cake

Since fresh chestnuts are available only from late fall until about Christmas time, this cake is a special seasonal treat.

To make one 8-inch [20-cm.] cake

2 lb.	chestnuts	1 kg.
12 tbsp.	butter, softened	180 ml.
1 cup	sugar	¼ liter
4	eggs, yolks separated from whites, whites stiffly beaten	4
2 tbsp.	rum	30 ml.
⅔ cup	heavy cream, whipped, lightly sweetened with sugar and flavored with vanilla extract	150 ml.
2 cups	thick chocolate icing (recipe, page 165)	½ liter

Prepare the chestnuts: Score the flat side of the chestnuts with the point of a sharp knife to break the skin. Place the nuts in a saucepan and cover with boiling water. Simmer for about an hour. To make certain they are done, peel one of the chestnuts and slice it in half. It should be dry and mealy and resemble a baked potato in texture. Cool the nuts in the water until you can handle them easily, but do not let them become cold or they will be really difficult to peel. Remove the shells and skins of the chestnuts. Put them through a food mill or a nut grater. Measure 2 cups [½ liter] of purée. To avoid packing the purée, use a light touch with your spoon when measuring.

Cream the butter with the back of a spoon until it is satiny (if you are using an electric mixer, beat at medium-low speed). Add the sugar gradually until it is well blended with the butter and the mixture is light and fluffy.

Beat the egg yolks in a separate bowl, then add them to the butter and mix well. Add the rum. Stir in the chestnut purée and mix until all the ingredients are thoroughly blended. Stir a third of the egg whites into the cake batter, then carefully fold in the rest. Be careful not to overmix or you will risk breaking down the egg whites. Spoon the mixture into two buttered and floured spring-form pans and bake in a preheated 350° F. [180° C.] oven for 30 minutes, or until a tester inserted in the middle comes out clean.

Remove the cakes from the oven. After a few minutes, slide a thin knife around the edge of the layers and slip off the pan rims. Set the layers on racks to cool. This is a rather fragile cake, so do not attempt to remove the cake-pan bottoms until the cakes are cold.

When the cake layers have cooled, spread one layer with the whipped cream, cover with the second layer, and dribble the chocolate icing over the top and sides.

EDNA LEWIS AND EVANGELINE PETERSON
THE EDNA LEWIS COOKBOOK

Flat Chestnut Cake

Castagnaccio

Castagnaccio can also be eaten cold, but do not keep it in the refrigerator.

To make one 9-inch [23-cm.] cake

3 tbsp.	raisins, soaked for ½ hour in ½ cup [125 ml.] lukewarm milk and drained	45 ml.
2 cups plus 2 tbsp.	chestnut flour	530 ml.
1 tbsp.	sugar	15 ml.
	salt	
2 tbsp.	pine nuts or walnuts, chopped	30 ml.
2 cups	cold milk	½ liter
3 tbsp.	olive oil	45 ml.
1 tbsp.	fresh rosemary	15 ml.

Sift all but 1 tablespoon [15 ml.] of the chestnut flour into a very large bowl. Add the sugar, a pinch of salt and the nuts. Mix very well with a wooden spoon, then add the cold milk a little at a time, stirring constantly and being careful to break up any lumps.

Flour the raisins with the reserved chestnut flour. Add the raisins to the batter, along with 1 tablespoon of the olive oil, and mix very well until smooth. Oil a deep cake pan, preferably tin-lined copper, with the entire second tablespoon of olive oil (do not remove the excess oil from the pan).

Pour the batter into the prepared pan and sprinkle the third tablespoon of olive oil and the rosemary over the top.

Bake in a preheated 425° F. [220° C.] oven for 40 to 50 minutes. (The time will be 10 minutes less if you are not using a copper pan.) Remove the cake from the oven and let it rest for 10 to 20 minutes before serving. Serve from the pan, sliced in the manner of a pie.

GUILIANO BUGIALLI
THE FINE ART OF ITALIAN COOKING

Black Walnut Cake

To make one 9-inch [23-cm.] tube cake

½ lb.	butter, softened	¼ kg.
2 cups	sugar	½ liter
1 cup	black walnuts, chopped (¼ lb. [125 g.])	¼ liter
3 cups	flour	¾ liter
2 tsp.	baking powder	10 ml.
1 cup	milk	¼ liter
5	egg whites, stiffly beaten	5
1 cup	glacé icing (recipe, page 165), flavored with a few drops of almond extract	¼ liter

Cream the butter and sugar. Dredge the nuts in a few spoonfuls of the flour. Sift together the remainder of the flour and the baking powder.

Add the flour mixture, alternately with the milk, to the creamed butter and sugar. Add the nuts and the egg whites, and beat the batter vigorously until all of the ingredients are well blended.

Pour the batter into a buttered and floured tube cake pan and bake in a preheated 325° F. [160° C.] oven for 45 to 60 minutes, or until a cake tester inserted in the middle comes out clean.

Cool the cake in the pan before turning it out onto an ovenproof plate. Pour the icing over the cake. Place the cake in a preheated 400° F. [200° C.] oven for a few seconds to glaze the icing.

HOPE ANDREWS AND FRANCES KELLY
MARYLAND'S WAY

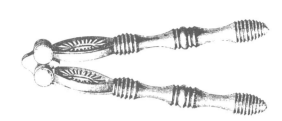

Nut-Glazed Cake

To make one cake 9 inches [23 cm.] square

3 tbsp.	butter	45 ml.
⅓ cup	brown sugar	75 ml.
1 tbsp.	water	15 ml.
¾ cup	walnuts, chopped	175 ml.
2 oz.	unsweetened chocolate	60 g.
½ cup	vegetable shortening	125 ml.
1¼ cups	sugar	300 ml.
2	eggs	2
1¾ cups	sifted flour	425 ml.
¾ tsp.	baking soda	4 ml.
1 tsp.	salt	5 ml.
1 cup	sour milk or buttermilk	¼ liter
	heavy cream, stiffly whipped (optional)	

Melt the butter in the bottom of the cake pan, and mix in the brown sugar and water. Then sprinkle the walnut pieces over the mixture.

Melt the chocolate in a bowl set over a pan of simmering water. Remove the bowl from the heat and let the chocolate cool for a few minutes, taking care that it does not harden.

In another bowl, cream the vegetable shortening with the sugar until it is fluffy. Then add the eggs, one at a time, beating thoroughly after each addition. Beat in the melted chocolate. Sift together the flour, baking soda and salt and, alternately with the sour milk, blend the dry ingredients into the creamed mixture. Spoon the resulting batter over the walnuts in the cake pan.

Bake the cake in a preheated 350° F. [180° C.] oven for about 50 minutes, or until a tester inserted into the center of the cake comes out clean. Let the cake cool in the pan for five minutes. Carefully turn the cake out onto a serving plate; serve warm, either plain or with whipped cream.

BRITISH COLUMBIA WOMEN'S INSTITUTES
ADVENTURES IN COOKING

Coffee and Walnut Cake

Torta Rustica di Noci al Caffé

To make one 8-inch [20-cm.] cake

7 tbsp.	butter, softened	105 ml.
1¼ cups	superfine sugar	300 ml.
2	eggs, lightly beaten	2
1¾ cups	flour, sifted with 1 tbsp. [15 ml.] baking powder	425 ml.
⅓ to ⅔ cup	strong black coffee	75 to 150 ml.
1¾ cups	walnuts, very finely chopped (about 7 oz. [200 g.])	425 ml.

Cream the butter and sugar until fluffy, then beat in the eggs. Add the flour alternately with the coffee until the mixture is smooth. Add the nuts. Pour the mixture into a buttered and floured cake pan and bake in a preheated 350° F. [180° C.] oven for one hour, or until a tester inserted in the center comes out clean. Cool the cake on a wire rack.

MARIÙ SALVATORI DE ZULIANI
LA CUCINA DI VERSILIA E GARFAGNANA

Nut and Anisette Cake

Brustengolo

To make one 8-by-12-inch [20-by-30-cm.] cake

3 cups	cornmeal	¾ liter
4 cups	lightly salted boiling water	1 liter
1	apple, peeled, cored and thinly sliced	1
1	lemon, peel grated, juice strained	1
¾ cup	pine nuts	175 ml.
1¾ cups	walnuts, coarsely chopped (about 7 oz. [200 g.])	425 ml.
7 tbsp.	sugar	105 ml.
⅓ cup	olive oil	75 ml.
¼ cup	anise-flavored liqueur	50 ml.

Put the cornmeal into a bowl. Gradually pour in the water, stirring the mixture all the time with a wooden spoon to make a smooth paste.

Sprinkle the apple with the lemon juice. Mix the apple, lemon peel, pine nuts and walnuts; flavor with the sugar, oil and liqueur. Mix these ingredients into the cornmeal.

Pour the batter into a buttered baking pan, spreading it out evenly. Bake in a preheated 350° F. [180° C.] oven for about 40 minutes, or until the top of the cake is golden brown. Serve cold.

LUIGI VOLPICELLI AND SECONDINO FREDA
L'ANTIARTUSI: 1000 RICETTE

Spirit, Spice and Sugar Cakes

Kentucky Bourbon Cake

To make one 9-inch [23-cm.] cake or one 10-inch [25-cm.] tube cake

1½ cups	sifted flour	375 ml.
1 tsp.	baking powder	5 ml.
1¼ lb.	pecans (about 5 cups [1¼ liters])	600 g.
1 cup	raisins	¼ liter
2 tsp.	freshly grated nutmeg	10 ml.
½ cup	bourbon	125 ml.
8 tbsp.	butter	120 ml.
1 cup	sugar	¼ liter
3	eggs, yolks separated from whites, whites stiffly beaten	3
	candied cherries	

Sift together 1 cup [¼ liter] of the flour and the baking powder. Break 1 pound [½ kg.] of the pecans into pieces with your fingers and combine them with the raisins in a bowl. Stir the remaining ½ cup [125 ml.] of flour into this mixture. Mix well, making sure that the raisins and nuts are thoroughly coated with flour; this flouring will prevent them from sinking to the bottom of the cake.

Combine the nutmeg and bourbon. Beat the butter until soft, then gradually add the sugar, beating well after each addition. Beat in the egg yolks, one at a time.

Stir the 1 cup of flour and the spiced bourbon alternately into the egg mixture, beginning and ending with flour. With a heavy wooden or metal spoon, stir in the raisin mixture until it is well distributed throughout the batter, scooping up batter from the bottom of the bowl as you stir. Carefully fold the beaten egg whites into the batter. Turn the batter into a spring-form or tube cake pan that has been buttered and lined with buttered brown paper. Let the cake stand at room temperature for 10 minutes. Meanwhile, decorate the top of the cake with the remaining ¼ pound [125 g.] of pecans, halved, and the candied cherries. Bake in a preheated 325° F. [160° C.] oven for about one and one quarter hours, or until the top of the cake is firm. Do not overbake; the cake should be on the moist side.

Cool the cake in the pan for 30 minutes. Remove the cake from the pan carefully and, holding the cake decorated side up, peel the paper from the bottom and sides. Cool the cake completely on a rack, keeping the decorated side up. Let it stand for one day before cutting. Store the cake in an airtight container.

NIKA HAZELTON
AMERICAN HOME COOKING

Wild Rice-Bourbon Cake

To make one 10-inch [25-cm.] tube cake

4 cups	sifted flour	1 liter
½ tsp.	salt	2 ml.
2 tsp.	baking powder	10 ml.
½ cup	bourbon	125 ml.
½ cup	milk	125 ml.
1 tsp.	vanilla extract	5 ml.
1 lb.	butter, softened	½ kg.
2 cups	sugar	½ liter
8	eggs, at room temperature	8
½ cup	wild rice, cooked in water only until the grains pop (about 30 minutes) and drained well	125 ml.

Sift the flour with the salt and baking powder. Set aside. Combine the bourbon, milk and vanilla, and set aside.

Cream the butter and sugar together until light and fluffy. Add the eggs, one at a time, beating well after each addition. Add one third of the flour mixture at a time, alternately with one third of the bourbon mixture. Blend in the wild rice, mixing thoroughly.

Pour the batter into a buttered and floured fluted tube cake pan, and bake in a preheated 300° F. [150° C.] oven for one and one quarter to one and one half hours, or until a tester inserted near the center comes out clean. Set the cake on a wire rack and cool it in the pan for about 10 minutes. Then turn the cake out of the pan onto the rack.

To maintain maximum moistness in the cake, place it, not yet quite cooled, on a cake plate and cover it with a kitchen towel. The cake is especially good served when it is still warm to the touch but cool enough to slice well.

BETH ANDERSON
WILD RICE FOR ALL SEASONS COOKBOOK

Rum Barada

Cadju nut is another name for cashew nut.

If made some time before it is to be used, the *barada* should be covered over with parchment paper while it is chilling in the refrigerator.

To make one 8-inch [20-cm.] tube cake

8 tbsp.	butter, softened	120 ml.
½ cup plus 1 tbsp.	superfine sugar	140 ml.
2	eggs, beaten	2
1 cup	flour, sifted 3 times with 1 tsp. [5 ml.] baking powder	¼ liter
¼ tsp.	vanilla extract	1 ml.
3 tbsp.	rum	45 ml.
2 tbsp.	apricot jam, strained	30 ml.
	candied cherries	
	candied angelica, cut into leaves	

Vanilla filling

4 tbsp.	butter	60 ml.
¼ cup	superfine sugar	50 ml.
2 tbsp.	rum (optional)	30 ml.
1	egg yolk	1
½ cup	almonds or cadju nuts, ground and mixed with a few drops of almond extract	125 ml.
2 tbsp.	heavy cream	30 ml.
1	large piece candied ginger, finely chopped (optional)	1

Beat the butter and ½ cup [125 ml.] of the sugar together to a pale cream. Beat in first the beaten eggs, then the sifted flour, baking powder and vanilla extract. Put the mixture into a buttered and floured tube cake pan and bake in a preheated 350° F. [180° C.] oven for about 30 minutes, or until the cake is pale golden brown on top and begins to ease away from the sides of the pan. Cool the cake for 10 minutes in the pan, then turn it onto a wire rack placed over foil to cool completely.

With a small-pronged fork, prick the cake all over on the underside, and here and there on the top and sides. Dissolve the remaining 1 tablespoon [15 ml.] of sugar in 2 tablespoons [30 ml.] of water and add 2 tablespoons of the rum. Spoon this mixture over the surface of the cake so that it runs into the pricked holes. Place the cake on a serving dish.

In a small saucepan, thoroughly mix the apricot jam and the remaining rum. Set the mixture over very low heat and stir very gently until it is hot and clear. Use a clean, dry pastry brush to coat the whole of the outside crust of the cake—including that of the center cavity—with the apricot mixture. The cake should now have a clear jellied appearance. Chill the cake thoroughly in the refrigerator.

To make the filling, beat the butter until soft. Add the sugar, and cream the mixture together for a few minutes until light and fluffy, then, if using, beat in the rum by degrees. Beat all together until the mixture is pale in color and thick. Add the egg yolk, mix well, then add the ground nuts and cream and beat again for a few minutes. If the chopped ginger is used, it should be added now. Chill the mixture in the refrigerator, then pile it up in the hollow center of the cake, rounding the top nicely.

Fill a pastry bag with any remaining mixture and, with a large No. 5 closed star tube, pipe a neat decoration on top of the cake around the edge of the center filling. Decorate the bottom edge of the cake in the same manner. Garnish the cake with cherries and angelica leaves, and arrange a cluster of cherries and angelica leaves on top of the center filling. Refrigerate until required, and serve ice-cold.

HILDA DEUTROM (EDITOR)
CEYLON DAILY NEWS COOKERY BOOK

Cider Cake

This recipe is from Somerset. The cake has a subtle flavor of cider and is particularly good served with a purée of apples and with plenty of cream, or at a picnic with apples and with cider to drink.

To make one cake 7 inches [18 cm.] square

8 tbsp.	butter, softened	120 ml.
½ cup	sugar	125 ml.
2	eggs, beaten	2
2 cups	flour	½ liter
1 tsp.	baking soda	5 ml.
1 tsp.	grated nutmeg	5 ml.
⅔ cup	hard cider	150 ml.

Cream the butter and the sugar, add the beaten eggs, and then half of the flour, sifted with the soda and the nutmeg.

Pour in the cider and beat the batter thoroughly until the acid of the cider acts on the alkali of the soda and makes the mixture froth. Then stir in the remaining flour and quickly pour the mixture into a well-buttered and floured cake pan. Bake in a preheated 350° F. [180° C.] oven for 40 minutes, or until the cake shrinks slightly from the sides of the pan. Turn the cake out onto a wire rack to cool it.

ELISABETH AYRTON
THE COOKERY OF ENGLAND

Cornmeal Cake

Dolce di Polenta

This cake is even better when served the day after it is made.

To make one 4-by-7-inch [10-by-16-cm.] cake

1 cup	flour	¼ liter
¾ cup	cornmeal	175 ml.
½ cup	sugar	125 ml.
6 tbsp.	butter, melted and cooled	90 ml.
1	egg yolk	1
	powdered saffron	
1 cup	dry white wine	¼ liter
½ cup	bread crumbs	125 ml.
½ cup	confectioners' sugar	125 ml.

Mix the flour and cornmeal in a bowl. Make a well in the center and place the sugar and butter in it. Stir the contents of the well thoroughly, incorporating the sugar—but not the flour that forms the sides of the well—into the butter. Add the egg yolk and a pinch of saffron to the sugar and butter, then begin incorporating the flour mixture little by little, at the same time adding the wine a little at a time.

When all the ingredients are well combined, stir for 10 to 12 minutes more in order to have a very soft dough.

Dust a buttered fluted jelly mold with the bread crumbs. Pour the dough mixture into the prepared mold and bake in a preheated 375° F. [190° C.] oven for about one hour and 20 minutes, or until the cake shrinks from the sides of the pan. (If the top of the cake appears to be browning too quickly, place a piece of aluminum foil over it.) Remove the cake from the oven, let it rest for 10 minutes, then turn it out onto a serving dish.

Sprinkle the confectioners' sugar over the cake and let it rest until it is completely cold.

GIULIANO BUGIALLI
THE FINE ART OF ITALIAN COOKING

Mother's Cake

Pastel de la Madre

To make one 8-inch [20-cm.] cake

1 cup	sugar	¼ liter
7 tbsp.	butter, softened	105 ml.
2	eggs	2
2 cups	flour, sifted with 2 tsp. [10 ml.] baking powder	½ liter
1 cup	muscatel	¼ liter
¾ cup	strawberry jam	175 ml.

Barely warm a pan over low heat, then remove it from the heat and put in the sugar and butter. Beat steadily until the mixture is creamy, then add the eggs and beat until fluffy. Add the flour and baking powder; stir in the muscatel. Pour the mixture into a buttered and floured cake pan and bake in a preheated 350° F. [180° C.] oven for 35 minutes, or until the top of the cake is springy. Cool the cake before removing it from the pan. Spread the top with strawberry jam.

CANDIDO LÓPEZ
EL LIBRO DE ORO DE LA GASTRONOMÍA

Porter Cakes

Porter is a form of stout, a dark brown ale, heavier and more bitter than beer.

To make two 7-inch [18-cm.] cakes

½ lb.	butter	¼ kg.
1½ cups	sugar	375 ml.
1 cup	stout	¼ liter
2	eggs, well beaten	2
4 cups	dried currants	1 liter
4 cups	flour	1 liter
1 tsp.	baking soda	5 ml.
½ tsp.	ground mixed spices	2 ml.

Melt the butter over very low heat without letting it foam. Remove the pan from the heat and stir in the sugar, stout and eggs. Transfer the mixture to a large bowl. Mix the dried currants with the flour and stir them into the stout mixture. Last, add the baking soda and the mixed spices. Stir thoroughly for several minutes so that all of the ingredients are well incorporated. Divide the mixture equally between two buttered and floured cake pans that have been lined with parchment paper, and bake in a preheated 350° F. [180° C.] oven for at least two hours, or until a tester inserted into the center of the cakes comes out clean. Cool the cakes for 10 minutes in the pans and turn them out onto wire racks to cool completely.

ANN PASCOE
CORNISH RECIPES OLD AND NEW

Gingerbread

To make one cake 8 or 9 inches [20 or 23 cm.] square

4 tbsp.	butter, softened	60 ml.
½ cup	brown sugar	125 ml.
1	egg	1
½ cup	molasses	125 ml.
1½ cups	sifted flour	375 ml.
1 tsp.	baking soda	5 ml.
½ tsp.	ground cinnamon	2 ml.
1 tsp.	ground ginger	5 ml.
⅛ tsp.	ground cardamom	½ ml.
½ cup	buttermilk	125 ml.
1 cup	heavy cream, whipped	¼ liter

Cream the butter and sugar until the mixture is light and fluffy. Add the egg, then the molasses; beat well.

Sift the flour with the baking soda and spices, and add them alternately with the buttermilk to the creamed mixture. Pour the batter into a buttered and floured pan. Bake in a preheated 350° F. [180° C.] oven for 30 minutes.

Serve hot or cold with the whipped cream.

MC CORMICK'S SPICES OF THE WORLD COOKBOOK

Lady Constance Howard's Ginger Cake

To make one 6-by-12-inch [15-by-30-cm.] loaf cake

5 cups	flour	1¼ liters
1 tbsp.	baking powder	15 ml.
8 tbsp.	butter	120 ml.
½ cup	sugar	125 ml.
2 tbsp.	ground ginger	30 ml.
2 cups	raisins	½ liter
2	eggs, well beaten	2
⅔ cup	dark molasses	150 ml.
⅔ cup	milk	150 ml.

Mix the flour and the baking powder; rub in the butter; add the sugar, the ginger and the raisins. Add to the eggs, the molasses and milk; then mix the whole well together, and put it in the oven at once in a buttered and floured loaf pan lined with buttered parchment paper. Bake in a preheated 350° F. [180° C.] oven for about two hours, or until the cake shrinks slightly from the sides of the pan.

W. T. FERNIE
KITCHEN PHYSIC

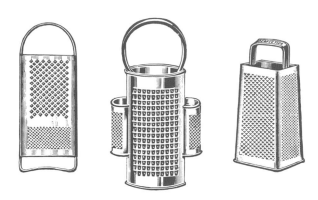

Mount Vernon Gingerbread

The techniques for making gingerbread are demonstrated on pages 64-65.

Gingerbread was one of Martha Washington's favorite desserts. The following is a modern adaptation of an old recipe. No topping is necessary, but sweetened whipped cream can be added.

To make one 9-by-14-inch [23-by-35-cm.] cake

2¾ cups	sifted flour	675 ml.
2½ tsp.	ground ginger	12 ml.
1 tsp.	salt	5 ml.
1 tsp.	baking soda	5 ml.
½ tsp.	ground cinnamon	2 ml.
½ tsp.	grated nutmeg	2 ml.
½ tsp.	ground cloves	2 ml.
1 cup	light molasses	¼ liter
½ cup	light brown sugar	125 ml.
8 tbsp.	butter or shortening	120 ml.
¾ cup	buttermilk or sour milk	175 ml.
¼ cup	strained fresh orange juice, or brandy	50 ml.
2	eggs, lightly beaten	2

Sift together the first seven ingredients. In a saucepan, combine the molasses, brown sugar, and butter or shortening, and bring the mixture to a simmer, stirring it two or three times. Cool the molasses mixture until lukewarm, and stir it and the buttermilk or sour milk into the dry ingredients. Add orange juice or brandy and the eggs, stirring until the batter is smooth.

Pour the batter into a well-buttered and floured pan, and bake in a preheated 350° F. [180° C.] oven for 30 to 35 minutes, or until a tester inserted in the center comes out clean. Serve warm or cold.

JAN MC BRIDE CARLTON
THE OLD-FASHIONED COOKBOOK

Fresh Ginger Cake

To make one cake 9 inches [23 cm.] square

1½ cups	sifted flour	375 ml.
1 tsp.	baking soda	5 ml.
¼ tsp.	salt	1 ml.
7 tbsp.	vegetable oil	105 ml.
½ cup plus 1 tbsp.	apple juice	140 ml.
½ cup	brown sugar	125 ml.
¼ cup	light molasses	50 ml.
¼ cup	dark corn syrup	50 ml.
1	egg	1
3 tbsp.	grated fresh ginger	45 ml.
	heavy cream, whipped (optional)	
	candied ginger, finely chopped (optional)	

Sift together the flour, baking soda and salt.

In a mixing bowl, combine the oil and the apple juice. Beat in the sugar, molasses and corn syrup. Beat in the egg. Add the grated fresh ginger and the flour mixture, and mix well. Pour the batter into a buttered and floured pan. Bake in a preheated 350° F. [180° C.] oven for 30 to 35 minutes, or until the cake is firm to the touch in the center and has pulled away slightly from the sides of the pan. Cool the cake in the pan for five minutes, then turn it out onto a wire rack.

Cut the cake into squares and serve it still warm or at room temperature. For special occasions, serve topped with whipped cream and finely chopped candied ginger.

THE GREAT COOKS' GUIDE TO CAKES

Shoofly Cake

To make one 9-by-13-inch [23-by-32½-cm.] cake

4 cups	flour	1 liter
2 cups	light brown sugar	½ liter
½ lb.	vegetable shortening	¼ kg.
¼ tsp.	ground cinnamon	1 ml.
1 cup	dark corn syrup	¼ liter
1 tbsp.	baking soda	15 ml.
2 cups	boiling water	½ liter

Mix together the flour and the sugar, then cut in the shortening to make crumbs, as for pastry. Reserve 1 cup [¼ liter] of these crumbs to use on top of the cake. Add the ground cinnamon to the remaining crumbs and then stir in the syrup.

Dissolve the baking soda in a little of the boiling water and slowly add it, with the rest of the boiling water, to the crumbs-and-syrup mixture.

Pour the mixture into a buttered and floured baking pan and sprinkle the reserved crumbs over the top. Bake in a preheated 375° F. [180° C.] oven for 45 minutes, or until a tester inserted in the middle comes out clean.

EDNA EBY HELLER
THE ART OF PENNSYLVANIA DUTCH COOKING

Oatmeal Ambrosia Cake

To make one 9-by-13-inch [23-by-32½-cm.] cake

1¼ cups	water	300 ml.
8 tbsp.	butter	120 ml.
1 cup	quick-cooking rolled oats	¼ liter
2	eggs, beaten	2
1 cup	granulated sugar	¼ liter
1 cup	dark brown sugar	¼ liter
½ tsp.	salt	2 ml.
1 tsp.	baking soda	5 ml.
1 tsp.	baking powder	5 ml.
½ tsp.	grated nutmeg	2 ml.
1 tsp.	ground cinnamon	5 ml.
1½ cups	flour	375 ml.

Coconut topping

2 cups	simple butter cream (recipe, page 166)	½ liter
3½ oz.	freshly grated coconut (about 1 cup [½ liter])	105 g.

Bring the water to a boil. Put 8 tablespoons [120 ml.] of the butter and the oats in a mixing bowl, and pour the boiling water over them. Stir for a few seconds and set the bowl aside for 20 minutes.

Add to the oatmeal the beaten eggs, sugars, salt, baking soda, baking powder, nutmeg and cinnamon. Mix these ingredients together thoroughly and add the flour. Beat again, and pour the batter into a buttered and floured baking pan.

Bake the cake in a preheated 375° F. [190° C.] oven for 40 to 45 minutes, until a tester inserted into the center comes out clean.

While the cake is baking, prepare the simple butter cream and stir in the grated coconut.

Spread the topping on the cake as soon as it is removed from the oven. Put the cake under a preheated broiler for one or two minutes, or just until the butter melts and the coconut browns a little.

CAROL CUTLER
THE SIX-MINUTE SOUFFLÉ AND OTHER CULINARY DELIGHTS

Old-fashioned Spicecake

To make one 9-by-13-inch [23-by-32½-cm.] cake

2 cups	sugar	½ liter
4 tbsp.	butter, softened	60 ml.
4 tbsp.	lard	60 ml.
3	eggs, beaten	3
2½ cups	flour	625 ml.
½ tbsp.	cocoa powder	7 ml.
½ tbsp.	baking soda	7 ml.
½ tsp.	ground cloves	2 ml.
½ tsp.	ground allspice	2 ml.
1 tsp.	ground cinnamon	5 ml.
1 cup	buttermilk	¼ liter

Cream together the sugar, butter and lard. Add the eggs and beat the mixture until it is light.

Sift together the flour, cocoa powder, baking soda and spices, and add them to the mixture alternately with the buttermilk. Beat the batter for two minutes.

Pour the mixture into a buttered and floured baking pan. Bake the cake in a preheated 350° F. [180° C.] oven for 40 to 45 minutes. The cake is done when a tester inserted in the middle comes out clean. Cool the cake for 10 minutes in the pan, then turn out onto a cake rack to cool completely.

EDNA EBY HELLER
THE ART OF PENNSYLVANIA DUTCH COOKING

French Spicecake

Pain d'Épice

To make one 5-by-9-inch [13-by-23-cm.] loaf or two 3-by-5-inch [8-by-13-cm.] loaves

1 tsp.	anise seeds	5 ml.
1½ cups	water	375 ml.
1 cup	honey	¼ liter
1¼ cups	sugar	300 ml.
1 tsp.	baking soda	5 ml.
6 cups	flour	1½ liters
½ tsp.	ground cinnamon	2 ml.
½ tsp.	grated nutmeg	2 ml.
¼ cup	mixed candied orange and lemon peel, chopped	50 ml.
	salt	

Cover the anise seeds with the water and bring the water to a boil. Add the honey and sugar and stir until both are dis-solved. Remove the mixture from the heat and add the baking soda. Sift the flour, spices and a pinch of salt into a large bowl. Add the candied peel. Strain the liquid to remove the anise seeds and, stirring all the time, add it to the dry ingredients. Beat until the mixture is smooth. Pour into one large or two small buttered and floured loaf pans, and bake in a preheated 350° F. [180° C.] oven for one hour, or until the cake just begins to shrink from the sides of the pan.

THEODORA FITZGIBBON
A TASTE OF PARIS

Molasses Cake

To make one cake 10 inches [25 cm.] square

7 to 8 cups	flour	1¾ to 2 liters
½ lb.	butter	¼ kg.
1 cup	sugar	¼ liter
2 tbsp.	ground ginger	30 ml.
1 tbsp.	baking soda	15 ml.
3 tbsp.	warm water	45 ml.
1 cup	sour milk	¼ liter
2 cups	molasses	½ liter

Put 7 cups [1¾ liters] of the flour in a large bowl and rub in the butter until the mixture is quite smooth; mix in the sugar and the ginger. Dissolve the baking soda in the warm water and stir it, along with the sour milk and molasses, into the flour mixture to make a fairly sticky dough. Work the dough thoroughly. If it is a little too stiff, more water can be added, or, if not stiff enough, a little more flour. Put the dough in a buttered and floured cake pan and bake in a preheated 375° F. [190° C.] oven for 50 minutes, or until a tester inserted into the center of the cake comes out clean. When cut, the interior should be quite dark.

OSCAR TSCHIRKY
THE COOK BOOK BY "OSCAR" OF THE WALDORF

Marble Cake

Gâteau Marbré

To make one 8-inch [20-cm.] cake

White batter

4	egg whites	4
1 cup	sugar	¼ liter
8 tbsp.	butter, softened	120 ml.
2 cups	flour	½ liter
2 tsp.	baking powder	10 ml.
½ tsp.	salt	2 ml.
½ cup	milk	125 ml.
1 tsp.	vanilla extract	5 ml.

Brown batter

8 tbsp.	butter, softened	120 ml.
⅔ cup	brown sugar	150 ml.
4	egg yolks	4
½ tsp.	baking soda	2 ml.
⅔ cup	molasses	150 ml.
2 cups	flour	½ liter
2 tsp.	baking powder	10 ml.
½ tsp.	salt	2 ml.
½ tsp.	grated nutmeg	2 ml.
1 tsp.	ground cinnamon	5 ml.
1 tsp.	ground ginger	5 ml.
4 tbsp.	milk	60 ml.

To prepare the white part of the cake, beat the egg whites to soft peaks, add half of the sugar, and continue beating until the whites are stiff. Cream the butter with the rest of the sugar. Sift the flour, baking powder and salt together and add this mixture to the butter a little at a time, alternating with the milk. Add the vanilla extract. Fold the egg whites into the batter.

To prepare the brown part of the cake, cream the butter with the sugar. Beat in the egg yolks. In a saucepan set over low heat, dissolve the baking soda in the molasses. Sift the flour with the baking powder, the salt and the spices. Combine all of these ingredients and add them to the butter little by little, alternating with the milk, and mix well.

Butter and flour a cake pan 3 inches [8 cm.] deep, and place heaped tablespoons of the white and brown mixtures alternately in the pan to create a marbled effect.

Bake in a preheated 350° F. [180° C.] oven for one hour or more, until an inserted tester comes out clean.

LA SOCIÉTÉ ST. THOMAS D'AQUIN
LA CUISINE ACADIENNE

Nutmeg Cake with Lemon Sauce

To make one cake 9 inches [23 cm.] square

2 cups	sifted cake flour	½ liter
2 cups	brown sugar	½ liter
8 tbsp.	butter	120 ml.
1 tsp.	baking soda	5 ml.
1 tsp.	grated nutmeg	5 ml.
1	egg	1
1 cup	sour cream	¼ liter
½ cup	pecans, chopped	125 ml.

Tangy lemon sauce

¾ cup	sugar	175 ml.
1½ tbsp.	cornstarch	22½ ml.
⅛ tsp.	salt	½ ml.
1 cup	water	¼ liter
2 tbsp.	strained fresh lemon juice	30 ml.
1 tsp.	grated lemon peel	5 ml.
	ground mace	
2 tbsp.	butter	30 ml.
	yellow food coloring	

Combine the cake flour and the brown sugar in a bowl. Using a pastry blender, cut in the butter until coarse crumbs form. Press half of this crumb mixture into a buttered pan.

Add the baking soda and the grated nutmeg to the remaining crumb mixture; mix well. Stir in the egg and the sour cream. Spread this mixture over the crumbled lining in the pan. Sprinkle with the pecans. Bake the cake in a preheated 350° F. [180° C.] oven for 35 minutes, or until a tester inserted in the center comes out clean. Cool the cake for 10 minutes in its pan on a cake rack.

Meanwhile, combine the sugar, cornstarch and salt in a 2-quart [2-liter] saucepan; mix well. Stir in the water and lemon juice, and cook the mixture over medium heat, stirring constantly, until it thickens and comes to a boil. Boil it for one minute, remove the saucepan from the heat, and stir in the grated lemon peel, a pinch of mace, the butter and a drop of food coloring. Cut the warm cake into squares, and spoon this sauce over each square.

ELISE W. MANNING
FARM JOURNAL'S COMPLETE HOME BAKING BOOK

Seedcake

To make one 7-inch [18-cm.] cake

8 tbsp.	butter, softened	120 ml.
⅔ cup	superfine sugar	150 ml.
2	eggs	2
1¼ cups	sifted flour	300 ml.
¼ cup	cornstarch	50 ml.
½ tsp.	baking powder	2 ml.
2 tsp.	caraway seeds	10 ml.
3 tbsp.	finely chopped candied cherries	45 ml.
½ tsp.	vanilla extract	2 ml.

Beat the butter and sugar together until white, then add each egg separately. Sift together the flour, cornstarch and baking powder, and stir the mixture—along with the caraway seeds, cherries and vanilla extract—into the creamed butter. Pour the batter into a buttered and floured cake pan lined with parchment paper and bake in a preheated 325° F. [170° C.] oven for one and one quarter hours, or until a tester inserted into the center of the cake comes out clean. Turn the cake onto a wire rack to cool.

FREDA MURRAY
LACOCK TEA TIME RECIPES

Colonial Caraway Cake

To make one 10-inch [25-cm.] tube cake

5	eggs, yolks separated from whites	5
¼ tsp.	salt	1 ml.
1½ cups	sugar	375 ml.
½ lb.	butter, softened	¼ kg.
2 tsp.	caraway seeds	10 ml.
¾ tsp.	orange extract	4 ml.
1⅔ cups	flour	400 ml.
	confectioners' sugar (optional)	

Combine the egg whites and salt in a large mixing bowl. Beat until the mixture is frothy. Gradually beat in ½ cup [125 ml.] of the sugar, beating until stiff peaks are formed.

Cream together the butter and remaining sugar until light and fluffy. Add the egg yolks, one at a time, beating well after each addition. Beat in the caraway seeds and orange extract. Blend the flour into the creamed mixture just until it is smooth. Fold half of the egg whites into the batter. Gently fold in the remaining egg whites. Turn the mixture into a buttered and lightly floured tube cake pan. Cut care-

fully through the batter with a spatula or knife three or four times to eliminate any large air bubbles. Bake in a preheated 300° F. [150° C.] oven for 60 to 70 minutes, or until the cake shrinks slightly from the sides of the pan. Cool the cake in the pan for 10 minutes. Remove the cake from the pan and cool it on a wire rack. If desired, sprinkle the cake with confectioners' sugar before serving.

HYLA O'CONNOR
THE EARLY AMERICAN COOKBOOK

Honey Cake

This cake will keep for as long as 10 days in the refrigerator.

To make one 8-inch [20-cm.] cake

1 cup	honey	¼ liter
10 tbsp.	butter	150 ml.
3	eggs	3
2¼ cups	flour	550 ml.
	baking soda	

Melt the honey and butter over low heat. Pour the mixture into a deep bowl and set it aside to cool. Using an electric beater or a whisk, beat the honey mixture briefly until it looks foamy, then add the eggs one at a time, beating well after each addition.

Sift the flour and a pinch of baking soda together into the honey and eggs, a third at a time. Beat well after each addition of flour, and when all is incorporated, beat well for one minute. Pour the batter into a buttered and floured cake pan, scraping all of it in. Place aluminum foil over the top of the cake pan and bake for one hour in a preheated 350° F. [180° C.] oven. Remove the foil and bake for another 20 to 30 minutes, or until the top is nicely browned and the cake pulls away from the sides of the pan. A tester plunged into the center should come out dry. Another test is to watch the ring of soft, slightly sunken batter in the center. As the cake bakes toward the center the moist area will disappear.

Cool for 10 minutes in the pan, then remove to a wire rack to cool completely.

CAROL CUTLER
THE SIX-MINUTE SOUFFLÉ AND OTHER CULINARY DELIGHTS

Ukrainian Honey Cake

To make one 7-inch [18-cm.] cake

1 cup	honey, warmed by setting the pot or bowl in a pan of hot water	¼ liter
4	eggs, beaten	4
1½ cups	flour	375 ml.
1 tsp.	baking powder	5 ml.

Beat the honey until it is frothy, then add the eggs, flour and baking powder. Pour into a buttered and floured cake pan, and bake for 15 to 20 minutes in a preheated 375° F. [190° C.] oven. Check the cake after 15 minutes; if it is done, it will shrink slightly from the pan. Turn it out and cool it. Store the cake in an airtight container for a day or so before using.

BRITISH COLUMBIA WOMEN'S INSTITUTES
ADVENTURES IN COOKING

Honey Cakes

Thick honey is also called set or granulated honey to distinguish it from the clear, syrupy type.

This recipe dates from about 1872. An alternative finish is to serve these light little cakes hot with warm honey.

To make about twenty-four 2-inch [5-cm.] cakes

8 tbsp.	butter	120 ml.
4 cups	flour	1 liter
3 tbsp.	superfine sugar	45 ml.
2 tbsp.	honey	30 ml.
1½ tsp.	baking powder	7 ml.
1	egg, yolk separated from white, white lightly beaten, plus 1 yolk	1
1 cup	milk	¼ liter
	salt	

Honey topping

1 cup	thick heather honey	¼ liter
3 tbsp.	almonds, blanched, peeled and ground	45 ml.

In a bowl, rub the butter into the flour. In another bowl, beat the egg yolks into the milk. In a saucepan over low heat, gently heat the sugar and honey, stirring them until they are well mixed. Then stir in the baking powder.

Alternately add the honey mixture and the milk mixture to the butter and flour, mixing the ingredients very well. Add a pinch of salt and mix again. Put the resulting dough on a floured board and roll it very lightly to a thickness of about ½ inch [1 cm.]. Cut out about 24 rounds. Place the rounds on a buttered baking sheet and bake in a preheated 350° F. [180° C.] oven for about 20 minutes, or until they are

lightly browned. Remove the cakes to a rack and immediately brush their tops with the egg white.

Mix the thick honey with the ground almonds and spread this topping on the cakes. Put the rack of cakes into a very cool—250° F. [130° C.]—oven for no longer than five minutes to set. The cakes may be served either hot or cold.

THEODORA FITZGIBBON
A TASTE OF SCOTLAND

Burnt-Sugar Cake

Burnt sugar, which is made by heating sugar until it turns brown, is another name for caramel.

To make one 8-inch [20-cm.] cake

2⅓ cups	sifted flour	575 ml.
2 tsp.	baking powder	10 ml.
½ tsp.	salt	2 ml.
8 tbsp.	butter, softened	120 ml.
1½ cups	sugar	375 ml.
3	eggs, yolks separated from whites, whites stiffly beaten	3
1 cup	water	¼ liter
2 cups	simple butter cream (recipe, page 166), flavored with 2 tbsp. [30 ml.] of burnt-sugar syrup	½ liter
	salted peanuts, finely chopped (optional)	

Burnt-sugar syrup

½ cup	sugar	125 ml.
½ cup	boiling water	125 ml.

Sift the flour with the baking powder and salt. Cream the butter in a large mixing bowl. Gradually add the sugar to the butter, then beat the mixture with an electric mixer at high speed until it is light and fluffy. At medium speed, blend in the egg yolks; beat well. At low speed, add the sifted dry ingredients alternately with the water, beginning and ending with dry ingredients. Blend well after each addition.

To make burnt-sugar syrup, melt the sugar in a heavy skillet over low heat until the sugar is golden brown. Remove from the heat. Gradually add the boiling water, a few drops at a time at first, stirring constantly, to dissolve the caramel. Blend all but 2 tablespoons [30 ml.] of this syrup into the batter. Then fold in the egg whites.

Pour the batter into two buttered and floured layer-cake pans. Bake in a preheated 350° F. [180° C.] oven for 30 to 35 minutes, or until the cake springs back when lightly touched in the center. Cool the layers on a wire rack. Flavor the butter cream with the remaining burnt-sugar syrup. Stack the cake layers, filling and frosting them with the butter cream. Sprinkle the frosted cake with finely chopped salted peanuts, if desired.

THE PILLSBURY FAMILY COOKBOOK

Maple Upside-down Cake

To make one 6-by-10-inch [15-by-25-cm.] cake

1 cup	pure maple syrup	¼ liter
2 tbsp.	butter, softened	30 ml.
3 tbsp.	sugar	45 ml.
1	large egg, well beaten	1
1 cup	sifted flour	¼ liter
2 tsp.	baking powder	10 ml.
¼ tsp.	salt	1 ml.
½ cup	milk	125 ml.
6	pecans, halved	6
1 cup	heavy cream	¼ liter

Heat the syrup to boiling and pour it into a rectangular ovenproof glass dish 2 inches [5 cm.] deep. Cream the butter and sugar until they are fluffy, and beat in the egg. Sift the flour, baking powder and salt, then sift the mixture into the bowl containing the butter, sugar and egg, alternating it with additions of milk. Pour the batter onto the hot syrup.

Bake in a preheated 375° F. [190° C.] oven for 25 to 30 minutes, or until the cake is brown and a tester inserted in the center comes out clean. Let the cake cool for 10 minutes; run a knife around the edge to loosen it. Then flip it onto a hot platter. Dot the cake with the pecan halves and cut it into portions. Serve the pieces while still warm, accompanied by the cream, lightly whipped, if you like.

JUNE PLATT
JUNE PLATT'S NEW ENGLAND COOK BOOK

Maple Sugar Cake

To make one 8-inch [20-cm.] cake

1 cup	maple sugar	¼ liter
¼ cup	vegetable shortening	50 ml.
2	egg yolks	2
1½ cups	flour	375 ml.
1 tsp.	salt	5 ml.
2 tsp.	baking powder	10 ml.
1 cup	milk	¼ liter
1 cup	nuts, chopped (¼ lb. [125 g.])	¼ liter
Maple icing		
¾ cup	maple syrup	175 ml.
¼ cup	granulated sugar	50 ml.
1	egg white, stiffly beaten	1

Cream together the maple sugar and the shortening until light and fluffy. Beat in the egg yolks. Sift together the flour,

salt and baking powder. Add the flour mixture to the batter alternately with the milk, then fold in the nuts. Spoon the batter into two buttered and floured layer-cake pans and bake in a preheated 350° F. [180° C.] oven for 25 minutes, or until a tester inserted into the center of a layer comes out clean. Cool the cake on a rack.

Meanwhile, make the icing. Place the syrup and sugar in a small pan and heat until the mixture reaches the small-thread stage—217° to 220° F. [103° to 105° C.] on a candy thermometer. Immediately pour the syrup slowly into the beaten egg white, continuing to beat until the mixture is cold. Fill and cover the cooled cake with the maple icing.

JEAN HEWITT
THE NEW YORK TIMES NEW ENGLAND HERITAGE COOKBOOK

Grecian Sugar Cake

Ravaní

This delicious concoction is based on farina, a meal milled from hard wheat available at health-food stores. The result is a light, fluffy, truly sweet cake, and one you can make ahead for company.

To make one 10-by-14-inch [25-by-36-cm.] cake

½ lb.	unsalted butter	¼ kg.
¾ cup	sugar	175 ml.
5	eggs, beaten	5
2 cups	flour sifted with 1 tsp. [5 ml.] baking soda and 2 tsp. [10 ml.] baking powder	½ liter
1 cup	farina	¼ liter
3 tsp.	baking powder	15 ml.
2 tsp.	vanilla extract	10 ml.
2 cups	sugar syrup (recipe, page 164) flavored with 1 tbsp. [15 ml.] strained fresh lemon juice	½ liter
	heavy cream, whipped (optional)	
	chopped nuts (optional)	

Melt the butter over low heat (do not brown). Transfer the butter to a large bowl and add the sugar. Cream until light, then beat in the eggs.

Stir the farina with the flour and baking powder. Combine them thoroughly with the egg-and-sugar mixture. Add the vanilla extract. Mix well with a beater or wooden spoon. The batter will be golden yellow with the consistency of oatmeal at this point.

Pour the batter into a buttered baking pan. The batter needs at least 1 inch [2½ cm.] of space to rise in the pan. Smooth the batter out in the pan and place it on the middle shelf of a preheated 350° F. [180° C.] oven.

Bake for 30 to 35 minutes. The cake should be brown on top, and a tester should come out clean when inserted into the cake. Cut the hot cake into squares or diamond shapes right in the pan. Pour some cooled syrup over the hot cake, slowly and evenly. When it has been absorbed pour a little more over the cake. Repeat until the syrup is used up.

Allow the cake to cool before serving. Room temperature is best. Whipped cream and chopped nuts can be used for topping, but are not necessary.

ANNE THEOHAROUS
COOKING THE GREEK WAY

Chocolate Cakes

Black Bottom Cupcakes

To make 18 cupcakes

6 oz.	cream cheese	175 g.
1	egg	1
1⅓ cups plus 2 tbsp.	sugar	355 ml.
	salt	
6 oz.	semisweet chocolate, broken into bits	175 g.
1½ cups	sifted flour	375 ml.
¼ cup	cocoa powder	50 ml.
1 tsp.	baking soda	5 ml.
1 cup	water	¼ liter
⅓ cup	vegetable oil	75 ml.
1 tbsp.	vinegar	15 ml.
1 tsp.	vanilla extract	5 ml.
½ cup	walnuts, chopped	125 ml.

Using an electric mixer set at medium speed, beat the cream cheese in a bowl until it is smooth. Add the egg, ⅓ cup [75 ml.] of the sugar and a pinch of salt. Beat the mixture until it is well blended, then stir in the chocolate pieces.

Sift together into a separate bowl the flour, 1 cup [¼ liter] sugar, the cocoa powder, baking soda and ½ teaspoon [2 ml.] of salt.

Combine the water, oil, vinegar and vanilla extract in a small bowl; mix well. Add the oil mixture to the flour-and-powder mixture. Beat until well blended. Spoon the batter into paper-lined, 2½-inch [6-cm.] muffin-pan cups, filling each cup about one third full. Place a large teaspoonful of the cheese mixture on top of the batter in each cup.

Combine the remaining sugar and the walnuts; mix well. Sprinkle each cupcake with the sugar-walnut mixture.

Bake in a preheated 350° F. [180° C.] oven for 35 minutes, or until a tester inserted in the center of a cupcake comes out clean. Remove the cupcakes from the pans to cool on racks.

ELISE W. MANNING
FARM JOURNAL'S COMPLETE HOME BAKING BOOK

Brownie Cupcakes

To make 24 cupcakes

4 oz.	unsweetened chocolate	125 g.
½ lb.	butter	¼ kg.
1½ cups	pecans, finely chopped (6 oz. [175 g.])	375 ml.
1¾ cups	sugar	425 ml.
1 cup	sifted flour	¼ liter
4	eggs	4
1 tsp.	vanilla extract	5 ml.
2 cups	chocolate fudge frosting *(recipe, page 166)*	½ liter

Melt the chocolate and the butter over very low heat. Add the pecans and stir them until they are coated.

In a separate bowl, combine the sugar, flour, eggs and vanilla extract; mix until the ingredients are well blended, but do not beat. Add the chocolate mixture and stir carefully. Pour the mixture evenly into a muffin tin that has been buttered and floured or lined with paper cups. Bake in a preheated 325° F. [160° C.] oven for 25 to 30 minutes, or until a tester inserted in the middle of each cake comes out faintly moist but clean; do not overcook. Cool the cakes in the pans for five minutes before turning them out onto a rack to cool completely. Cover the cupcakes with the frosting.

THE JUNIOR LEAGUE OF FAYETTEVILLE
THE CAROLINA COLLECTION

Chocolate Cake

Gâteau au Chocolat

To make one 8-inch [20-cm.] cake

5	eggs, yolks separated from whites, whites stiffly beaten	5
1 cup	superfine sugar	¼ liter
8 tbsp.	butter, softened	120 ml.
4 oz.	semisweet chocolate, grated	125 g.
1 cup	sifted flour	¼ liter

Beat the egg yolks with the sugar until the mixture is thick and pale and forms a ribbon. Add the butter and chocolate, and gradually beat in the flour. Fold in the egg whites, and pour the mixture into a buttered and floured cake pan. Bake in a preheated 350° F. [180° C.] oven for 30 minutes, or until a tester inserted in the center of the cake comes out clean.

FERNAND POINT
MA GASTRONOMIE

A Small Chocolate Cake

This cake may be baked and frozen , but should not be frosted until after it has thawed. It may be frosted and refrigerated a day ahead, but it should be brought to room temperature for two or three hours before it is served.

To make one 6-inch [15-cm.] cake

4 oz.	unsweetened chocolate	125 ml.
6 tbsp.	butter, softened	90 ml.
2 tbsp.	flour	30 ml.
½ cup	sugar	125 ml.
3	eggs, yolks separated from whites, yolks beaten until lemon-colored, whites stiffly beaten	3
1 cup	thick chocolate icing (recipe, page 165), flavored with 1 tbsp. [15 ml.] dark rum	¼ liter

Melt the chocolate over hot water. Let it cool slightly. Mix the butter with the flour and sugar, then the egg yolks. Mix in the chocolate. Fold in the egg whites. Spoon the batter into a buttered pan that has been sprinkled with sugar, and bake in a preheated 350° F. [180° C.] oven for 35 minutes. The cake will have a thin crust on top and will seem to be soft and insufficiently cooked, but this is the way it should be. It will get firmer as it cools. Let the cake cool in the pan, then turn it out onto a cake rack. Cover the sides and top of the cooled cake with the chocolate icing before serving.

MAURICE MOORE-BETTY
THE MAURICE MOORE-BETTY COOKING SCHOOL BOOK OF FINE COOKING

Chocolate-Praline Cake

Schokoladentorte

Chocolate pralines can be bought in specialty food stores. If not available, chocolate shavings (demonstration, page 17) can be substituted.

To make one 7-inch [18-cm.] cake

3½ oz.	semisweet chocolate	105 g.
7 tbsp.	butter, softened	105 ml.
1¼ cups	confectioners' sugar	300 ml.
7	eggs, yolks separated from whites, whites stiffly beaten	7
1¼ cups	flour	300 ml.
3 tbsp.	apricot jam	45 ml.
½ cup	heavy cream, lightly whipped	125 ml.
2 oz.	chocolate pralines	60 g.

Put the chocolate into a heatproof dish and place it in a preheated 325° F. [170° C.] oven to melt. Put the butter into a bowl and beat in the confectioners' sugar, egg yolks and the softened chocolate. Beat for 20 minutes, or until the mixture is smooth and creamy. Fold in the egg whites and the flour.

Pour the batter into a buttered and floured cake pan, and bake the cake in a preheated 350° F. [180° C.] oven for about 40 minutes, or until the cake shrinks slightly from the sides of the pan and a tester inserted into the center comes out clean. Cool the cake in the pan for 10 minutes and then turn it onto a rack to cool completely.

Cut the cake in half horizontally. Spread the bottom layer with apricot jam and spread half of the cream over the jam. Replace the top half of the cake and cover it with the remaining cream. Garnish with the chocolate pralines.

MÁRIA HAJKOVÁ
MÚČNIKY

Chocolate Fudge Cake

To make one 9-inch [23-cm.] tube cake

½ cup	cocoa powder	125 ml.
1 cup	boiling water	¼ liter
8 tbsp.	butter	120 ml.
2 cups	sifted flour	½ liter
2 cups	sugar	½ liter
1½ tsp.	baking soda	7 ml.
1 tsp.	salt	5 ml.
2	eggs	2
½ cup	sour cream	125 ml.
1 tsp.	vanilla extract	5 ml.

Chocolate cream-cheese frosting

4 oz.	cream cheese, softened	125 g.
2½ cups	confectioners' sugar	625 ml.
½ cup	cocoa powder	125 ml.
1 tsp.	vanilla extract	5 ml.
2 tbsp.	sour cream	30 ml.

Mix ½ cup [125 ml.] of cocoa powder, the boiling water and the butter, stirring well to dissolve the cocoa powder. Let the mixture cool. Sift together the flour, sugar, baking soda and salt, and slowly mix the dry ingredients into the cooled cocoa mixture. Add the eggs, one at a time, beating well after each addition. Add the sour cream and the vanilla extract. Pour the batter into a buttered and floured tube pan, and bake in a preheated 350° F. [180° C.] oven for 35 to 40 minutes, or until a tester inserted into the center comes out clean.

Cool the cake on a cake rack. Combine the ingredients for the frosting, blending very well. Spread the frosting over the cooled cake.

JOAN NATHAN
THE JEWISH HOLIDAY KITCHEN

Chocolate Cake with Almonds

Gâteau au Chocolat et aux Amandes

To make one 7-inch [18-cm.] cake

⅓ cup	water	75 ml.
8 oz.	semisweet chocolate	¼ kg.
4	eggs, yolks separated from whites, whites stiffly beaten	4
1 cup	sugar	¼ liter
8 tbsp.	butter, softened and cut into pieces	120 ml.
1 cup	almonds, blanched, peeled and ground (about ¼ lb. [125 g.])	¼ liter
⅔ cup	flour	150 ml.

Heat the water to a simmer, and in it melt the chocolate. Remove the mixture from the heat and stir in the egg yolks, one at a time, then the sugar and the butter. When the butter has melted, stir in the almonds and the flour. Last of all, fold in the stiffly beaten egg whites. Pour the mixture into a buttered and floured cake pan and bake it in a preheated 350° F. [180° C.] oven for 45 to 50 minutes, or until a warm tester inserted into the cake comes out clean.

GINETTE MATHIOT
JE SAIS FAIRE LA PÂTISSERIE

Chocolate Pancake

Galette au Chocolat

To make one 7-inch [18-cm.] cake

4 tbsp.	butter, softened	60 ml.
½ cup	sugar	125 ml.
3	eggs, yolks separated from whites, whites stiffly beaten	3
4 oz.	semisweet chocolate, melted	125 g.
2 tbsp.	flour	30 ml.

In a bowl, cream the butter and sugar together until light and fluffy. Gradually beat in the egg yolks, then the chocolate and flour. Fold in the egg whites.

Put the mixture into a buttered and floured cake pan; the batter should be 1 inch [2½ cm.] deep. Bake for 10 minutes in a preheated 425° F. [220° C.] oven. When the top is nicely golden, invert another buttered and floured pan of the same size over the cake. Turn the pans over, holding them together, so that the pancake is inverted into the second pan. Place this pan in the oven and bake for another 10 minutes. The inside of the cake should remain soft. Cool the cake in the pan and serve cold from the pan.

X. MARCEL BOULESTIN
SIMPLE FRENCH COOKING FOR ENGLISH HOMES

Triple Chocolate Cake

Gâteau au Chocolat de la Maréchale de Lannes

To make one 7-inch [18-cm.] cake

4	eggs, yolks separated from whites, whites stiffly beaten	4
¾ cup plus 2 tbsp.	superfine sugar	205 ml.
3 oz.	semisweet chocolate, melted in 1 tablespoon [15 ml.] of water	90 g.
¾ cup plus 2 tbsp.	flour	205 ml.
2 cups	rich butter cream *(recipe, page 166),* flavored with 4 oz. [125 g.] semisweet chocolate	½ liter
	Rich chocolate glaze	
2 oz.	semisweet chocolate	60 g.
1 tbsp.	butter	15 ml.
1	egg yolk, lightly beaten	1

To prepare the cake, whisk the egg yolks and sugar to a pale foam that forms a slowly dissolving ribbon when the whisk is lifted from the bowl.

Gradually fold in the melted chocolate and flour, then gently fold in the egg whites. Blend thoroughly and pour the batter into a buttered and floured cake pan 3 inches [8 cm.] deep. Bake in a preheated 350° F. [180° C.] oven for approximately 30 minutes; the cake is baked when a tester inserted in the middle comes out dry. Remove the cake from the pan and set it on a rack to cool.

When the cake is cool, cut it horizontally into three layers. Spread thick layers of chocolate butter cream between the slices and reassemble the cake.

To make the glaze, melt the chocolate and butter over low heat, stirring. Remove the pan from the heat and bind the glaze with the beaten egg yolk. Carefully pour the icing over the top of the cake so that it is evenly glazed.

LES PETITS PLATS ET LES GRANDS

Chocolate Roll

Roulade au Chocolat

To make one rolled cake 17 inches [43 cm.] long

6 oz.	semisweet chocolate	175 g.
½ cup	granulated sugar	125 ml.
¼ cup	water	50 ml.
6	eggs, yolks separated from whites, whites stiffly beaten	6
1 tbsp.	very strong coffee, or 1 tsp. [5 ml.] instant-coffee crystals	15 ml.
1½ cups	heavy cream	375 ml.
2 tbsp.	confectioners' sugar	30 ml.
½ tsp.	vanilla extract	2 ml.
2 tsp.	kirsch	10 ml.
1 tbsp.	cocoa powder	15 ml.

Melt the chocolate in a double boiler over simmering water or in a preheated 200° F. [100° C.] oven. Mix the granulated sugar and water in a saucepan. Bring the liquid to a boil and cook for two minutes over medium heat. Meanwhile, place the egg yolks in a bowl.

Slowly pour the hot sugar syrup over the yolks, beating vigorously with a whisk. Continue whisking the mixture for about five minutes, until it is light, smooth and pale yellow in color. Mix in the melted chocolate and the coffee. Add about one third of the whites to the chocolate mixture and mix vigorously with the whisk. Add the remaining whites and fold in with a spatula—mix just enough to combine the ingredients. Do not overwork.

Spread the batter in a buttered jelly-roll pan lined with buttered and floured parchment paper. The mixture will be about ½ inch [1 cm.] thick.

Bake the cake in a preheated 375° F. [190° C.] oven for 15 minutes, until the cake is springy to the touch. Initially, cool at room temperature; then cover with plastic wrap and allow to cool for at least two more hours.

Start whipping the cream; when thick but not stiff, add the confectioners' sugar, vanilla extract and kirsch. Continue beating until the cream is firm.

Now begin rolling the cake. This is a delicate operation. Remove the plastic wrap, and slide a knife all around the edges of the pan to loosen the cake. Spread the whipped cream on the cake. Starting on one long side, begin rolling the cake with the paper still on, peeling the paper off, then rolling a little. Avoid pressing down on the cake as you roll so that the whipped cream is not squeezed out. Continue rolling and removing the paper. Try to have the end of the cake underneath so that the cake looks smooth on top. Use two large spatulas to slide the cake onto a serving platter. Place the cocoa powder in a sieve and shake it over the cake to coat the top. Refrigerate.

JACQUES PÉPIN
A FRENCH CHEF COOKS AT HOME

Chocolate Cake with Cinnamon

Torta de Chocolate

This Chilean recipe is adapted from *El Cocinero Chileno*, originally published in Spanish in 1875.

To make one 12-inch [30-cm.] cake

6 oz.	unsweetened chocolate, melted	175 g.
2 cups	sugar	½ liter
4 tsp.	ground cinnamon	20 ml.
1 tsp.	ground cloves	5 ml.
14	eggs, yolks separated from whites, whites stiffly beaten	14
2½ cups	fresh black-bread crumbs	625 ml.

Mix together the chocolate, sugar, cinnamon and cloves. Beat in the egg yolks, one at a time, and then beat the mixture until it becomes very thick and forms a ribbon. Fold in the egg whites and then the bread crumbs. Pour the mixture into a cake pan that has been greased with unsalted butter. Place the cake immediately in a preheated 300° F. [150° C.] oven and bake for about one hour, or until a tester inserted into the center of the cake comes out clean. Cool the cake in the pan before turning it out onto a flat plate.

MARTHA VON ZOBELTITZ
DAS KASSEROL: ABSONDERLICHE GAUMENLETZEN AUS ALLER ZEIT

The Prior's Chocolate Cake

Gâteau au Chocolat du Prieur

To make one 9-inch [23-cm.] cake

7	eggs	7
1 cup	sugar	¼ liter
1 tsp.	vanilla extract	5 ml.
4 oz.	semisweet chocolate	125 g.
3 tbsp.	water	45 ml.
1¾ cups	sifted flour	425 ml.
½ cup	clarified butter, cooled	125 ml.
1½ cups	rich butter cream (recipe, page 166), flavored with 1 tbsp. [15 ml.] strong black coffee	375 ml.
1½ cups	rich butter cream (recipe, page 166), flavored with 4 oz. [125 g.] semisweet chocolate and 2 tbsp. [30 ml.] rum	375 ml.
2 cups	fondant icing (recipe, page 164), flavored with 3 oz. [90 g.] semisweet chocolate	½ liter

Break up the eggs with the sugar lightly with a fork in a large bowl. Place the bowl over, but not touching, simmering water and beat with a wire whisk until the mixture feels hot to the finger. Remove from the heat and beat with a rotary beater or an electric mixer for about 15 minutes, until the mixture is completely cool, has tripled in bulk, and forms a ribbon when dropped from a spoon. Melt the chocolate with the 3 tablespoons [45 ml.] of water in a saucepan, allow it to cool, and beat the chocolate mixture into the egg mixture. Beat in the vanilla extract.

Very gently fold in the flour alternately with the clarified butter, adding a little of each at a time. Bake the chocolate *génoise* batter in two buttered and floured layer-cake pans in a preheated 350° F. [180° C.] oven for about 30 minutes, until the layers begin to shrink from the sides of the pans. When the layers are baked, remove them from the pans and let them cool on a rack.

Cut each cooled layer into three very thin slices, and spread each slice alternately with one of the two butter creams. Stack the slices, alternating the butter-cream fillings, and cover the cake with the chocolate-flavored fondant icing. Refrigerate it until serving time.

RAYMOND OLIVER
LA CUISINE

Devil's Food Layer Cake

This recipe can also be made into 12 cupcakes as demonstrated on pages 58-59. To make cupcakes, bake the batter in buttered and floured muffin pans for 20 minutes. The cupcakes or the cake can be frosted with whipped cream. Other good choices for filling and frosting include boiled icing (recipe, page 164), seven-minute icing (recipe, page 165) and rich butter cream (recipe, page 166).

To make one 9-inch [23-cm.] cake

10 tbsp.	butter, softened	150 ml.
1½ cups	sugar	375 ml.
3	eggs, yolks separated from whites, whites stiffly beaten	3
⅔ cup	cocoa powder, dissolved in ½ cup [125 ml.] hot water	150 ml.
½ tsp.	baking soda	2 ml.
1 cup	buttermilk	¼ liter
2 cups	sifted cake flour	½ liter
2 tsp.	baking powder	10 ml.
1 tsp.	vanilla extract	5 ml.

Cream together the butter and the sugar. Beat the egg yolks well and stir them into the creamed mixture. Dissolve the soda in the buttermilk. Sift together the flour and baking powder, then add the flour to the creamed mixture alternately with the dissolved cocoa and the buttermilk mixture. Add the vanilla extract. Fold in the egg whites. Divide the batter evenly between two buttered and floured layer-cake pans. Bake in a preheated 350° F. [180° C.] oven for 30 to 35 minutes, or until the top of the cake is springy to the touch. When the cake is cool, fill and frost it as desired.

THE JUNIOR LEAGUE OF HOUSTON
HOUSTON JUNIOR LEAGUE COOK BOOK

Devil's Food Cake

Coffee-flavored simple butter cream (recipe, page 166) may be used for this cake instead of the boiled icing. Add baking powder for a fluffier cake; omit it for a denser, moister cake.

To make one 8-inch [20-cm.] cake

1⅔ cups	brown sugar	400 ml.
12 tbsp.	butter, softened	180 ml.
3	eggs	3
⅔ cup	boiling water	150 ml.
3 oz.	semisweet chocolate, broken into pieces	90 g.
2½ cups	flour	625 ml.
¼ tsp.	baking powder (optional)	1 ml.
1½ tsp.	baking soda	7 ml.
⅔ cup	sour cream	150 ml.
1 tsp.	vanilla extract	5 ml.
2 cups	boiled icing (recipe, page 164), flavored with 1 tbsp. [15 ml.] strong black coffee	½ liter

Cream the butter. Add the sugar, a little at a time, to the butter. Beat until light and fluffy. Add the eggs, one at a time, beating well. Pour the boiling water over the broken-up chocolate in a heavy pan. Stir this mixture over low heat until it is smooth and thick. Cool the chocolate a little, add it to the creamed mixture, and blend well. Sift the flour with the baking powder, if using, and the baking soda. Add these dry ingredients to the batter alternately with the sour cream and vanilla extract.

Pour the batter into three buttered and floured layer-cake pans, and bake in a preheated 375° F. [190° C.] oven for about 25 minutes, or until the cakes shrink slightly from the sides of the pans. Turn the cakes out of the pans onto wire racks to cool completely. Spread the icing between the layers, stack the layers, and spread the icing over the top and sides of the cake.

MARGARET COSTA
MARGARET COSTA'S FOUR SEASONS COOKERY BOOK

Dutch Chocolate Cake
Holländische Schokoladentorte

To make one 8-inch [20-cm.] cake

12 tbsp.	butter, softened	180 ml.
¾ cup	sugar	175 ml.
8	eggs, yolks separated from whites, whites stiffly beaten	8
4 oz.	semisweet or unsweetened chocolate, grated	120 g.
1 tsp.	ground cinnamon	5 ml.
1	small lemon, peel grated, juice strained	1
½ lb.	almonds, ground (about 2 cups [½ liter]), or ¼ lb. [125 g.] almonds, ground (about 1 cup [¼ liter]), mixed with ¼ lb. of ladyfingers or other dried cake, broken into small pieces to give the same volume	¼ kg.

Chocolate cream filling

1½ cups	milk	375 ml.
⅓ cup	sugar	75 ml.
3	egg yolks	3
½ cup	cocoa powder	125 ml.
3 tbsp.	butter, cut into small pieces	45 ml.

Chocolate glaze

3 oz.	semisweet chocolate	90 g.
¾ cup	sugar	175 ml.
½ cup	water	125 ml.

Put the butter into a bowl and beat in the sugar and egg yolks. Beat by hand for about 30 minutes or for five minutes in the electric mixer, or until the mixture is foamy. Melt the chocolate with 2 tablespoons [30 ml.] of hot water and spoon it into the foamy butter-and-egg mixture. Mix well. Then add the cinnamon, lemon peel and juice, and almonds, and fold in the stiffly beaten egg whites.

Bake the cake in a buttered and floured pan in a preheated 350° F. [180° C.] oven for about one hour, or until the edges shrink slightly from the sides of the pan and a cake tester inserted in the center comes out clean. Let the cake cool, and then cut it horizontally into three layers.

To make the filling, put the milk, sugar, egg yolks, cocoa and butter in a double boiler over hot water or in a bowl standing in a saucepan of hot water, and stir until you have a thick cream. Stack the layers of cake, spreading filling between the layers.

To make the glaze, melt the chocolate in a bowl set over a pan of hot water. In a small saucepan, boil the sugar and

water together until the syrup reaches a temperature of 234° to 240° F. [112° to 116° C.] on a candy thermometer—the soft-ball stage. Cool the syrup slightly, then stir it into the chocolate. Remove the mixture from the heat. When the glaze is still warm, but beginning to thicken, spread it on the top and sides of the cake.

HERMINE KIEHNLE AND MARIA HÄDECKE
DAS NEUE KIEHNLE-KOCHBUCH

French Chocolate Cake

Candied violets are sold at candy and specialty food stores.

To make one 8-inch [20-cm.] cake

4 oz.	unsweetened chocolate	125 g.
¼ cup	water or coffee	50 ml.
½ cup	sugar	125 ml.
8 tbsp.	butter, cut into pieces	120 ml.
4	eggs, yolks separated from whites, whites stiffly beaten	4
⅓ cup	almonds, blanched, peeled and finely ground	75 ml.
1½ tsp.	vanilla extract or 1 tbsp. [15 ml.] brandy, rum or kirsch	7 ml.
⅓ cup	sifted flour	75 ml.
1 cup	heavy cream, whipped with 1 tbsp. [15 ml.] sugar	¼ liter
	candied violets	

Put the chocolate in the top of a double boiler over hot—not boiling—water, add the water or coffee and the sugar, and let the chocolate melt completely, stirring frequently. Remove the double boiler from the heat, but keep the top over the hot water. Stir the butter, piece by piece, into the chocolate, letting each piece melt completely before adding the next. Remove the top of the double boiler from the bottom and cool the contents. Add the egg yolks, one at a time, beating well after each. Blend in the nuts and the flavoring. Gradually stir in the flour and mix well. Gently fold in the egg whites.

Spoon the batter into two buttered and floured layer-cake pans. Bake in a preheated 350° F. [180° C.] oven for about 20 minutes, or until a tester inserted in the middle of the cake comes out clean. Do not overbake; the cake should be on the moist side. Cool the layers in their pans for approximately five minutes; turn the layers out of the pans and cool completely.

Just before serving time, spread about one third of the whipped cream on one layer, then top with the other. Spread the remaining whipped cream over the top and sides of the cake. Decorate with the candied violets.

NIKA HAZELTON
I COOK AS I PLEASE

A Very Rich Chocolate Cake with Cherries

Le Montmorency

For the cherries in this recipe, you may substitute a purée of fresh figs; or chopped dried-and-pitted prunes or apricots, plumped in water and a little kirsch, and flavored with orange marmalade. To do the cake full justice, it must be made a day ahead, or even two or three. Then all the flavors of chocolate and fruit will rest and ripen, and be even richer.

To make one 9-inch [22-cm.] cake

14 oz.	semisweet chocolate, broken into bits	425 g.
2 tbsp.	instant-coffee crystals	30 ml.
½ cup	kirsch	125 ml.
4	eggs, yolks separated from whites	4
12 tbsp.	unsalted butter, softened	180 ml.
⅓ cup	flour	75 ml.
	salt	
⅔ cup	sugar	150 ml.
4 cups	cherries, pitted	1 liter
3 tbsp.	water	45 ml.

In a saucepan over low heat, melt 8 ounces [250 g.] of the chocolate with 1 tablespoon [15 ml.] of the coffee and half of the kirsch, stirring occasionally until smooth. Off the heat, stir in the egg yolks one at a time, then return the pan to the heat and stir the mixture briefly until the yolks are warmed and have thickened the chocolate slightly. Off the heat, beat in the butter by tablespoonfuls, stirring after each addition until the mixture is smooth. Stir in the flour.

Beat the egg whites with a pinch of salt until they form soft peaks. Sprinkle on ⅓ cup [75 ml.] of the sugar and beat until the whites form stiff peaks. Fold the chocolate mixture into this meringue and turn the batter into a deep cake pan that has been buttered and lined with buttered wax paper. Bake in a preheated 375° F. [190° C.] oven for 25 to 30 minutes, or until a tester inserted in the center comes out with a slightly creamy coating. Set the cake pan on a rack to cool for at least 45 minutes before turning out the cake. As it cools, the cake will fall and the surface will crack slightly.

While the cake is baking and cooling, place the cherries in a saucepan with the remaining sugar and 2 tablespoons [30 ml.] of the remaining kirsch. Reserve a few cherries for decoration, if desired. Cook the mixture over medium-low heat, partially covered, for 30 to 40 minutes, stirring occasionally. Uncover the pan for the last 10 minutes or so; the cherries should reduce to a thick compote. Let the cherries cool, then chop them coarse.

Invert the cake pan onto a serving platter, remove it from the cooled cake and remove the paper.

Using a large spoon, trace a 5-inch [13-cm.] circle in the center of the cake, then scoop out the top part of the circle, leaving at least ½ inch [1 cm.] of cake at the bottom. Crumble the scooped-out cake into the cherries and stir together well. Spoon the mixture into the cake, smoothing it nicely.

Melt the remaining chocolate with the rest of the coffee and kirsch and the 3 tablespoons [45 ml.] of water, stirring occasionally until smooth. Let the mixture cool slightly, then spread it evenly over the top and sides of the cake. Refrigerate the cake until 30 minutes before serving. Serve the cake garnished with the reserved cherries.

SIMONE BECK AND MICHAEL JAMES
NEW MENUS FROM SIMCA'S CUISINE

Black Forest Cake

Schwarzwaelder Kirschtorte

To poach cherries, pit the fruit, then drop it into 1 cup [¼ liter] of boiling water. Reduce the heat and simmer the cherries until tender, about three to four minutes. Add ½ cup [125 ml.] of sugar and cook a few more minutes. Cool and drain.

To make two 7-inch [18-cm.] cakes

5 tbsp.	butter, softened	75 ml.
¼ cup	vegetable shortening	50 ml.
1¼ cups	sugar	300 ml.
4	eggs	4
2 oz.	unsweetened chocolate	60 g.
1 cup	buttermilk	¼ liter
2 cups	sifted cake flour	½ liter
½ tsp.	baking powder	2 ml.
2 cups	heavy cream, whipped and slightly sweetened with sugar	½ liter
¾ cup	sour cherries, poached and drained	175 ml.
¼ cup	kirsch	50 ml.
3 oz.	semisweet chocolate, grated	90 g.

Using an electric mixer, beat the butter, shortening, sugar and eggs together until fluffy. Melt the chocolate over hot water, then let it cool almost to room temperature. Beat the chocolate into the batter. Sift together the flour and baking powder and fold them, alternately with the buttermilk, into the batter. Divide the batter between two buttered and floured cake pans. Bake in a preheated 375° F. [190° C.] oven for 35 minutes. Turn the cakes out onto a rack to cool.

Cut horizontally through the center of each cooled cake to make four round layers; this will give you two double-layer cakes. Cover the bottom layers with 2 inches [5 cm.] of whipped cream and divide the cherries between them. Cover each half with a top layer and sprinkle with kirsch.

Frost the tops and sides of the cakes with the remaining whipped cream and sprinkle grated chocolate over the top. Let the cakes stand for several hours before cutting.

EVE BROWN
THE PLAZA COOKBOOK

Sacher Cake
Sachertorte
To make one 9-inch [23-cm.] cake

14 tbsp.	butter, softened	210 ml.
¾ cup	sugar	175 ml.
10	eggs, yolks separated from whites, whites stiffly beaten	10
10 oz.	semisweet chocolate	300 g.
1¼ cups	sifted flour	300 ml.
¾ cup	rusk or zwieback crumbs	175 ml.
	apricot jam	

Cream the butter. Add the sugar and egg yolks alternately, beating for 30 minutes, or until the mixture is fluffy.

Put 7 ounces [200 g.] of the chocolate in a double boiler or in a bowl set over hot water, and heat gently until the chocolate is melted. Beat it into the butter mixture. Fold in the flour and ½ cup [125 ml.] of the rusk or zwieback crumbs. Finally, fold in the beaten egg whites.

Dust a buttered cake pan with the remaining crumbs, pour the batter into it, and bake in a preheated 350° F. [180° C.] oven for one hour, or until the cake shrinks slightly from the pan. Cool the cake for 10 minutes in the pan, then turn it out onto a rack to cool overnight.

The following day, spread the top and sides of the cake with apricot jam. Let it set. Melt the remaining chocolate over hot water and spread it evenly over the jam coating. The cake becomes smooth and shiny if it is put very briefly into a warm oven (325° F. [160° C.]) for a minute or two after the chocolate is spread on it.

ELIZABETH SCHULER
MEIN KOCHBUCH

Chocolate Poppy-Seed Torte
Schokoladen Mohntorte
To make one 9-inch [23-cm.] cake

7 tbsp.	unsalted butter, softened	105 ml.
⅓ cup	sugar	75 ml.
4	eggs, yolks separated from whites, whites stiffly beaten	4
1¾ cups	ground poppy seeds	425 ml.
2½ oz.	semisweet chocolate, grated	75 g.
¼ to ⅓ cup	apricot jam	50 to 75 ml.
	confectioners' sugar	
	heavy cream, whipped (optional)	

Cream the butter and the sugar until the mixture is light and fluffy. Add the egg yolks, and continue to beat until the mixture is light. Mix the poppy seeds with the chocolate. Gently fold the chocolate mixture and the beaten egg whites into the batter, blending until all lumps have been absorbed.

Pour the batter into a buttered and floured spring-form pan. Bake the cake in a preheated 350° F. [180° C.] oven for about 30 to 40 minutes, or until a cake tester inserted into the center of the cake comes out dry.

When the cake is completely cool, preferably the next day, slice it into two equal layers. Spread one layer with apricot jam and place the other layer on top. Refrigerate. Before serving, sprinkle the cake with confectioners' sugar. This cake is especially good served with whipped cream.

LILLY JOSS REICH
THE VIENNESE PASTRY COOKBOOK

Black-Bread Torte
To make one 9-inch [23-cm.] cake

¼ cup	rum	50 ml.
2 cups	fresh black-bread crumbs	½ liter
6	eggs, yolks separated from whites	6
	salt	
1 cup	sugar	¼ liter
1 tsp.	vanilla extract	5 ml.
¼ cup	walnuts, finely ground	50 ml.
3½ oz.	semisweet chocolate, grated	105 g.
1½ cups	heavy cream, whipped lightly with sugar and rum	375 ml.

Pour the rum over the bread crumbs and set them aside. Beat the egg whites with a pinch of salt until they hold soft peaks. Add the sugar, a tablespoonful [15 ml.] at a time, beating well after each addition. Beat for at least five minutes, or until the egg whites are very firm.

Stir the yolks with a fork to break them up. Add the vanilla extract. Fold a quarter of the whites into the yolks. Pour this mixture over the remaining whites. Add the bread-crumb mixture, nuts and chocolate. Carefully fold all these ingredients together. Pour the batter into a spring-form pan that has been buttered on the bottom but not on the sides.

Bake in an oven preheated to 350° F. [180° C.] for 50 to 60 minutes, or until the cake is brown and springy to the touch. Let it cool in the pan before removing. It will shrink quite a bit. Serve with the rum-flavored whipped cream.

PAULA PECK
THE ART OF FINE BAKING

Dead Man's Cake
Pan di Mort

Demerara sugar, a partially refined light brown sugar from England, is available in specialty food stores. Turbinado sug-

ar most closely resembles this product and is obtainable from health-food stores.

To make about twenty 1½-by-4-inch [4-by-10-cm.] cakes

2⅓ cups	demerara sugar	575 ml.
½ cup	cocoa powder	125 ml.
2 oz.	semisweet chocolate, melted	60 g.
¾ cup	dry white wine	175 ml.
1 tbsp.	honey	15 ml.
2½ cups	flour	625 ml.
2½ cups	almonds, blanched, peeled and coarsely chopped (about 10 oz. [300 g.])	625 ml.
⅔ cup	mixed candied fruit peel	150 ml.
¾ cup	pine nuts	175 ml.
1 tbsp.	ground allspice	15 ml.
	confectioners' sugar	

In a large bowl, knead all of the ingredients except the confectioners' sugar. Form the mixture into 20 small loaves. Arrange them on a buttered baking sheet, lined with buttered parchment paper if desired, and bake in a preheated 350° F. [180° C.] oven for one hour, or until the cakes feel firm. Sprinkle with confectioners' sugar while still hot.

OTTORINA PERNA BOZZI
VECCHIA MILANO IN CUCINA

Claricinha Coffee-flavored Cake

Bôlo de Café Claricinha

To make one 10-inch [25-cm.] cake

1 cup	strong black coffee	¼ liter
2	eggs, lightly beaten	2
¾ cup plus 2 tbsp.	sugar	205 ml.
1 cup	honey	¼ liter
1 tbsp.	butter, softened	15 ml.
1 cup	mixed candied fruit, chopped	¼ liter
1¼ cups	raisins	300 ml.
4 oz.	semisweet chocolate, grated	125 g.
1 tsp.	ground cinnamon	5 ml.
1	clove, crushed	1
1 tbsp.	baking powder	15 ml.
3 cups	flour	¾ liter

Mix all the ingredients together and beat them well. Put the mixture into a buttered and floured cake pan, and bake in a

preheated 350° F. [180° C.] oven for one and one half hours, or until the cake shrinks slightly from the sides of the pan. Cool the cake on a wire rack.

DONA TITA
RECEITAS EXPERIMENTADAS

Dutch Mocha Cake

To make one 9-inch [23-cm.] cake

3 cups	sifted cake flour	¾ liter
1 tsp.	baking soda	5 ml.
½ tsp.	salt	2 ml.
¾ cup	cocoa powder	175 ml.
2¾ cups	sugar	675 ml.
1 cup	hot coffee	¼ liter
½ lb.	butter, softened	¼ kg.
1 cup	sour cream	¼ liter
2 tsp.	vanilla extract	10 ml.
5	egg whites	5
1½ cups	pastry cream (recipe, page 166)	375 ml.
2 cups	rich butter cream (recipe, page 166) flavored with 1 tbsp. [15 ml.] strong black coffee, 1 tsp. [5 ml.] vanilla extract and 3 oz. [90 g.] semisweet chocolate	½ liter
1 cup	heavy cream, whipped and flavored with 1 tsp. [5 ml.] vanilla extract	¼ liter

Combine the flour, baking soda and salt. Sift these three times. Combine the cocoa powder, ½ cup [125 ml.] of the sugar and the hot coffee. Cool. Cream the butter and 1½ cups [375 ml.] of sugar until light and fluffy. Add the cocoa mixture, sour cream and vanilla extract to the sweetened butter. Add the flour mixture, stirring until smooth. Beat the egg whites with the remaining sugar until stiff and fold them into the batter. Divide the batter among three layer-cake pans that have been buttered, floured and lined with parchment paper. Bake in a preheated 350° F. [180° C.] oven for 25 to 30 minutes, or until a cake tester inserted in the middle comes out clean. Cool the cakes in the pans for five minutes before turning them out onto wire racks.

Fold the whipped cream into the pastry cream. Spread the filling between the cooled cake layers. Spread the butter cream over the top and sides of the cake.

THE JUNIOR LEAGUE OF FAYETTEVILLE
THE CAROLINA COLLECTION

Yeast Cakes

German Apple Boy

Apfelbuwele

This recipe makes a double portion of dough. The extra dough can be used for a second Apfelbuwele if you double the amounts of ingredients in the filling recipe.

To make one 10-inch [25-cm.] ring cake

8 cups	flour	2 liters
two ¼ oz.	packages active dry yeast or two ⅗ oz. [18 g.] cakes fresh yeast	two 7½ g.
1 tsp.	salt	5 ml.
1 cup	tepid milk or water	¼ liter
1 cup	sugar	¼ liter
8 tbsp.	butter or shortening	120 ml.
1 tsp.	vanilla extract	5 ml.
2 tsp.	grated lemon peel	10 ml.
3	eggs, plus 2 egg yolks	3
	Apple filling	
6	medium-sized apples, peeled, cored and diced (about 7 cups [1¾ liters])	6
½ cup	raisins	125 ml.
¾ cup	sugar	175 ml.
½ tsp.	ground cinnamon	2 ml.
1 tbsp.	butter, cut into small pieces	15 ml.
	ice cream (optional)	
	heavy cream, whipped (optional)	

The day before cooking, put the flour in the mixing bowl and place the bowl in a warm place such as a gas oven heated only by its pilot light. The next day remove 1 cup [¼ liter] of flour from the bowl and reserve it. Make a well in the remaining flour. Mix the yeast and about 1 tablespoon [15 ml.] of the tepid milk or water. Pour the mixture into the well and, without stirring, sprinkle on the sugar. Melt the butter in the remaining tepid milk or water.

Add the vanilla extract, lemon peel, eggs, egg yolks, butter mixture and salt to the well. Mix the ingredients together, then knead the dough by hand until it is shiny and smooth, adding the reserved flour as needed to make the mixture cohere. Or divide the dough into three parts and whirl each third in a food processor fitted with a steel blade, until the dough is shiny and forms a ball; combine the thirds

into one ball. Put the kneaded ball of dough in a bowl, cover the bowl with plastic wrap and let the dough rise in a warm place for two hours, or until it has doubled in bulk.

Divide the dough in half and, on a floured board, roll out one half to make a rectangle about 18 by 24 inches [45 by 60 cm.]. The dough should be about ⅛ inch [3 mm.] thick. Gently pull the corners of the rectangle with your hands to make the dough still thinner.

To make the filling, mix the apples, raisins, sugar and cinnamon. Spread the filling over the dough rectangle, leaving a 1-inch [2½-cm.] border around the edges. Dot the filling with the butter.

Carefully roll the dough, jelly-roll fashion, tucking the ends under. When the roll is completed, shape it into a ring and place it, seam side up, in a buttered 10-inch [25-cm.] round pan 3 inches [8 cm.] deep. Bake in a preheated 350° F. [180° C.] oven for 30 minutes, or until golden. As the *Apfelbuwele* starts to cook, the juice from the apples will begin to accumulate in the pan. Occasionally brush the juice onto the top crust to form a glaze.

When the cake is finished, let it sit for a few minutes and then, using a spatula, carefully loosen it from the pan. Cover the pan with a plate and invert the pair together. Tap the pan and the *Apfelbuwele* should fall out. Turn it once again so that the glazed side is upward. Serve warm, with ice cream or whipped cream if you like.

JOAN NATHAN
THE JEWISH HOLIDAY KITCHEN

Apple Cake

Torta di Mele

To make one 12-inch [30-cm.] cake

4 tbsp.	lard	60 ml.
5	medium-sized McIntosh apples	5
1½ tbsp.	strained fresh lemon juice	22½ ml.
1½ cups	flour	375 ml.
two ¼ oz.	packages active dry yeast or two ⅗ oz. [18 g.] cakes fresh yeast	two 7½ g.
¼ cup	tepid water	50 ml.
⅔ cup	sugar	150 ml.
2 tsp.	grated lemon peel	10 ml.
2	eggs	2
½ cup	raisins, soaked in warm water for 20 minutes and drained	125 ml.

Melt the lard in a saucepan and let it cool. Cut the apples in quarters and remove the cores and skin, then cut the flesh into thin slices. Place the apple slices in a bowl and sprinkle the lemon juice over them. Place 1 cup [¼ liter] of the flour in a second bowl and make a well in it. Dissolve the yeast in the water and pour it into the well; stir with a wooden spoon. Add the sugar, melted lard, grated lemon peel and eggs, and when these ingredients are all well incorporated, sprinkle in the remaining flour. Stir very well until the dough is homogeneous and very soft, then add the soaked raisins and half of the apple slices to the dough, incorporating them well.

Place the dough in an oiled cake mold or spring-form pan and arrange the remaining apple slices on top. Cover with a cotton dish towel and let the dough rise until it is almost doubled in bulk.

When the dough has risen, remove the towel and bake in a preheated 400° F. [200° C.] oven for 35 to 40 minutes, or until the top of the cake is golden brown. Let the cake cool for 30 minutes, then turn it out and serve.

GIULIANO BUGIALLI
THE FINE ART OF ITALIAN COOKING

Applesauce Cake

To make the applesauce required for this recipe, wash, quarter and core 1 pound [½ kg.] of apples, and put them in a saucepan with about ¼ cup [50 ml.] of water. Simmer the apples until tender, then purée them through a vegetable mill.

To make one 6-by-12-inch [15-by-30-cm.] cake

¼ oz.	package active dry yeast	7½ g.
⅓ cup	tepid sweet cider	75 ml.
¼ cup	honey	50 ml.
¼ cup	vegetable oil	50 ml.
1	egg, lightly beaten	1
1 cup	applesauce	¼ liter
2 cups	mixed whole-grain flours such as rye, buckwheat, corn, oatmeal, wheat	½ liter
¼ tsp.	salt	1 ml.
1 cup	dates, pitted and chopped	¼ liter
1 cup	chopped nuts (¼ lb. [125 g.])	¼ liter
1 tsp.	ground cinnamon	5 ml.
1 tsp.	ground allspice	5 ml.
1 tsp.	grated nutmeg	5 ml.

Soften the yeast in the tepid cider. Mix the honey, oil, egg and applesauce, and combine with the softened yeast. Stir in the flour and the salt, then add the remainder of the ingredients. Blend them thoroughly. Turn the batter into a buttered and floured loaf pan. Cover the pan and set it in a warm place to let the cake rise for 30 minutes. Bake the cake in a preheated 350° F. [180° C.] oven for 45 to 55 minutes, until a tester inserted in the middle comes out clean.

BEATRICE TRUM HUNTER
THE NATURAL FOODS COOKBOOK

Savarin

Apricot juice may replace the water in the sugar syrup used in this recipe.

If desired, just before serving, heat 2 tablespoons [30 ml.] of rum, ignite it and pour it over the savarin; bring the cake to the table flaming. The center of a large savarin may be filled with ice cream or piled high with fruit such as pitted black cherries, berries, or sliced bananas, apricots or peaches. Small savarins may be filled with fruit, ice cream or sweetened whipped cream—whipped cream lightly flavored with sugar and vanilla. Or, if desired, sprinkle the top with chopped pistachio nuts and sprinkle chopped toasted blanched almonds all around the sides at the bottom of the savarin.

To make one 8½-inch [21-cm.] ring cake or eight individual 2½-inch [6-cm.] cakes

¼ oz.	package active dry yeast	7½ g.
¼ cup	tepid water	50 ml.
1 tbsp.	sugar	15 ml.
¼ cup	tepid milk	50 ml.
2 cups	sifted flour	½ liter
4	eggs	4
½ tsp.	salt	2 ml.
10 tbsp.	butter, melted	150 ml.
¾ cup	sugar syrup (recipe, page 164), flavored with 1 tsp. [5 ml.] strained fresh lemon juice and ¼ cup [50 ml.] rum	175 ml.

Soften the yeast in the tepid water with 1 teaspoon [5 ml.] of the sugar. When the mixture is foamy—after about 10 minutes—add the remaining sugar and the tepid milk. Stir in the flour and the eggs and beat about two minutes. Cover the bowl, and let the dough rise in a warm place until it has doubled in bulk. Punch down the dough, add the salt and melted butter, and work these ingredients into the dough. Put the dough into a well-buttered ring mold, filling it two thirds full, or put it into eight individual buttered ring molds or baking cups, filling each two thirds full. Cover the dough and let it rise until it fills the mold or molds. Bake in a preheated 400° F. [200° C.] oven. A large ring will need about 25 minutes; small cakes about 15. Either can be tested for doneness by inserting a tester into the center; when it comes out clean, the cake is done.

Invert the hot savarin onto a serving plate and pour the rum syrup over it.

HENRI PAUL PELLAPRAT
THE GREAT BOOK OF FRENCH CUISINE

Baba au Rhum

To make twelve 2½-inch [6-cm.] babas

1½ cups	flour	375 ml.
¼ oz.	package active dry yeast	7½ g.
2 tbsp.	tepid water	30 ml.
1 tsp.	salt	5 ml.
2 tbsp.	sugar	30 ml.
2	eggs	2
4 tbsp.	butter, melted and cooled	60 ml.
2 cups	sugar syrup (*recipe, page 164*), flavored with ½ cup [125 ml.] rum	½ liter
¼ cup	apricot jam glaze (*recipe, page 167*)	50 ml.

Put the flour in a deep mixing bowl, make a well in the center and put the yeast in the well. Add the tepid water and let it stand a few seconds to activate the yeast. Add the salt, sugar and eggs to the well. Using the tips of your fingers, blend together the ingredients in the center, then gradually incorporate the flour. When all of the ingredients have been worked together, knead the dough for at least five minutes. Knead in the butter.

Place the dough in a greased bowl, cover it with plastic wrap or a cloth and let it stand in a warm place for one and one half to two hours, or until the dough has doubled in bulk. Test for sufficient rising by pressing your finger into the top of the dough; the depression should remain. Deflate the dough by kneading gently with your finger tips.

Break off enough dough to fill 12 buttered baba molds, custard cups or muffin-tin cups one third full. Press the dough lightly into the bottom of the molds. Place the molds, uncovered, in a warm place and let the dough rise again until it expands ½ inch [1 cm.] above the top of the molds. Bake at once in a preheated 375° F. [190° C.] oven for about 15 minutes, or until the babas are nicely browned and have shrunk slightly from the sides of the molds.

Before the babas have cooled completely, turn them out of the molds, prick the top and sides of the warm cakes with a skewer and place them in a deep dish. Pour the sugar syrup over the cakes and let them stand for one hour, basting occasionally. (A bulb baster works well for this.)

Drain the babas and brush the apricot glaze over the tops. Babas are best eaten the day they are prepared, but will keep in the refrigerator for a day or two.

THE GREAT COOKS' GUIDE TO CAKES

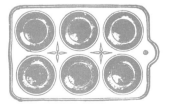

Baba au Rhum with Whipped Cream and Strawberries

To make one 9½-inch [24-cm.] cake

Baba

¼ oz.	package active dry yeast or one ⅗ oz. [18 g.] cake fresh yeast	7½ g.
2 tbsp. plus 2 tsp.	sugar	40 ml.
2 cups	flour	½ liter
½ cup	tepid milk	125 ml.
1 tsp.	salt	5 ml.
3	eggs, lightly beaten	3
12 tbsp.	unsalted butter, softened	180 ml.
¼ cup	almonds, blanched, peeled and slivered	50 ml.
½ cup	sugar syrup (*recipe, page 164*), boiled with a lemon slice and flavored with ⅓ cup [75 ml.] dark rum	125 ml.
1½ cups	apricot jam glaze (*recipe, page 167*)	375 ml.
½ cup	strawberries	125 ml.

Whipped-cream filling

1½ cups	heavy cream, whipped and lightly sweetened with sugar	375 ml.
2 tbsp.	rum or vanilla extract	30 ml.

To make the baba, place the yeast, 2 teaspoons [10 ml.] of sugar and 2 tablespoons [30 ml.] of flour in a 2- to 3-quart [2- to 3-liter] bowl and mix well. Sprinkle the tepid milk over it and set the bowl in a warm, draft-free place until the mixture becomes foamy, which will take about 15 to 20 minutes.

As soon as it reaches this stage, mix in the remaining flour, the salt and the eggs. Stir well until the batter becomes smooth (about five minutes). Again, set the bowl in a warm place and let the dough rise until it doubles in bulk. This will take about an hour.

Gently stir down the dough. Add the softened butter and the remaining sugar. Mix well and pour into a buttered and floured ring mold. Return the mixture to the warm, sheltered spot until the dough rises to within ½ inch [1 cm.] of the top of the mold, which will take from 20 to 30 minutes.

Set the mold on a cookie sheet and bake in the middle of a preheated 375° F. [190° C.] oven for 25 minutes, or until the cake is nicely browned and begins to shrink from the sides of the mold. Let the cake rest in the mold for 10 to 12 minutes.

Place a round platter over the baba, invert the mold and the platter, and remove the cake. Cover the baba with a light, clean cloth.

About one hour before serving, spoon the sugar syrup over the baba—the syrup must be hot in order to soak in properly. (If you like, you can at this point press the slivered almonds onto the top and sides of the cake.)

Pour the apricot jam glaze—boiling hot—over the baba. It is always interesting to see how beautifully the preserves adhere to the baba when poured this way, giving the baba a perfect glaze.

Next, move the baba to a serving dish by sliding two wide spatulas under it. Fill the center with the whipped-cream filling and place whole strawberries around the edge. Serve it immediately.

EDNA LEWIS AND EVANGELINE PETERSON
THE EDNA LEWIS COOKBOOK

❦

Easter Baba

Babka Wielkanocna

To make two 9-inch [23-cm.] tube cakes

two ¼ oz.	packages active dry yeast	two 7½ g.
⅔ cup	sugar	150 ml.
1 cup	tepid light cream	¼ liter
4 cups	sifted flour	1 liter
6	egg yolks	6
1 tbsp.	vanilla extract	15 ml.
1 tsp.	almond extract	5 ml.
1 tbsp.	grated lemon peel	15 ml.
8 tbsp.	butter, melted	120 ml.
⅓ cup	raisins	75 ml.
1 cup	glacé icing (recipe, page 165), flavored with 2 tbsp. [30 ml.] lemon juice or rum	¼ liter

Place the yeast in a small bowl. Add 2 tablespoons [30 ml.] of sugar and the cream, stir, and let the mixture stand for five minutes. Add 1 cup [¼ liter] of the flour and stir to make a yeast sponge. Let the sponge stand in a warm place until it has doubled in bulk. Beat the egg yolks with the rest of the sugar very well. Add the rest of the flour, the yeast sponge, the vanilla and almond extracts, and the lemon peel. Knead the dough for five minutes and add the butter in small portions. Knead for another five minutes until smooth. Add the raisins and knead some more.

Divide the dough between two buttered and floured fluted tube pans. Cover the cakes with clean towels, and place the pans in a warm place such as a gas oven heated only by the pilot light, leaving the oven door half-open. Let the cakes stand for one hour, or until they have at least doubled in bulk. Bake in a preheated 350° F. [180° C.] oven for 45 minutes. Cool the cakes; remove them from the pans. Spread the icing over the cakes, letting it drip down the sides.

ALINA ŻERAŃSKA
THE ART OF POLISH COOKING

Traditional Butter Cake of Brittany

Kouign Amann

To make one 8- or 9-inch [20- or 23-cm.] cake

1 cup plus 7 tbsp.	flour	355 ml.
1 tbsp.	cornstarch	15 ml.
½ tsp.	orange-flower water	2 ml.
	salt	
½ tbsp.	active dry yeast (½ of a ¼ oz. [7½ g.] package)	7 ml.
½ cup	tepid water	125 ml.
10 tbsp.	butter	150 ml.
½ cup	sugar	125 ml.
1	egg yolk, lightly beaten	1

Put the flour and cornstarch in a bowl; add the orange-flower water, a pinch of salt, the yeast and the tepid water. Work the mixture into a soft dough and flatten it into a round ½ inch [1 cm.] thick and 6 inches [15 cm.] in diameter. Set the round on a lightly buttered plate. Cover the dough with plastic wrap and let it rise until it has doubled in bulk.

Knead the butter with your thumb or fingers to make sure that it is soft and pliable. Flatten the dough into a small 6-inch [15-cm.] square. Spread the butter over the dough and let it rest for five minutes. Roll the dough into a rectangle 12 inches [30 cm.] long and 4 inches [10 cm.] wide. Sprinkle it with one third of the sugar. Pass the rolling pin over the sugar to impress it into the surface of the dough. Fold one end of the dough toward the center, then fold the other end in to cover the first. Cover the dough with plastic wrap and store in the crisper of the refrigerator for at least 20 minutes.

Take the dough out of the crisper, turn the dough by 90 degrees so that it will now look like a book ready to be opened, and roll it out again. Sprinkle the dough with the second third of the sugar and fold it again. Repeat the turning, rolling, sprinkling and folding a third time, using the last third of the sugar less 1 teaspoon [5 ml.]. Refrigerate the dough for another half hour. Give it a last rolling and folding, and then, with the rolling pin, tease the dough into a round cake as close as possible to the circumference of your cake pan. Transfer the dough to a buttered and floured cake pan, which should be one at least 3 inches [8 cm.] deep. Dock (slash) the top of the cake in a crisscross pattern, cutting at least ¼ inch [6 mm.] deep into the dough.

Keep the cake at room temperature and let the dough rise within ¼ inch of the rim of the cake pan. Brush the top with the egg yolk and sprinkle it with the last teaspoon of sugar. Bake in a preheated 375° F. [190° C.] oven for 25 minutes. The top of the cake should be nice and brown and, on the bottom, a lovely buttered caramel layer will build.

MADELEINE KAMMAN
WHEN FRENCH WOMEN COOK

Golden Dumpling Cake

Aranygaluska

To make one 9-inch [23-cm.] tube cake

¼ oz.	package active dry yeast	7½ g.
1 cup	tepid milk	¼ liter
2 tbsp.	sugar	30 ml.
4 cups	flour	1 liter
6	egg yolks	6
	salt	
about ½ lb.	unsalted butter, melted	about ¼ kg.
2 tbsp.	cake or cookie crumbs	30 ml.
1 cup	walnuts, finely ground (¼ lb. [125 g.])	¼ liter
1 tbsp.	grated lemon peel	15 ml.
½ cup	thick apricot jam	125 ml.
¼ cup	vanilla sugar	50 ml.

Mix the yeast, ¼ cup [50 ml.] tepid milk, ½ tablespoon [7 ml.] sugar and 3 tablespoons [45 ml.] flour. Let this starter mixture rest for 10 minutes. Mix the remaining tepid milk, the egg yolks, the salt, and the remaining sugar and flour. Mix thoroughly and stir into the starter mixture to make a firm dough.

Gradually add 4 tablespoons [60 ml.] of the melted butter, kneading it into the dough until it is incorporated and the dough becomes blistered and separates easily from hand or spoon. Let the dough rise about one hour.

Put the dough on a floured board and stretch it into a sheet ½ inch [1 cm.] thick. Cut the dough into rounds with a cookie cutter 1 to 1½ inches [2½ to 4 cm.] in diameter. Sprinkle a buttered fluted tube pan with the cake or cookie crumbs. Dip the little dough rounds in the remaining melted butter and pack a layer of them tightly on the bottom of the mold. Sprinkle with some of a mixture of the walnuts and the grated lemon peel.

Arrange more buttered dough rounds to make a second layer. Put ½ teaspoon [2 ml.] of jam in the center of each round. Continue this way, alternating rounds with ground walnuts and rounds with jam, until the mold is filled. Cover the top with the remaining melted butter. Bake in a preheated 375° F. [190° C.] oven for 35 to 40 minutes, until the cake is golden brown. Turn the cake out of the mold, sprinkle it with vanilla sugar, and serve.

GEORGE LANG
THE CUISINE OF HUNGARY

Dresdner Stollen

To make one cake 12 inches [30 cm.] long

½ cup	diced mixed candied fruit	125 ml.
¼ cup	golden raisins	50 ml.
¼ cup	dried currants	50 ml.
2 tbsp.	candied citron	30 ml.
3 tbsp.	rum	45 ml.
¼ oz.	package active dry yeast	7½ g.
⅓ cup plus 1 tsp.	granulated sugar	80 ml.
2 tbsp.	tepid water	30 ml.
⅓ cup	milk	75 ml.
6 tbsp.	unsalted butter	90 ml.
½ tsp.	salt	2 ml.
2¾ to 3 cups	flour	650 to 700 ml.
1	egg, plus 1 egg yolk, lightly beaten	1
1 tsp.	grated lemon peel	5 ml.
⅓ cup	almonds, blanched, peeled and chopped	75 ml.
4 tbsp.	melted butter	60 ml.
	confectioners' sugar	

In a bowl, combine the mixed fruit, raisins, dried currants, citron and rum. Toss the fruits and let them stand for one hour. Drain the fruits, reserving the liquid.

In a small bowl, soften the yeast with 1 tsp. [5 ml.] of the sugar in the tepid water for 10 minutes. Heat the milk with the butter, the ⅓ cup [75 ml.] of sugar and the salt until the butter melts and the sugar dissolves. Let the mixture cool until lukewarm.

In a large bowl, combine 2½ cups [625 ml.] of the flour with the milk mixture, yeast, whole egg, egg yolk, rum and lemon peel. Mix the ingredients well to form a dough.

Turn the dough onto a lightly floured board and knead for 10 minutes, adding 1 to 2 tablespoons [15 to 30 ml.] flour, if necessary, to produce a smooth and elastic dough. Toss the fruits and the almonds with 1½ tablespoons [22.5 ml.] of the flour. Knead these ingredients into the dough, a little at a time, until they are evenly distributed.

Place the dough in a large, buttered bowl, and turn so that it is lightly coated with butter. Cover the bowl with a towel and let the dough rise in a warm place for two hours, or until it has doubled in bulk. Turn the dough onto a lightly floured board and punch it down with a lightly floured rolling pin. Roll it into an 8-by-12-inch [20-by-30-cm.] oval.

Brush the dough with 2 tablespoons [30 ml.] of the melted butter. Fold one side lengthwise over the center of the oval and press it down lightly. Fold in the other side, overlapping the first side by 1 inch [2½ cm.], and press the edge down. Transfer the roll, seam-side down, to a buttered baking sheet, cover it with a towel, and let it rise in a warm place for one and one half hours, or until the roll has almost doubled in bulk.

Bake the *Stollen* in a preheated 400° F. [200° C.] oven for 10 minutes, reduce the heat to 350° F. [180° C.], and bake it for 25 to 30 minutes longer, or until it sounds hollow when it is tapped on the bottom. Transfer it to a rack, brush it with the remaining 2 tablespoons of melted butter, and let it cool. When cool, sprinkle with confectioners' sugar.

THE GREAT COOKS' GUIDE TO CAKES

Panettone

This dough may be baked in two 1-quart [1-liter] charlotte molds; in that case, bake the cakes in the bottom third of a preheated 400° F. [200° C.] oven for 10 minutes; reduce the temperature to 350° F. [180° C.] and bake the cakes for 40 minutes longer. If the surfaces of the panettones turn dark brown before baking is completed, cover them with sheets of parchment paper.

To make four 8-inch [20-cm.] cakes

three ¼ oz.	packages active dry yeast	three 7½ g.
¾ cup	tepid water	175 ml.
1¾ cups	sugar	425 ml.
¾ cup	milk	175 ml.
about 10 tbsp.	unsalted butter	about 150 ml.
2½ tsp.	salt	12 ml.
2 tbsp.	grated lemon peel	30 ml.
4 tsp.	vanilla extract	20 ml.
8 cups	flour	2 liters
5	eggs, plus 1 egg, separated	5
⅔ cup	golden raisins, soaked in warm water for 15 minutes, drained and squeezed dry	150 ml.
½ cup	candied citron, cut in slivers	125 ml.
1 tsp.	sugar mixed with 1 tsp. [5 ml.] water	5 ml.

Mix the yeast into the tepid water in a quart jar along with 2 tablespoons [30 ml.] of the sugar. Let the mixture stand in a warm place for 10 minutes, or until it has nearly tripled its original bulk.

Scald the milk; add 8 tablespoons [120 ml.] of the butter and stir until the butter has melted, then add the salt and the rest of the sugar. Transfer the milk-butter mixture to a large bowl. Stir in the lemon peel and the vanilla extract, and let the mixture cool for a few moments.

With a hand-held electric mixer or a dough hook, beat in 2 cups [½ liter] of the flour. Beat in the yeast mixture. Beat in another 2 cups flour, the five whole eggs, one by one, and the white of the sixth egg. Beat until smooth.

If you are not using a dough hook, put aside the mixer and begin working the mixture with a wooden spoon: Add 3 more cups [¾ liter] of the flour and mix until the resulting dough becomes unwieldy.

Scoop the dough out onto a floured work surface and add ½ cup [125 ml.] of the flour. Knead with your hands, adding more flour until all the remaining flour is absorbed. The dough will now be soft, elastic, smooth and still a bit sticky.

Place the dough in an oiled 3-quart [3-liter] or larger bowl, and twirl the dough around until it glistens with oil. Cover the bowl with a dry dish towel, and place in a warm corner until it rises to nearly three times its original bulk—three to four hours.

When the dough has risen, punch it down and knead in the raisins and citron. Cut the dough into four equal parts.

Butter four casseroles or soufflé dishes. Fix a collar of double-folded and buttered aluminum foil around the inside of each dish. Put a piece of dough in each pan, mark a cross in the center of the dough with a sharp knife, and put the pans back into the same warm place. Cover all four vessels with a dish towel. Let the dough rise until more than doubled in size—a little more than an hour should do.

Mix the yolk of the last egg with the sugar-and-water solution until smooth, and brush the tops of the panettones with the mixture.

Bake in a preheated 400° F. [200° C.] oven for 10 minutes. Put ½ tablespoon [7 ml.] of butter in the center of each cross, lower the heat to 375° F. [190° C.], and bake for 10 more minutes. Lower the heat to 350° F. [170° C.], and bake 30 minutes longer, or until the panettones are crusty and golden brown on top and a cake tester comes out clean after being inserted in the centers of the cakes.

Cool the cakes completely before removing from pans. Let stand for a day before cutting.

MARGARET AND G. FRANCO ROMAGNOLI
THE NEW ITALIAN COOKING

161

Moravian Sugar Cake

To make two 11-by-16-inch [28-by-40-cm.] cakes

2 cups	water	½ liter
2	medium-sized boiling potatoes, peeled and quartered	2
½ lb.	butter, cut into ½-inch [1-cm.] bits	¼ kg.
¼ oz.	package active dry yeast	7½ g.
1 cup plus 1 tsp.	granulated sugar	255 ml.
about 6½ cups	unsifted flour	about 1½ liters
1 tsp.	salt	5 ml.
2	eggs	2
2¼ cups	light brown sugar	550 ml.
2 tsp.	ground cinnamon	10 ml.

Bring the water to a boil in a small, heavy saucepan, drop in the potatoes, and boil briskly, uncovered, until they can be easily mashed against the side of the pan with the back of a fork. Drain the potatoes in a sieve set over a bowl, pat them dry with paper towels, and return them to the pan. Measure and reserve 1 cup [¼ liter] of the potato water.

Mash the potatoes to a smooth purée with the back of a fork. (You should have 1 cup of purée.) Beat in half the butter bits and cover the pan to keep the purée warm.

When the reserved potato water has cooled until tepid (110° to 115° F. [42° to 45° C.]), pour ¼ cup [50 ml.] of it into a shallow bowl. Add the yeast and 1 teaspoon [5 ml.] of the granulated sugar. Let the mixture stand for two or three minutes, then stir well. Set the bowl in a warm, draft-free place for about five minutes, or until the yeast bubbles up and the mixture almost doubles in volume.

Combine 6 cups [1½ liters] of flour, the remaining granulated sugar and the salt in a deep mixing bowl; make a well in the center. Add the potato purée, the yeast mixture, the eggs and the remaining potato water. With a large spoon, mix the ingredients together, and stir until the dough is smooth and can be gathered into a soft ball. Place the ball on a lightly floured surface and knead it, pushing the dough down with the heels of your hands, pressing it forward, and folding it back on itself. As you knead, sprinkle additional flour over the ball, 1 tablespoon [15 ml.] at a time, to make a firm dough. Continue to knead for about 10 minutes, or until the dough is smooth, shiny and elastic; gather it into a ball.

Place the ball in a deep, buttered mixing bowl, and turn it around to butter the entire surface of the dough. Drape the bowl loosely with a kitchen towel and put it in the draft-free place for about one and one half hours, or until the dough has doubled in bulk.

Punch the dough down with a single blow of your fist and divide it in half. On a lightly floured surface, roll each half into an 11-by-16-inch [28-by-40-cm.] rectangle, about ½

inch [1 cm.] thick. Place the rectangles in two buttered jelly-roll pans and set them aside in the draft-free place to rise again for about 45 minutes, or until doubled in bulk.

Stir the brown sugar and cinnamon together in a bowl. With your forefinger, make parallel rows of small indentations in the top of each cake, spacing the indentations about 1½ inches [4 cm.] apart and pressing down almost to the bottom of the pan. Drop the remaining butter bits into the indentations and fill the holes with some of the brown-sugar mixture. Scatter the rest of the brown-sugar mixture over the surface of the cakes, dividing it evenly between them.

Bake the cakes in the middle of a preheated 350° F. [180° C.] oven for 25 to 30 minutes, or until the topping is golden brown and crusty. Transfer the Moravian sugar cakes to a platter and serve them warm or at room temperature.

FOODS OF THE WORLD/AMERICAN COOKING: THE EASTERN HEARTLAND

Mixed-Grain Fruitcake

To make one cake 8 inches [20 cm.] square

three ¼ oz.	packages active dry yeast	three 7½ g.
½ cup	tepid sweet cider	125 ml.
½ cup	honey	125 ml.
½ cup	vegetable oil	125 ml.
3	eggs	3
1 cup	cold sweet cider	¼ liter
1 cup	buckwheat flour	¼ liter
¼ cup	whole-wheat flour	50 ml.
1¾ cups	rye flour	425 ml.
1 tsp.	salt	5 ml.
1 cup	prunes, pitted and chopped	¼ liter
1 cup	dried apricots, chopped	¼ liter
1 cup	raisins, figs or dates, chopped	¼ liter
½ tsp.	anise seeds, crushed	2 ml.
½ cup	sesame seeds, toasted	125 ml.
½ cup	sunflower seeds, hulled	125 ml.

Soften the yeast in the tepid cider. Blend together the honey and oil. One at a time, add the eggs to the honey mixture. Combine the mixture with the softened yeast and the cold cider. Stir in the flours and the salt. Mix the fruits and the seeds, and blend thoroughly with the batter. Turn the mixture into a buttered pan. Cover the pan, and set it in a warm place until the dough has risen slightly; then bake the cake at 350° F. [180° C.] for about one hour, until the cake begins to shrink from the sides of the pan.

BEATRICE TRUM HUNTER
THE NATURAL FOODS COOKBOOK

Greek Anise Cake
Peta

Masticha is an anise-flavored liqueur made from mastic, the small crystals of a resinous shrub grown chiefly on the Greek island of Chios. It can be bought in stores where Greek specialty foods are sold. Another anise-flavored liqueur such as ouzo may be substituted for the masticha.

To make two 9-inch [23-cm.] cakes

two 1/4 oz.	packages active dry yeast or two 3/5 oz. [18 g.] cakes fresh yeast	two 7 1/2 g.
1/4 cup	tepid water	50 ml.
14 cups	flour	3 1/2 liters
2 tsp.	baking soda	10 ml.
2 tsp.	ground cinnamon	10 ml.
1 tsp.	masticha	5 ml.
1 lb.	butter, melted and cooled	1/2 kg.
3 1/2 cups	sugar	875 ml.
2 1/2 cups	water	625 ml.
1	egg, beaten	1
	sesame seeds	
	almonds, blanched and peeled	

Soften the yeast in the tepid water. Beat in enough of the flour to make a thin batter, and let the batter rise for about two hours in a draft-free place. In a large mixing bowl combine the remaining flour, the baking soda, cinnamon and *masticha*. Stir in the butter. Dissolve the sugar in the water, and stir the solution into the flour mixture together with the yeast. Turn the dough out onto a lightly floured board and knead until it is smooth and elastic. Put the dough into a buttered bowl, cover, and let the dough rise in a warm place for about one and one half hours, or until doubled in bulk.

Divide the dough in half. Mold the halves into cakes and put the cakes into oiled pans 3 inches [8 cm.] deep. Cover each pan with a towel, and again let the dough rise until doubled in bulk. Brush the tops of the risen dough with beaten egg, sprinkle with sesame seeds, and decorate with almonds. Press the cakes around the edges with the tines of a fork to give a fluted effect. Cover the tops of the cakes with parchment paper or foil to prevent them from overbrowning and place them in a preheated 350° F. [180° C.] oven. After half an hour of baking, remove the parchment paper or foil. Bake half an hour more, or until golden.

ST. PAUL'S GREEK ORTHODOX CHURCH
THE ART OF GREEK COOKERY

Sweet Carnival Cake
Schiacciata Unta di Berlingaccio

This Italian dessert is traditional during the spring festival of Carnival. It is named for the Commedia dell'Arte character Berlingaccio, a fat, red-faced man frequently represented in Carnival parades.

Low like a *schiacciata*, this dessert pastry contains lard and is flavored with orange, vanilla, nutmeg and saffron. It is this last, with the lard, that gives it its antique flavor.

To make one 11-by-16-inch [28-by-40-cm.] cake

1/4 oz.	package active dry yeast or 3/5 oz. [18 g.] cake fresh yeast	7 1/2 g.
1 cup	tepid water	1/4 liter
2 1/3 cups	flour	575 ml.
	salt	
2 tbsp.	grated orange peel	30 ml.
1 tsp.	ground saffron	5 ml.
	vanilla extract	
	grated nutmeg	
2	eggs	2
2/3 cup	sugar	150 ml.
3/4 cup	lard	175 ml.
	confectioners' sugar	

In a small bowl, mix the yeast into the water. Put 2 cups [1/2 liter] of the flour and a pinch of salt in a large bowl. Make a well in the center and put in the yeast mixture. Stir the yeast mixture with a wooden spoon, gradually incorporating half of the surrounding flour.

Cover the bowl with a dish towel and let it rest in a warm place until the mixture—called a sponge—foams and doubles in size, about one hour. While the sponge is rising, put orange peel into a small bowl and add the saffron, a few drops of vanilla extract, a pinch of nutmeg, the eggs and the sugar; mix very well with a wooden spoon.

Melt all but 1 tablespoon [15 ml.] of the lard in a saucepan, then remove the pan from the heat and let the lard stand for 10 to 12 minutes, until lukewarm. When the sponge has risen, add the orange-peel mixture to it and stir with a wooden spoon until all the ingredients are well amalgamated. Add the lukewarm lard and keep stirring, using a motion pushing up from the bottom rather than a rotary one.

Add the remaining flour a little at a time, incorporating each addition before stirring in the next. Continue to mix, using the method described, for 10 minutes more. The resulting dough will have the consistency of a very thick batter.

Grease a jelly-roll pan with the remaining lard. Pour the dough into the pan, cover it with a dish towel and let it rise until it has almost doubled in size, about one hour.

When the dough has risen, place the pan in a preheated 400° F. [200° C.] oven; bake for 35 minutes, then remove the cake from the oven and let it cool. Sprinkle the cake with confectioners' sugar before serving.

GIULIANO BUGIALLI
THE FINE ART OF ITALIAN COOKING

Standard Preparations

Sugar Syrup

Sugar syrup boiled to the small-thread stage *(page 9, Step 2)* is used for rich butter cream and to thin fondant icing; sugar syrup boiled to the soft-ball stage *(page 9, Step 3)* is used for boiled icing and to make fondant.

For fruit-flavored sugar syrup, substitute ¼ cup [50 ml.] of strained fresh lemon or orange juice for ¼ cup of the water. To flavor sugar syrup with extracts or liqueurs, stir the flavoring in after the syrup has been removed from the heat.

To make about 2 cups [½ liter] syrup

2 cups	sugar	½ liter
1 cup	water	¼ liter

Stir the sugar and water together in a deep, heavy saucepan set over medium heat until the sugar dissolves. During this period, use a dampened pastry brush to wipe down any stray sugar crystals that cling to the sides of the pan.

When the sugar has dissolved, bring the syrup to a boil. It is now ready for use for poaching fruit or for brushing on cakes. For more condensed syrups, place a candy thermometer in the pan and boil the syrup without stirring until it reaches the required temperature: 217° to 220° F. [103° to 105° C.] for the small-thread stage or 234° to 240° F. [112° to 116° C.] for the soft-ball stage. To make caramel, continue to boil the syrup until it is golden brown—345° F. [173° C.] on a candy thermometer.

As soon as the syrup reaches the required temperature, remove the pan from the heat and briefly dip its base in ice water to arrest the cooking.

Fondant Icing

To flavor melted fondant icing, stir in 1 tablespoon [15 ml.] of flavoring extract, liqueur or strong black coffee; for chocolate fondant, stir in 3 tablespoons [45 ml.] of grated unsweetened chocolate. You can add nuts, freshly grated coconut or candied fruits in amounts equal to the amount of fondant. Food colorings may be added, a small amount at a time, in the same manner as liquid flavorings.

To make about 2 cups [½ liter] icing

2 cups	sugar	½ liter
⅔ cup	water	150 ml.
	cream of tartar	
¼ to ½ cup	sugar syrup *(recipe, above)*, cooked to the small-thread stage	50 to 125 ml.

In a saucepan set over medium heat, stir the sugar and water together until the sugar dissolves. Stir in a pinch of cream of tartar and bring the syrup to a boil. Let it boil without stirring until its temperature reaches 238° F. [115° C.] on a candy thermometer—the soft-ball stage. Immediately pour the syrup out onto a cool, oiled marble slab or baking sheet. Let it cool and thicken a few moments, then fold the pool of syrup over on itself several times, using a pastry scraper. When the syrup is cool enough to handle, knead it well with your hands until it is stiff, smooth and opaque.

The fondant thus formed may be placed in an airtight container and stored in the refrigerator for several months. To make the fondant into icing, place it in a bowl, set the bowl in a pan of hot water and place the pan over low heat. When the fondant begins to melt, thin it with the small-thread-stage sugar syrup, stirring until the mixture has the consistency of thick cream; then add the food coloring or flavoring desired.

Boiled Icing

To make coffee-flavored icing, add 2 tablespoons [30 ml.] of instant-coffee crystals to the sugar syrup before pouring it into the egg whites. To make fruit-flavored icing, substitute fruit juice for all or part of the water in the sugar syrup and eliminate the vanilla extract. To make liqueur-flavored icing, substitute liqueur to taste for the vanilla extract. To make chocolate-flavored icing, melt 1 to 2 ounces [30 to 60 g.] of unsweetened chocolate in a double boiler over hot water; let the chocolate cool slightly, then fold it into the prepared icing. To color the icing, add food coloring by the drop until the desired color is achieved.

To make about 2 cups [½ liter] icing

2 cups	sugar	½ liter
½ tsp.	strained fresh lemon juice	2 ml.
¾ cup	water	175 ml.
2	egg whites, stiffly beaten	2
1 tsp.	vanilla extract	5 ml.

Combine the sugar, water and lemon juice in a saucepan set over medium heat. Stir the mixture until the sugar dissolves and the liquid comes to a boil. Boil the mixture without stirring until its temperature reaches 234° to 240° F. [112° to 116° C.] on a candy thermometer—the soft-ball stage. Cover the saucepan and cook the syrup for three minutes. Cool it slightly, then very slowly beat it into the beaten egg whites. Add the vanilla extract and beat until the icing is cool.

Seven-Minute Icing

For fruit-flavored seven-minute icing, substitute strained fresh fruit juice for part or all of the water, according to taste. To flavor the icing, you may also substitute praline powder, strong black coffee, brandy or liqueur to taste for the vanilla extract. To color the icing, add food coloring by the drop until the desired color is achieved.

To make about 2 cups [½ liter] icing

1¼ cups	sugar	300 ml.
¼ cup	water	50 ml.
2	egg whites	2
2 tsp.	corn syrup	10 ml.
	salt	
1 tsp.	vanilla extract	5 ml.

Combine the sugar, water, egg whites, corn syrup and a pinch of salt in the top of a double boiler over hot water. Beating constantly, cook the mixture for seven minutes, until it forms soft peaks. Remove the mixture from the heat and stir in the vanilla extract. Beat the icing for three to five minutes longer, until it forms stiff peaks and is tepid.

Royal Icing

This icing may be stored for a week in the refrigerator; press a layer of plastic wrap against the surface of the icing to prevent a crust from forming, then cover the container. The icing can be colored with a small amount of food coloring, but it cannot be flavored.

To make about 2½ cups [625 ml.] icing

3½ cups	confectioners' sugar	875 ml.
3	egg whites	3
1 tbsp.	strained fresh lemon juice	15 ml.

Beat 2 cups [½ liter] of the sugar, the egg whites and lemon juice together for about 10 minutes, or until the mixture is smooth and white and stands in soft peaks. Add the remaining sugar and continue to beat until the mixture is stiff.

Glacé Icing

For fruit-flavored icing, replace the water with strained fresh fruit juice. To make coffee-flavored icing replace the water with strong black coffee. Once it is made, plain glacé icing may be flavored to taste with vanilla, almond or peppermint extract, or with a liqueur. Liqueur must be added in larger amounts than more concentrated extracts; if you use liqueur, reduce the amount of water used in the icing by about 1 tablespoon [15 ml.]. For chocolate-flavored icing,

melt 2 ounces [60 g.] of semisweet chocolate in the top of a double boiler over hot water. Let the chocolate cool slightly, then stir it into the prepared icing.

To make about 1 cup [¼ liter] icing

2 cups	sifted confectioners' sugar	½ liter
2 tbsp.	warm water	30 ml.

Stir the warm water and the confectioners' sugar together until the sugar dissolves completely and the icing is smooth. The icing should be thick enough to coat the back of a spoon. If it is too thick, add more liquid; if too thin, add a little sugar. The icing should be used at once.

Thin Chocolate Icing

Thin chocolate icing may be whipped until it is almost doubled in volume. Both types of icing should be used as soon as they are made; otherwise they harden and become impossible to spread. If this should happen, thin chocolate icing may be reheated to liquefy it; whipped frosting must be melted over low heat, chilled, and whipped again.

To make about 2 cups [½ liter] unwhipped icing

8 oz.	semisweet chocolate	¼ kg.
1 cup	heavy cream	¼ liter

Combine the chocolate and the cream in a saucepan and set the pan over medium heat. Stirring constantly, cook the mixture until the chocolate melts and the liquid comes to a boil. Remove the pan from the heat and let the mixture cool slightly before using. If you wish to make whipped chocolate frosting, chill the mixture for one hour before whipping.

Thick Chocolate Icing

Thick chocolate icing may be whipped until it is almost doubled in volume. Both types of icing should be used as soon as they are made; otherwise they harden and become impossible to spread. If this should happen, thick chocolate icing may be reheated to liquefy it; whipped frosting must be melted over low heat, chilled, and whipped again.

To make about 2 cups [½ liter] unwhipped icing

½ lb.	semisweet chocolate	¼ kg.
½ lb.	unsalted butter, softened	¼ kg.

Melt the chocolate in the top of a double boiler over hot water. When the chocolate is soft, add the butter. Swirl the butter and chocolate until they are completely dissolved and all lumps have disappeared. Let the icing cool slightly before pouring it over the cake. To make whipped chocolate frosting, chill the mixture for one hour, then whip it until it has doubled in volume.

Fudge Frosting

This recipe is for chocolate-flavored fudge frosting. To make caramel-flavored fudge frosting, use 1 cup [¼ liter] of granulated sugar and 1 cup of dark brown sugar, and eliminate the chocolate.

To make about 3 cups [¾ liter] frosting

2 cups	sugar	½ liter
½ cup	milk	125 ml.
2 tbsp.	butter, softened	30 ml.
3 oz.	semisweet chocolate, grated	90 g.
1 tsp.	vanilla extract	5 ml.

Put the sugar, milk, butter and grated chocolate into a saucepan and, stirring constantly, cook over low heat until the sugar has dissolved and the chocolate has completely melted. Do not allow the mixture to come to a boil. When the mixture is well blended, increase the heat and boil until its temperature reaches 234° to 240° F. [112° to 116° C.] on a candy thermometer—the soft-ball stage. Remove the fudge from the heat, let it cool for five minutes, then stir in the vanilla extract and beat the fudge until its surface is not shiny and it is cool enough to spread. Use it immediately.

Pastry Cream

To make chocolate pastry cream stir 4 ounces [125 g.] of melted and cooled semisweet chocolate into the finished pastry cream. You may also substitute 3 tablespoons [45 ml.] of rum, brandy or liqueur for the vanilla bean; stir these ingredients into the pastry cream after you remove it from the heat. To flavor the finished cream with coffee, add 2 tablespoons [30 ml.] of instant-coffee crystals that have been dissolved in 2 tablespoons of hot water.

To make about 2 cups [½ liter] pastry cream

½ cup	sugar	125 ml.
5 or 6	egg yolks	5 or 6
⅓ cup	flour	75 ml.
	salt	
2 cups	milk	½ liter
2-inch	piece vanilla bean	5-cm.

Mix the sugar and egg yolks together with a spoon, beating until the mixture is thick and cream-colored. Gradually work in the flour, and season with a pinch of salt.

Heat the milk with the vanilla bean to the boiling point. Stirring constantly, pour the hot milk into the egg mixture in a thin stream. Turn the pastry-cream mixture into a saucepan and, stirring vigorously, cook over medium heat until the mixture comes to the boiling point. Boil for about two minutes. Strain the pastry cream and allow it to cool, stirring occasionally to prevent a skin from forming. The cream may be stored, covered, in a refrigerator for two days.

Simple Butter Cream

To flavor this butter cream, you may replace the vanilla extract with other extracts, cocoa powder, praline powder *(recipe, opposite)*, liqueurs, strong black coffee or fruit juices; add these flavoring agents by teaspoonfuls until the butter cream is flavored to taste. To make a chocolate-flavored butter cream, melt 2 ounces [60 g.] of unsweetened chocolate in the top of a double boiler over hot water. Let the chocolate cool slightly, then fold it into the prepared butter cream. To color butter cream, mix in food coloring in small amounts until the desired color is achieved.

To make about 2 cups [½ liter] butter cream

9 tbsp.	unsalted butter, softened	135 ml.
4½ cups	confectioners' sugar	1,125 ml.
6 tbsp.	light cream	90 ml.
1½ tsp.	vanilla extract	7 ml.

Beat the butter until it is fluffy. Gradually beat the sugar into the butter, alternately with the cream, until the sugar is absorbed. Beat in the vanilla extract. The butter cream should be of spreading consistency. If it is too thin, beat in a little more sugar; if it is too thick, beat in a little more cream.

Rich Butter Cream

This butter cream will be yellow in color. To make ivory butter cream, replace four of the egg yolks with stiffly beaten egg whites. For white butter cream, replace all the egg yolks with stiffly beaten egg whites. To flavor the butter cream, you may substitute praline powder *(recipe, opposite)*, strong black coffee, brandy or liqueur for the vanilla extract. To make chocolate butter cream, melt 3 ounces [90 g.] of unsweetened chocolate in a double boiler over hot water; let the chocolate cool, then fold it into the prepared butter cream.

To make about 2 cups [½ liter] butter cream

1 cup	sugar	¼ liter
½ cup	water	125 ml.
5	egg yolks, beaten	5
½ lb.	butter, softened	¼ kg.
1 tbsp.	vanilla extract	15 ml.

Stir the sugar and water together in a saucepan set over medium heat until the sugar dissolves and the liquid comes to a boil; let this syrup boil, without stirring, until its temperature reaches 234° to 240° F. [112° to 116° C.] on a candy thermometer — the soft-ball stage. Remove the syrup from the heat. Whisking vigorously, pour the hot syrup into the egg yolks and continue to beat until the mixture is cool, light and fluffy. Cream the butter until it is very soft, then beat the butter and the vanilla extract into the yolk mixture until the mixture is shiny and firm enough to spread.

Molding Butter Cream

Molding butter cream is used to make the flower-type cake decorations demonstrated on pages 24-27. To color molding butter cream, add a small amount of food coloring to the butter cream and stir until the color is evenly distributed.

To make about 5 cups [1 1/4 liters] butter cream

1 1/3 cups	vegetable shortening	325 ml.
4 or 5 tbsp.	hot water	60 or 75 ml.
5 cups	confectioners' sugar	1 1/4 liters
1 tsp.	vanilla extract	5 ml.

Beat the vegetable shortening with an electric mixer until it is fluffy. Slowly beat in 4 tablespoons [60 ml.] of the hot water. Beating constantly, add the sugar, 1 cup [1/4 liter] at a time. Add the vanilla extract, and continue beating the mixture until the ingredients are thoroughly blended. The mixture should be the consistency of mashed potatoes; if it is too stiff, beat in the remaining water.

Jam Glaze

To make liqueur-flavored glaze, combine the jam or jelly with 1 tablespoon [15 ml.] of liqueur before melting it. This recipe produces enough glaze to fill and cover the top of a two-layer cake 9 inches [23 cm.] in diameter.

To make about 1 cup [1/4 liter] glaze

1 cup	jelly or jam	1/4 liter

In a saucepan set over medium heat, melt the jelly or jam until it is liquid. Melted jelly can be used immediately. Melted jam should be forced through a fine-meshed sieve to remove any lumps of fruit, and used while it is still liquid.

Meringue

This meringue may be spread on top of a prepared cake; the cake should then be placed in a preheated 375° F. [190° C.] oven for five minutes, until the meringue is a delicate golden brown. If the meringue is made with double the amount of sugar specified, it can be used to pipe decorations, as demonstrated on page 73. The decorations should be baked in a preheated 200° F. [100° C.] oven for three hours, until they are firm and dry.

To make about 2 1/2 cups [625 ml.] meringue

5	egg whites	5
2/3 cup	sugar	150 ml.

Beat the egg whites until soft peaks form, then gradually beat in the sugar. Continue to beat until the ingredients are well blended and the meringue stands in stiff peaks.

Praline Powder

To make about 3 cups [3/4 liter] powder

3/4 lb.	almonds	350 g.
2 cups	sugar	1/2 liter
2/3 cup	water	150 ml.

Spread the nuts on a baking sheet in one layer and warm them in a preheated 350° F. [180° C.] oven for about five minutes. Oil or butter a marble slab or a baking sheet.

In a heavy saucepan over medium heat, dissolve the sugar in the water, stirring constantly. Use a wet pastry brush to brush down any crystals that form on the sides of the pan. As soon as the sugar has dissolved, stop stirring and put a candy thermometer in the pan.

Bring the syrup to a boil over high heat and boil it to a light caramel color—320° to 330° F. [160° to 165° C.] on the candy thermometer. Remove the pan from the heat and dip the base into ice water to stop the cooking.

Immediately add the warmed nuts and gently stir them into the syrup. Pour the mixture onto the oiled or buttered slab or baking sheet, spreading it into a thin, even layer. Let it cool completely, then break it into pieces, put them in a plastic bag and crush them to a powder with a rolling pin. Alternatively, drop the pieces into the bowl of a food processor equipped with a metal blade, and grind them to a powder.

Almond Paste

This paste is used as an ingredient in some cake batters; it also can be rolled out into a sheet and used as a filling between cake layers or as a topping for cakes that are to be given thin coverings, such as royal icing or fondant icing. Rum, brandy or liqueur may be substituted for the vanilla extract. One whole egg or the whites of two eggs may be substituted for the egg yolks. Egg yolk produces a rich, yellow paste; egg white produces a paler, lighter paste. Almond paste may be wrapped in foil and stored in the refrigerator for up to two weeks.

To make about 6 cups [1 1/2 liters] paste

1 1/2 cups	sifted confectioners' sugar	375 ml.
1 1/2 cups	sifted superfine sugar	375 ml.
3/4 lb.	almonds, blanched, peeled and finely ground (about 3 cups [3/4 liter])	350 g.
2 tbsp.	strained fresh lemon juice	30 ml.
1 tsp.	vanilla extract	5 ml.
2	egg yolks, beaten	2

Mix the confectioners' sugar with the superfine sugar and the ground almonds. Stir in the lemon juice and the vanilla extract. Gradually mix in enough egg yolk to make a pliable but dry paste. If the mixture feels sticky add more confectioners' sugar. Knead the mixture thoroughly until smooth.

Recipe Index

All recipes in the index that follows are listed by their English titles except in cases where a food of foreign origin, such as Stollen, is universally recognized by its source name. Entries also are organized by the major ingredients specified in the recipe titles. Foreign recipes are listed by country or region of origin. Recipe credits appear on pages 173-175.

General Index/ Glossary

Included in this index to the cooking demonstrations are definitions, in italics, of special culinary terms not explained elsewhere in this volume. The Recipe Index begins on page 168.

Acid: activating baking soda, 6, 64; in baking powder, 6; in liquid sweeteners, 64; provided by buttermilk or sour milk, 58; tartaric, 6, 56

Almond paste: added to creamed-cake batter, 48, 49, 54-55; breaking up paste with mixer, 54; decorating almond-paste creamed cake, 55; grinding nuts, 18; kneading, 19; layering fruitcake with, 52; rolling out and layering with poundcake to make petits fours, 76

Almonds: blanching to remove inner skins, 18, 19; decorating spongecake, 39; in fruitcake, 52; grinding and kneading to make marzipan, 18-19; ground, in meringue cake, 42; ground, in a torte with chestnuts and rum, 46-47

Altitudes: adjustments for baking at high, 7

Angel food, 32-33; aerating egg whites, 32, 33; cooling upside down, 32; garnishing with fruit, 32, 33, 74; leavened by egg whites, 31, 32; lightness, 32; pans for, 32; sifting ingredients, 32-33; sugar bloom, 33

Angelica: *a native European herb, cultivated mostly for its roots, which are used in producing cordials and liqueurs such as chartreuse, and for its stalks, which are candied in sugar syrup when they are green. Candied angelica is available at most fine grocers.*

Apples: poaching in sugar syrup, 74; in upside-down cake, 62

Apricots: in fruitcake, 52; jam glaze, 53, 54, 55, 67, 75, 76

Assembled cakes: filling a hollowed-out spongecake with blackberries, 74-75; ice-cream cake made with layers of devil's food cake and layers of ice cream, 78-79; layering a butter spongecake filled with fresh fruit and whipped cream, 74-75; petits fours, 76-77; rolled cake, 72-73; wedding cake, 80-84

Baking powder: adjusting for baking at high altitudes, 7; in blended cakes, 62; in chiffon cake, 40; double-acting, 6, 62; as leavening, 6, 49, 56, 62; releasing carbon dioxide, 40, 49, 56, 62

Baking soda: activated by acid, 6, 58, 64; in gingerbread, 64; as leavening, 6, 58, 64

Bananas: decorating a fruit-filled spongecake, 75

Barley flour: *the low-gluten flour of milled barley, available in most health-food stores.*

Barsac: serving with cake, 7

Batter, 7; acid in, 58; angel food, 32; for blended cakes, 61, 62; butter-sponge, 36; chiffon cake, 40; creamed-cake, strengthened by almond paste, 48, 49, 54-55; creamed-cake, working by hand, 50-51; cupcakes, 58; for egg-foam cakes, 31; fruitcake, 52-53; gingerbread, 64; ingredients in, 7; made with large proportion of butter, 49; poundcake, layered with almond paste to create petits fours, 76; reducing amounts of butter and eggs in a layer-cake, 56-57; replacing flour with ground nuts or crumbs, 31, 44, 46; separated-egg spongecake, 34; spongecake baked in sheets, 71; using a mixer, 50; working a batter with almond paste in it, 54; yeast, 66; yeast cake made with low proportion of liquid (savarin), 61, 68

Beerenauslese: serving with cake, 7

Berries: preparing for use as cake filling, 74

Birthday cakes: history of, 6

Blackberries: filling a hollowed-out butter spongecake, 74-75

Blanching: almonds and pistachios, 18, 19

Blended cakes: baking powder in, 62; butter in, 61, 62; eggs, 61, 62; gingerbread, 64-65; leavening, 61, 62; proportions of ingredients, 62; toppings for, 62; upside-down cake, 62-63

Boiled icing: beating hot sugar syrup into egg whites, 8, 10-11; coloring and flavoring, 11; frosting a coconut cake, 56, 57

Borders: decorating tubes for, 21, 22; frosting for, 12, 20; piping with molding butter cream, 22-23; ribbon, 22; shells, 23, 38, 82, 83; stars, 22; two-strand, 22-23; on a wedding cake, 22, 82, 83

Brandy: flavoring sugar syrup, 38; in traditional fruitcake, 52

Bread crumbs: replacing flour in batter, 31, 44

Brown sugar: in gingerbread, 64; glaze for upside-down cake, 63

Bûche de Noël (yule log), 72-73; baking sheet cake, 72; fillings and garnishes, 72; rolling sheet of cake, 72, 73; warming jam for filling, 72

Butter: adjusting amount in recipe for baking at high altitudes, 7; in blended cakes, 61; in butter-cream frosting, 13; creaming, 50-51; inhibiting growth of yeast, 66; in layer-cake batter, 56; making a glaze of butter and chocolate, 14, 15; in poundcake, 50; role of, in batter, 49; in savarins, 66; temperature of, for creaming, 50; unsalted, 7

Butter cream, molding: adding coloring paste to, 13; applying decorations to cake, 24; coloring, 12,

Recipe Credits

The sources for the recipes in this volume are shown below. Page references in parentheses indicate where the recipes appear in the Anthology.

Adam, Hans Karl, *Das Kochbuch aus Schwaben.* © Copyright 1976 by Verlagsteam Wolfgang Hölker. Published by Verlag Wolfgang Hölker, Münster. Translated by permission of Verlag Wolfgang Hölker, Münster(123).

Adams, Charlotte, *The Four Seasons Cookbook.* Copyright © 1971 in all countries of the International Copyright Union by The Ridge Press, Inc. By permission of The Ridge Press and Crown Publishers, Inc.(90).

Anderson, Beth, *Wild Rice for All Seasons Cookbook.* © 1977 Minnehaha Publishing. Published by Minnehaha Publishing, 1977. By permission of Beth Anderson, Minnesota(137).

Andrews, Hope and Frances Kelly, *Maryland's Way.* Copyright © 1966 by Hammond-Harwood House Association. Reprinted by permission of the Hammond-Harwood House Association(109, 120, 135).

Ayrton, Elisabeth, *The Cookery of England.* © Copyright Elisabeth Ayrton, 1974. Published by Penguin Books Ltd., London. By permission of Penguin Books Ltd.(138).

Bartley, Mrs. J., *Indian Cookery General for Young House-Keepers.* Seventh Edition 1935. Eighth Edition 1946. Published by C. Murphy for Thacker & Co., Ltd., Bombay(134).

Bates, Margaret, *Talking about Cakes.* © Copyright 1964 Pergamon Press Ltd. Published by Pergamon Press Ltd. By permission of Pergamon Press Ltd.(114).

Beck, Simone and Michael James, *New Menus from Simca's Cuisine.* © Copyright 1979 by Simone Beck and Michael James. First published in Great Britain 1980 by John Murray, London. By permission of John Murray (Publishers) Ltd.(89, 153).

Bergeron, Victor J., *Trader Vic's Rum Cookery and Drinkery.* © Copyright 1974 by Victor J. Bergeron. Published by Doubleday and Company, Inc., New York, 1974. Reprinted by permission of the Harold Matson Company, Inc., New York(119).

Bertholle, Louisette, *Secrets of the Great French Restaurants.* Copyright © 1974 by Macmillan Publishing Co., Inc. Reprinted by permission of Macmillan Publishing Co., Inc.(86, 101).

Borer, Eva Maria, *Tante Heidi's Swiss Kitchen.* English text copyright © 1965 by Nicholas Kaye Ltd. Published by Kaye and Ward Ltd., London. First published as *Die Echte Schweizer Küche* by Mary Hahns Kochbuchverlag, Berlin W., 1963. By permission of Kaye and Ward Ltd.(98).

Boulestin, X. Marcel, *Simple French Cooking for English Homes.* Published by William Heinemann, Ltd., London 1923. By permission of A. D. Peters and Co., Ltd., Writers' Agents(149).

Bozzi, Ottorina Perna, *Vecchia Milano in Cucina.* © 1975 by Aldo Martello-Giunti Editore, S.p.A. Published by Aldo Martello-Giunti Editore, S.p.A. Translated by permission of Giunti Publishing Group, Florence(155).

British Columbia Women's Institutes, *Adventures in Cooking.* Published by British Columbia Women's Institutes, British Columbia, 1958. By permission of British Columbia Women's Institutes(136, 145).

Břizová, Joza, *The Czechoslovak Cookbook.* Translated and adapted by Adrienna Vahala. Copyright © 1965 by Crown Publishers, Inc. Reprinted by permission of Crown Publishers, Inc.(114, 134).

Brown, Eve, *The Plaza Cookbook.* Copyright © 1972 by Eve Brown. Published by Prentice-Hall, Inc. Reprinted by permission of Prentice-Hall, Inc.(153).

Brown, Marion, *The Southern Cook Book.* Copyright 1951 by The University of North Carolina Press. Published by The University of North Carolina Press, Chapel Hill. Reprinted by permission of The University of North Carolina Press(95, 126).

Bugialli, Giuliano, *The Fine Art of Italian Cooking.* Copyright © by Giuliano Bugialli. Published by Times Books, a division of Quadrangle/The New York Times Book Co., Inc. Reprinted by permission of the publisher(135, 139, 157, 163).

Byron, May, *May Byron's Cake Book.* Published by Hodder and Stoughton Ltd., London. By permission of Hodder and Stoughton Ltd.(117, 128).

Carlton, Jan McBride, *The Old-Fashioned Cookbook.* Copyright © 1975 by Jan McBride Carlton. Reprinted by permission of Holt, Rinehart and Winston, Publishers(140).

Carnacina, Luigi, *Luigi Carnacina Presents Italian Home Cooking.* Copyright © 1972 by Luigi Carnacina. Reprinted by permission of Doubleday & Company, Inc.(106).

Carnacina, Luigi and Vincenzo Buonassisi, *Il Libro della Polenta.* © Di Aldo Martello Editore, Milan. Published by Aldo Martello Editore, Milan, 1967. Translated by permission of Giunti Publishing Group, Florence(130).

Cascante, Maria Del Carmen, *150 Recetas de Dulces de Fácil Preparación.* © Editorial De Vecchi S.A., 1975. Published by Editorial De Vecchi, S.A. Translated by permission of Editorial De Vecchi, S.A.(93).

Chamberlain, Narcisse and Narcissa G. Chamberlain, *The Chamberlain Sampler of American Cooking in Recipes and Pictures.* Copyright © 1961 by Hastings House Publishers, Inc. Reprinted by permission of Hastings House Publishers, Inc.(92, 125).

Cohen, Rona (Editor), *Recipes to Rona.* Copyright © Sherman Distributors. Published by Kitchen Bazaar, Washington, D.C. Reprinted by permission of Sherman Distributors(122).

Comelade, Éliane Thibaut, *La Cuisine Catalane.* Copyright © Éditions CLT J. Lanore. Published by Éditions Jacques Lanore, Paris, 1978. Translated by permission of Éditions Jacques Lanore(92).

Costa, Margaret, *Margaret Costa's Four Seasons Cookery Book.* © Copyright Margaret Costa. First published in Great Britain by Thomas Nelson & Sons Ltd., 1970, also by Sphere Books Ltd., London, 1972, 1976. By permission of Margaret Costa(124, 151).

Cutler, Carol, *The Six-Minute Soufflé and Other Culinary Delights.* Copyright © 1976 by Carol Cutler. Published by Clarkson N. Potter, Inc. By permission of Carol Cutler(112, 141, 144).

Dannenbaum, Julie, *Menus for All Occasions.* © Copyright 1974 by Julie Dannenbaum. Published by Saturday Review Press/E. P. Dutton & Co., Inc., New York. By permission of John Schaffner, Literary Agent, New York(98, 100, 120).

D'Ermo, Dominique, *The Chef's Dessert Cookbook.* Copyright © 1976 by Dominique D'Ermo (New York: Atheneum, 1976). By permission of Atheneum Publishers (122, 125).

Deutrom, Hilda (Editor), *Ceylon Daily News Cookery Book.* Published by Lake House Investments Limited, Publishers, Sri Lanka. By permission of Lake House Investments Limited, Publishers(138).

de Zuliani, Mariù Salvatori, *La Cucina di Versilia e Garfagnana.* © Copyright by Franco Angeli Editore, Milano. Published 1969 by Franco Angeli Editore, Milan. Translated by permission of Franco Angeli Editore(136).

Dmochmowska-Gorska, J., *Domowe Ciasta i Desery.* Copyright © by the author. Originally published by Wydawnictwo "Watra," Warsaw, 1976. Translated by permission of Agencja Autorska, Warsaw, for the author(118).

Duckitt, Hildagonda J., *Hilda's "Where is it?" of Recipes.* Published by Chapman and Hall Ltd., London, 1903. By permission of Associated Books Publishers Ltd., London(105).

Fernie, W. T., *Kitchen Physic: At Hand for the Doctor, and Helpful for Homely Cures.* Published by John Wright and Co., Bristol, 1901. By permission of John Wright and Sons Ltd., Bristol(140).

FitzGibbon, Theodora, *A Taste of Paris.* Copyright © 1974 by Theodora FitzGibbon. Reprinted by permission of Houghton Mifflin Company, Boston(94, 103, 142). *A Taste of Scotland.* Copyright © Theodora FitzGibbon. Reprinted by permission of David Higham Associations, Ltd., London(145).

Foods of the World, *American Cooking: The Eastern Heartland; American Cooking: New England; The Cooking of Vienna's Empire; Pacific and Southeast Asian Cooking.* Copyright © 1971 Time-Life Books Inc.; Copyright © 1970 Time Inc.; Copyright © 1968, 1974 Time-Life Books Inc.; Copyright © 1970 Time Inc. Published by Time-Life Books, Alexandria(95, 110, 133, 162).

The Great Cooks' Guide To Cakes. Copyright © 1977 by Jay Rosengarten. Published by Random House, Inc. (113—Carol Cutler, 141—Emanuel and Madeline Greenberg, 158—Carol Cutler, 160—Bianca Brown).

Guinaudeau-Franc, Zette, *Les Secrets des Fermes en Périgord Noir.* © 1978, Éditions Serg, Paris. Published by Éditions Serg, Paris. Translated by permission of Madame Guinaudeau(122).

Hajková, Mária, *Múčniky.* © Mária Hajková 1974. Published by PRÁCA, Bratislava and Verlag für die Frau, Leipzig. German translation © 1974 by PRÁCA, Bratislava, CSSR and Verlag für die Frau, DDR-701, Leipzig. Translated by permission of PRÁCA, for the author(148).

Hazelton, Nika, *American Home Cooking.* Copyright © 1980 by Nika Hazelton. Published by The Viking Press. Reprinted by permission of Viking Penguin Inc.(137). *I Cook as I Please.* Copyright © by Nika Hazelton. Reprinted by permission of Grosset & Dunlap, Inc., New York(101, 152).

Heller, Edna Eby, *The Art of Pennsylvania Dutch Cooking.* Copyright © 1968 by Edna Eby Heller. Reprinted by permission of Doubleday & Company(128, 141, 142).

Hewitt, Jean, *The New York Times New England Heritage Cookbook.* Reprinted by permission of G. P. Putnam's Sons. Copyright © 1977 by The New York Times Company(111, 112, 124, 146).

Howe, Robin, *Greek Cooking.* Copyright © 1960 by Robin Howe. First published by André Deutsch Ltd. in 1960. Reprinted by permission of the author and Curtis Brown Ltd., London agents(107, 133).

Hunter, Beatrice Trum, *The Natural Foods Cookbook.* Copyright © by Beatrice Trum Hunter. Reprinted by permission of Simon & Schuster, a division of Gulf & Western Corporation(103, 157, 162).

The Junior Charity League of Monroe, Louisiana, *The Cotton Country Collection.* Copyright © 1972, Junior Charity League, Monroe, Louisiana. Published by the Junior Charity League of Monroe, Inc. Reprinted by permission of the publisher(97—Mrs. Wesley Shafto Sr.; 126—Mrs. W. J. Hodge Jr.; 132—Mrs. Cora Feathers).

The Junior League of Dallas, *The Dallas Junior League Cookbook.* Copyright © 1976 by the Junior League of Dallas, Inc. Reprinted by permission of the Junior League of Dallas(104, 109—Mrs. Julius Runge; 120—Mrs. W. T. Slayton).

The Junior League of Fayetteville, *The Carolina Collection.* Copyright © 1978 by the Junior League of Fayetteville, Inc., North Carolina. Published by the Junior League of Fayetteville. By permission of the publisher(107, 114, 147, 155).

The Junior League of Houston, *Houston Junior League Cook Book.* Copyright © 1968 Junior League of Houston, Inc. Reprinted by permission of the Junior League of Houston(151).

Kamman, Madeleine M., *The Making of a Cook.* © Copyright 1971 by Madeleine Kamman. Published by Atheneum Publishers, New York, 1971. By permission of Atheneum Publishers(89, 104, 132). *When French Women Cook.* Copyright © 1976 by Madeleine M. Kamman (New York: Atheneum, 1976). Reprinted by permission of Atheneum Publishers(102, 159).

Keller, Jean, *Les Pâtisseries et les Bonbons.* © Culture, Art, Loisirs 1979. Published by Culture, Art, Loisirs, Paris. Translated by permission of Culture, Art, Loisirs(87, 96).

Kiehnle, Hermine and Maria Hädecke, *Das Neue Kiehnle-Kochbuch.* © Walter Hädecke Verlag. (Vorm. Süddeutsches Verlagshaus) Weil der Stadt, 1960. Published by Walter Hädecke Verlag, Weil der Stadt. Translated by permission of Walter Hädecke Verlag(115, 152).

The Ladies Auxiliary of The Lunenburg Hospital Society, *Dutch Oven.* Published by The Ladies Auxiliary of The Lunenburg Hospital Society, Nova Scotia, 1953. By permission of The Ladies Auxiliary of The Lunenburg Hospital Society(113).

Landon School, *Landon's Favorite Desserts Cookbook.* Copyright © Landon School. Published by Landon School, Bethesda, Maryland. Reprinted by permission of the publishers(91, 105, 107, 117).

Lang, George, *The Cuisine of Hungary.* Copyright © 1971 by George Lang. (New York: Atheneum). Reprinted by permission of Atheneum Publishers(160).

Langseth-Christensen, Lillian, *Voyage Gastonomique.* Copyright © 1973 by Lillian Langseth-Christensen. Reprinted by permission of McIntosh and Otis, Inc., New York(114, 132).

Lenôtre, Gaston, *Lenôtre's Desserts and Pastries.* Copyright © 1977. Reprinted with the permission of Barron's Educational Series, Inc., Woodbury, New York(117).

Lewis, Edna and Evangeline Peterson, *The Edna Lewis Cookbook.* Copyright © 1972, by Edna Lewis and Evangeline Peterson. Reprinted by permission of the publisher, The Bobbs-Merrill Company, Inc.(108, 134, 158).

Leyel, Mrs. C. F., *Cakes of England.* First published by George Routledge and Sons, Ltd., London, 1936. By permission of Routledge and Kegan Paul Ltd., London(131).

López, Candido, *El Libro de Oro de la Gastronomía.* © 1979 by Candido López. Published by Plaza & Janes S.A., Barcelona. Translated by permission of Plaza & Janes S.A.(126, 131, 139).

McCormick's Spices of the World Cookbook. Copyright © 1964 by McCormick & Company, Inc. Published by McGraw-Hill Book Company. Reprinted by permission of McGraw-Hill Book Company(110, 140).

McCully, Helen, Jacques Pépin and William Jayme, *The Other Half of the Egg.* Copyright © 1967 by M. Barrows & Company, Inc. Reprinted by permission of William Morrow & Company, Inc.(93, 104).

Mann, Gertrude, *A Book of Cakes.* © Gertrude Mann, 1957. Published 1957 by André Deutsch Limited, London. By permission of André Deutsch Limited(129, 130).

Manning, Elise W., *Farm Journal's Complete Home Baking Book.* Copyright © 1979 Farm Journal, Inc. Reprinted by permission of Farm Journal, Inc.(123, 143, 147).

Mathiot, Ginette, *Je Sais Faire la Pâtisserie.* © Albin Michel, 1938, 1966. Published by Éditions Albin Michel, Paris. Translated by permission of Éditions Albin Michel(103,149).

Miller, Gloria Bley, *The Thousand Recipe Chinese Cookbook.* Copyright © by Gloria Bley Miller. Published by Grosset & Dunlap, Inc. Reprinted by permission of the author(93).

Moore-Betty, Maurice, *The Maurice Moore-Betty Cooking School Book of Fine Cooking.* Copyright © by Maurice Moore-Betty. Published by Arbor House Publishing Co., Inc. New York. Reprinted by permission of Maurice Moore-Betty(119, 148).

Murray, Freda, *Lacock Tea Time Recipes.* Published by Freda Murray. Edited by Peter Murray (Ed. RIBA Journal). By permission of Freda Murray(144).

Näslund, Görel Kristina, *Swedish Baking.* © Copyright ICA-Förlaget 1973, Västerås, Sweden. Published by ICA-Förlaget Västerås. By permission of ICA-Förlaget AB(91, 97).

Nathan, Joan, *The Jewish Holiday Kitchen.* Copyright © 1979 by Schocken Books, Inc. Published by Schocken Books, New York. Reprinted by permission of the publisher(102, 115, 148, 156).

Norberg, Inga, *Good Food from Sweden.* First published by Chatto and Windus, London, 1935. By permission of Curtis Brown Ltd., London(87).

Nouveau Manuel de la Cuisinière Bourgeoise et Économique. Published by Bernardin-Béchet, Libraire, Paris, 1868(132).

O'Connor, Hyla, *The Early American Cookbook.* Copyright © 1974 by Alan Landsburg Productions, Inc. Published by Prentice-Hall, Inc. Reprinted by permission of the publisher(118, 144).

Oliver, Raymond, *La Cuisine: Secrets of Modern French Cooking.* Translated and edited by Nika Standen Hazelton with Jack Van Bibber. Copyright © 1969 by Tudor Publishing Company, New York. Reprinted by permission of Leon Amiel, Publisher(150).

Paddleford, Clementine, *The Best in American Cooking.* Copyright © 1960, 1970 by Chase Manhattan Bank, Executors for the Estate of Clementine Paddleford (New York: Charles Scribner's Sons, 1970). Reprinted by permission of Charles Scribner's Sons(113, 121).

Pascoe, Ann, *Cornish Recipes Old and New.* Published by Tor Mark Press, a Division of D. Bradford Barton Ltd., Truro. By permission of Tor Mark Press(139).

Peck, Paula, *The Art of Fine Baking.* © Copyright 1961 by Paula Peck. Published by Simon & Schuster, a Division of Gulf & Western Corporation. By permission of John Schaffner Agency, Literary Agent, New York(154). *Paula Peck's Art of Good Cooking.* Copyright © 1961, 1966 by Paula Peck. Published by Simon & Schuster, a Division of Gulf & Western Corporation, New York. Reprinted by permission of the publisher(105).

Pellaprat, Henri Paul, *The Great Book of French Cuisine.* Copyright © 1966, 1971 by Rene Kramer Publishers, Castagnola/Lugano, Switzerland. Reprinted by permission of Harper & Row, Publishers, Inc.(90, 108, 116, 157).

Pépin, Jacques, *A French Chef Cooks at Home.* Copyright © 1975 by Jacques Pépin. Published by Simon & Schuster, a division of Gulf & Western Corporation. Reprinted by permission of the publisher(87, 150).

Les Petits Plats et les Grands. © 1977 by Éditions Denoël, Paris. Published by Éditions Denoël Sarl, Paris. Translated by permission of Éditions Denoël Sarl(149).

The Pillsbury Family Cook Book. Copyright © 1963 by The Pillsbury Company. Reprinted by permission of Harper & Row, Publishers, Inc.(118, 145).

Platt, June, *June Platt's New England Cook Book.* © 1971 by June Platt. Published by Atheneum Publishers, New York, 1971. By permission of Atheneum Publishers(146).

Point, Fernand, *Ma Gastronomie.* Translated and adapted by Frank Kulla and Patricia Shannon Kulla. English language edition © 1974, Lyceum Books, Inc., Wilton,

Connecticut. Published by Lyceum Books, Inc., Wilton, Connecticut. Translated by permission of Lyceum Books, Inc.(88, 147).

Read, Miss, *Miss Read's Country Cooking.* © 1969 by Miss Read. Published by Michael Joseph Ltd., London, 1969. By permission of Michael Joseph Ltd., for the author(106).

Reich, Lilly Joss, *The Viennese Pastry Cookbook.* Copyright © 1970 by Lilly Joss Reich. Published by Macmillan Publishing Co., Inc. Reprinted by permission of Macmillan Publishing Co., Inc.(96, 99, 154).

Romagnoli, Margaret and G. Franco, *The New Italian Cooking.* Copyright © by Margaret and G. Franco Romagnoli. Reprinted by permission of Little, Brown and Company in association with the Atlantic Monthly Press(161).

Rombauer, Irma S. and Marion Rombauer Becker, *The Joy of Cooking.* Copyright © 1931, 1936, 1941, 1942, 1943, 1946, 1951, 1952, 1953, 1962, 1963, 1964, 1975 by the Bobbs-Merrill Company, Inc. Published by the Bobbs-Merrill Company, Inc., Indianapolis/New York 1975. Reprinted from the 1975 edition by permission of the publisher(86).

St. Paul's Greek Orthodox Church, The Women of, *The Art of Greek Cookery.* Copyright © 1961, 1963 by St. Paul's Greek Orthodox Church of Hempstead, New York. Reprinted by permission of Doubleday & Company, Inc.(101, 163).

St. Stephen's Episcopal Church, *Bayou Cuisine.* Copyright © 1970 St. Stephen's Episcopal Church. Reprinted by permission of St. Stephen's Episcopal Church, Indianola, Mississippi(97, 116, 128).

Savarin, Mme. Jeanne (Editor), *La Cuisine des Familles* (Magazine), No. 24, December 3, 1905(100).

Schuler, Elizabeth, *Mein Kochbuch.* Copyright © 1948 by Schuler-Verlag, Stuttgart-N, Lenzhalde 28. Published by Schuler Verlagsgesellschaft, Stuttgart. Translated by permission of Schuler Verlagsgesellschaft mbH(154).

Seranne, Ann, *The Complete Book of Desserts.* Copyright © 1963 by Ann Seranne. Reprinted by permission of Doubleday & Company, Inc.(88).

The Settlement Cook Book. Copyright © 1965, 1976 by the Settlement Cook Book Co. Published by Simon & Schuster, New York. Reprinted by permission of Simon & Schuster, a Division of Gulf & Western Corporation(103).

La Société St. Thomas d'Aquin, *La Cuisine Acadienne (Acadian Cuisine).* Published by La Société St. Thomas d'Aquin, Succursale de Charlottetown, Île-du-Prince Edouard, Canada. Translated by permission of La Société St. Thomas d'Aquin(143).

Southern Railway Ladies Club Cookbook. Published by the Southern Company for the Southern Railway Ladies Clubs. By permission of the publisher(105—Beulah Shelley).

Stockli, Albert, *Splendid Fare: The Albert Stockli Cookbook.* Copyright © 1970 by Albert Stockli, Inc. Published by Alfred A. Knopf, Inc., New York. By permission of Alfred A. Knopf, Inc.(99).

Sultan, William J., *Modern Pastry Chef,* Vol. 1. Copyright © 1977 by The AVI Publishing Company, Inc., Westport, Connecticut. Reprinted by permission of AVI Publishing Company(94).

Taylor, Margaret and Frances McNaught, *The Early Canadian Galt Cook Book.* Copyright © by Coles Publishing Company. Reprinted by permission of Coles Publishing Co., Ltd., Toronto(109).

Theoharous, Anne, *Cooking the Greek Way.* © Copyright 1977 by Anne Theoharous. Published in Great Britain 1979 by Methuen Paperbacks Ltd., London. First published as *Cooking and Baking the Greek Way* by Holt, Rinehart and Winston, Inc., New York. By permission of Methuen Paperbacks Ltd., and Holt, Rinehart and Winston, Inc.(146).

Tibbot, S. Minwel, *Welsh Fare.* © National Museum of Wales (Welsh Folk Museum). Published by the National Museum of Wales (Welsh Folk Museum) Cardiff, 1976. By permission of the National Museum of Wales (131).

Tita, Dona, *Receitas Experimentadas.* 8th Edition. Published by Editôra e Encadernadora Lumen Ltda., Sao Paulo. Translated by permission of Editôra Rideel Ltda., Sao Paulo(155).

Toklas, Alice B., *The Alice B. Toklas Cookbook.* Copyright © 1954 by Alice B. Toklas. Reprinted by permission of Harper & Row, Publishers, Inc.(127).

Tracy, Marian (Editor), *Favorite American Regional Recipes by Leading Food Editors.* Copyright © 1952 by Indiana University Press. Published 1976 by Dover Publications, Inc. Reprinted by permission of the publisher(127).

Tschirky, Oscar, *The Cook Book by "Oscar" of the Waldorf.* Copyright 1896 by Oscar Tschirky. Published by The Werner Company, New York(142).

Volpicelli, Luigi and Secondino Freda, *L'Antiartusi: 1,000 Ricette.* © 1978 Pan Editrice, Milan. Published by Pan Editrice, Milan. Translated by permission of Pan Editrice(130, 136).

von Zobeltitz, Martha, *Das Kasserol: Absonderliche Gaumenletzen aus aller Zeit.* © by Albert Langen-Georg Müller Verlag München. Published by Albert Langen-Georg Müller Verlag, Munich 1923. Translated by permission of Albert Langen-Georg Müller Verlag GmbH(150).

Willan, Anne, *La Varenne's Paris Kitchen.* Copyright © 1981 by La Varenne U.S.A., Inc. Reprinted by permission of William Morrow & Co.(94).

Willinsky, Grete, *Kulinarische Weltreise.* © by Mary Hahns Kochbuchverlag, Berlin W. Published by Bûchergilde Gutenberg Frankfurt. Translated by permission of Mary Hahns Kochbuchverlag(129).

Wolcott, Imogene, *The Yankee Cook Book.* Copyright 1939, © 1963 by Imogene Wolcott. Published 1963 by Ives Washburn, Inc., New York(127).

Zenker, Hazel G., *Cake Bakery.* Copyright © 1973 by Hazel G. Zenker. Reprinted by permission of the publisher, M. Evans and Company, Inc., New York(86, 91, 92, 106).

Żerańska, Alina, *The Art of Polish Cooking.* Copyright © 1968 by Alina Żerańska. Reprinted by permission of Doubleday & Company, Inc.(99, 111, 159).

Acknowledgments

The indexes for this book were prepared by Louise W. Hedberg. The editors are particularly indebted to Jacqueline Cattani, Bethesda, Maryland; Barbara Jo Davis, Betty Crocker Food & Nutrition Center, Minneapolis, Minnesota; John De Keizer, Kitchens of Sara Lee, Deerfield, Illinois; Gail Duff, Kent, England; Ann O'Sullivan, Majorca, Spain; Jean Reynolds, London; Fran Wheat, Fran's Cake and Candy Supplies, Annandale, Virginia.

The editors also wish to thank: Julie Bailey, London; Caroline Baum, Yorkshire, England; JeanMarie Brownson, Chicago Tribune, Chicago; Sarah Bunney, London; Dr. M. Burge, Wendy Godfrey, Tate & Lyle, London; Marisa Centis, London; Joanne Cooper, Cheryl Reitz, Hershey Foods Technical Center, Hershey, Pennsylvania; Jennifer Davison, London; Marlene Di Cola, Marlene's Cake & Party Supplies, Alexandria, Virginia; Neyla Freeman, London; Maggie Heinz, London; Marion Hunter, Surrey, England; Frederica L. Huxley, London; Brenda Jayes, London; Maria Johnson, Hertfordshire, England; Wanda Kemp-Welch, Nottingham, England; Dr. N. Knowles, British Egg Information Service, London; Mary Jane Law, American Dairy Association, Rosemont, Illinois; Mrs. B. Morrison, Ranks Hovis McDougall Ltd., London; Dilys Naylor, Surrey, England; Jo Oxley, Surrey, England; Robert Rodriguez, American Institute of Baking, Manhattan, Kansas; Amy Rohr, Wilton Enterprises, Woodridge, Illinois; Michael Schwab, London; Cynthia A. Sheppard, London; Dr. R. H. Smith, Aberdeen, Scotland; Susan G. Smith, London; Anne Stephenson, London; Pat Tookey, London.

Picture Credits

The sources for the pictures in this book are listed below. Credits for each of the photographers and illustrators are listed by page number in sequence with successive pages indicated by hyphens; where necessary, the locations of pictures within pages are also indicated—separated from page numbers by dashes.

Photographs by Aldo Tutino: 4, 8—top, 9—top left, top center, 10-11, 12-13—bottom, 14—bottom, 15, 16—top, 17—top left, top center, 18—top, 19—top left, top center, 20-27, 28-29—bottom, 30-35, 36—bottom right, 37—bottom, 38-70, 74-84.

Other photographs (alphabetically): Tom Belshaw, 8—bottom, 9—top right, bottom left, bottom center, 13—top, 16—bottom, 17—right, 72—top right and bottom, 73. John Cook, 18—bottom, 19—bottom left, bottom center. Alan Duns, 9—bottom right, 17—bottom left, bottom center. John Elliott, 14—top, 28-29—top, 36—bottom left, bottom center, 37—top, 72—top left. Louis Klein, 2. Bob Komar, cover, 12—top. David Levin, 19—right. Illustrations: From The Mary Evans Picture Library and private sources and *Food & Drink: A Pictorial Archive from Nineteenth Century Sources* by Jim Harter, published by Dover Publications, Inc., 1979, 6-7, 86-164.

Endpapers: From The Mary Evans Picture Library and private sources.

Library of Congress Cataloguing in Publication Data
Main entry under title:
Cakes.
(The Good cook, techniques & recipes)
1. Cake. I. Time-Life Books. II. Series.
TX771.C27   641.8'653   81-9322
ISBN 0-8094-2916-0 (retail ed.)   AACR2
ISBN 0-8094-2918-7 (regular bdg.)
ISBN 0-8094-2917-9 (lib. bdg.)